UNCLASSIFIED

AIR BATTLE
A Paper Game
of Strategy, Search, and Destroy
Includes 80 Game Sheets
Ages 8-108

Printed by Amazon KDP Print

SMART SWITCH PUBLICATIONS

UNCLASSIFIED

MY AIRSPACE

	A ALPHA	B BRAVO	C CHARLIE	D DELTA	E ECHO	F FOXTROT	G GOLF	H HOTEL	I INDIA	J JULIETT	
1											1
2					F	F	F	F			2
3		C									3
4				A	A				B		4
5				A	A		B	B	B	B	5
6									B		6
7		S				T					7
8		S			T	T	T				8
9						T					9
10											10
	ALPHA A	BRAVO B	CHARLIE C	DELTA D	ECHO E	FOXTROT F	GOLF G	HOTEL H	INDIA I	JULIETT J	

GAIN SYM BRT CON

☒ HIT ◯ MISS

FOLD ALONG DOTTED LINE AND TEAR OUT GAME SHEET

DRAW YOUR AIRCRAFT

WHEN ENEMY GUESSES MARK
X= HIT
O= MISS

ENEMY AIRSPACE

	A ALPHA	B BRAVO	C CHARLIE	D DELTA	E ECHO	F FOXTROT	G GOLF	H HOTEL	I INDIA	J JULIETT	
1											1
2											2
3											3
4											4
5											5
6											6
7											7
8											8
9											9
10											10
	ALPHA A	BRAVO B	CHARLIE C	DELTA D	ECHO E	FOXTROT F	GOLF G	HOTEL H	INDIA I	JULIETT J	

GAIN SYM BRT CON

☒ HIT ◯ MISS

MARK YOUR GUESSES AT THE ENEMY HERE
X= HIT
O= MISS

FOLD ALONG DOTTED LINE AND TEAR

FOLD ALONG DOTTED LINE AND TEAR

Rules of Engagement:

1. Fold and tear out 1 game sheet for each player
   (Game sheet = one page = My Airspace & Enemy Airspace Grids)
2. On "My Airspace Grid" Draw Your 5 Airplane Groupings Plus 1 Civilian Aircraft :

- One 4-Ship of Fighters 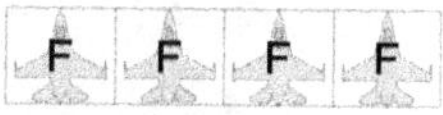

or 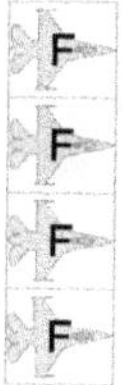

- One 4-Ship of Attack Aircraft 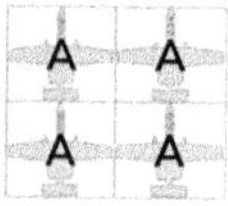

- One Bomber

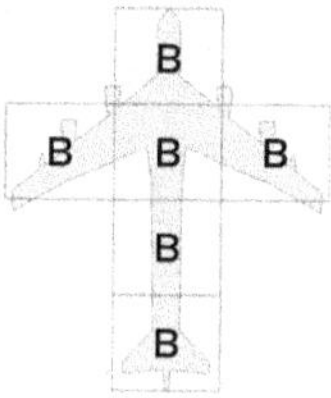

or 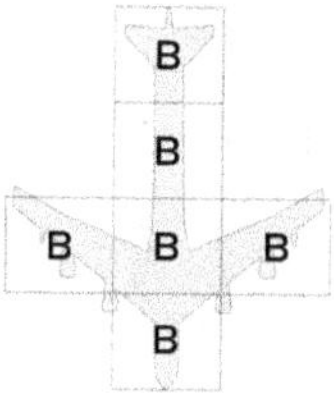

or 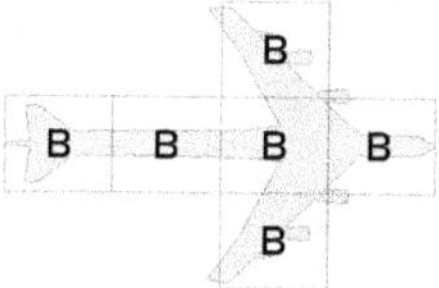

or 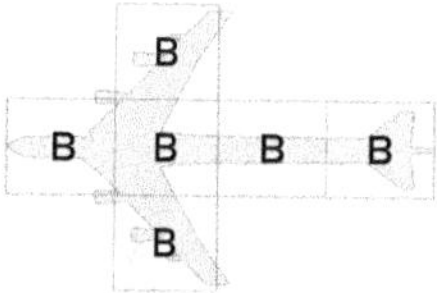

- One Tanker 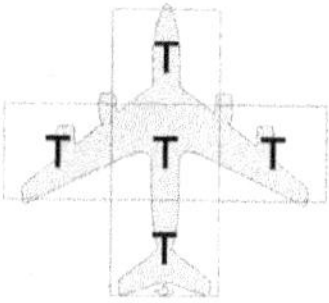

- One Stealth Fighter 

or 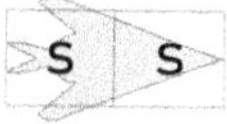

- One Civilian Aircraft 

3. Take turns guessing the position of Enemy Aircraft by calling grid positions

4. Tell the Other Player if it was a 'HIT' or 'MISS"
   Mark a "HIT" with an "X"
   Mark a "MISS" with an "O"

5. Let the Other Player know when an Airplane Grouping is shot down

6. If you Hit a "Civilian" C Aircraft - You lose your next Turn
   It is not required to hit the "Civilian" (C) aircraft to win, you should actually try to avoid it!

7. First Player to Shoot Down all 5 Enemy Groupings Wins

UNCLASSIFIED
farm
microwave tower
substation
NICOLAS
Stickney
Eagle
2110
Bijou Hills
farm
1695
Academy
CORSICA MUNI (D65)
1580 *L 34 122.9
PLATTE MUNI (1D3)
1618 *L 31 122.8
RP 32
IR509
VR 510
Harrison
New Holland
Corsica
Platte
LAKE ANDES MOA
Lucas
stockyard
2000
Geddes
2104
Lake Andes
Ravinia
LAKE ANDES MUNI (8D8)
1475 – 26 122.9
2000
2040
Herrick
St Charles
Bonesteel
(Pvt)
SELLE
1988 – 25
Fairfax
Pickstown
power plant
IR509
WAGNER MUNI
SOUTH DAKOTA
NEBRASKA
43°
99°
Naper
VR1521
1960
IR518
Marty
Gross
Anoka
Greenwood
Butte
VR1520
(Pvt)
HUFFY'S
1690 – 26
Spencer
Bristow
Lynch
(Pvt)
WOOLF BROTHERS
1395 – 26
IR508-509
(Pvt)
BAR LAZY B
1689 – 15
STUART-ATKINSON MUNI (8V2)
2131 *L 39 122.9
Stuart
AIR BATTLE

Fuel Up with Extra game sheets:

FOLD ALONG DOTTED LINE AND TEAR

FOLD ALONG DOTTED LINE AND TEAR

Call Sign: _____

KEY

MY AIRSPACE

FIGHTER				BOMBER
F	F	F	F	B

ATTACK

BOMBER: B B B / B / B

STEALTH: S S

TANKER: T T T / T

CIVILIAN: C

MY AIRSPACE

```
        A   B   C   D   E   F   G   H   I   J
     ALPHA BRAVO CHARLIE DELTA ECHO FOXTROT GOLF HOTEL INDIA JULIETT
  1                                              1
  2                                              2
  3                                              3
  4                                              4
  5                                              5
  6                                              6
  7                                              7
  8                                              8
  9                                              9
 10                                             10
     ALPHA BRAVO CHARLIE DELTA ECHO FOXTROT GOLF HOTEL INDIA JULIETT
        A   B   C   D   E   F   G   H   I   J
```

☒ HIT   ◯ MISS

Enemy Call Sign: _____

KEY

ENEMY AIRSPACE

FIGHTER				BOMBER
F	F	F	F	B

ATTACK: A A / A A

STEALTH: S S

TANKER: T / T T T / T

BOMBER: B B B / B

CIVILIAN: C

ENEMY AIRSPACE

```
        A   B   C   D   E   F   G   H   I   J
     ALPHA BRAVO CHARLIE DELTA ECHO FOXTROT GOLF HOTEL INDIA JULIETT
  1                                              1
  2                                              2
  3                                              3
  4                                              4
  5                                              5
  6                                              6
  7                                              7
  8                                              8
  9                                              9
 10                                             10
     ALPHA BRAVO CHARLIE DELTA ECHO FOXTROT GOLF HOTEL INDIA JULIETT
        A   B   C   D   E   F   G   H   I   J
```

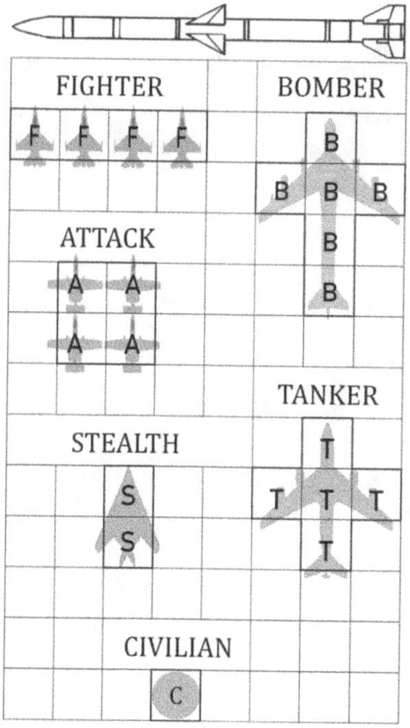

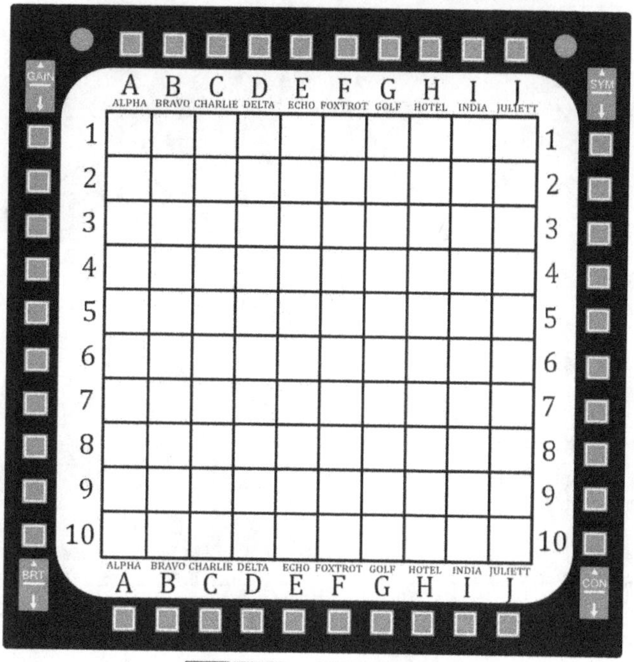

☒ HIT   ◯ MISS

FOLD ALONG DOTTED LINE AND TEAR

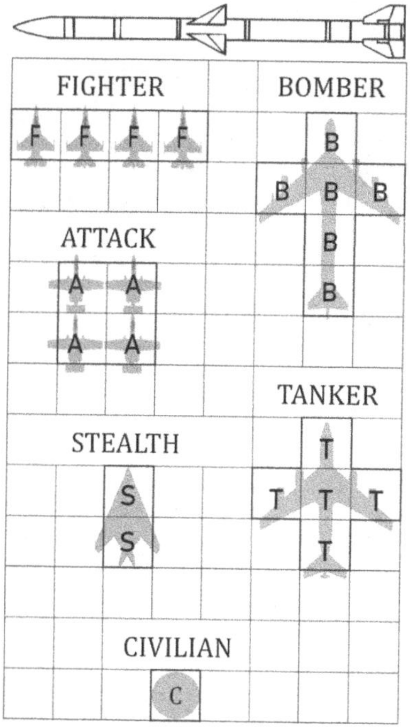

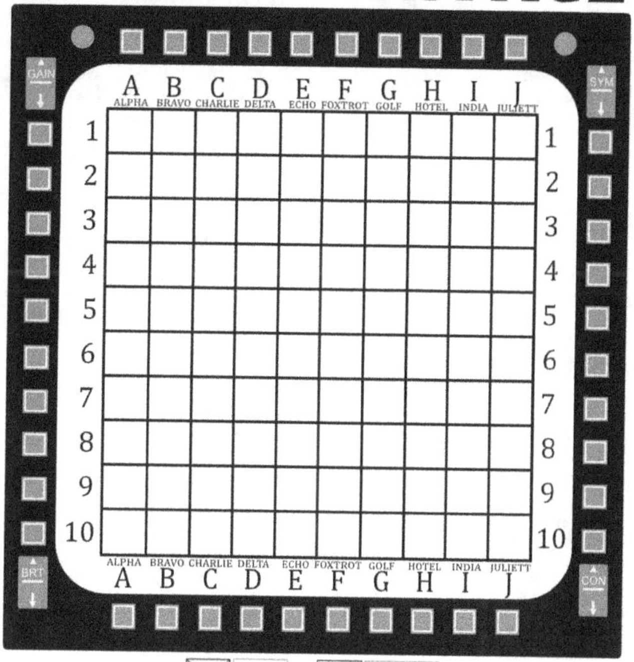

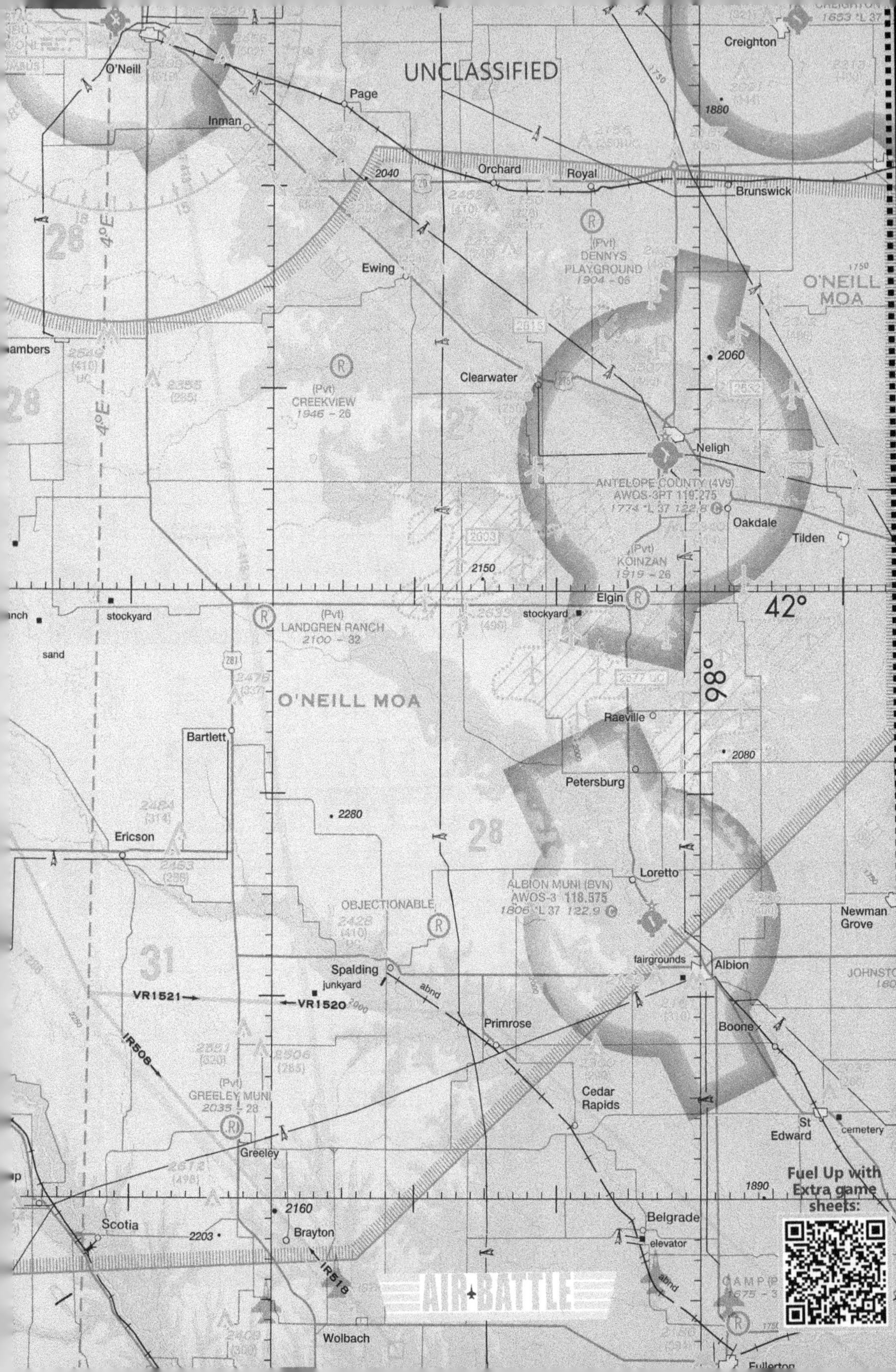
UNCLASSIFIED
O'Neill
Page
Inman
Creighton
1880
Orchard
Royal
Brunswick
2040
(Pvt)
DENNYS
PLAYGROUND
1904 - 06
Ewing
O'NEILL
MOA
2060
Clearwater
(Pvt)
CREEKVIEW
1946 - 26
Neligh
ANTELOPE COUNTY (4V9)
AWOS-3PT 119.275
1774 L 37 122.8
Oakdale
Tilden
(Pvt)
KOINZAN
1919 - 26
2150
Elgin
42°
stockyard
(Pvt)
LANDGREN RANCH
2100 - 32
stockyard
sand
O'NEILL MOA
98°
Raeville
Bartlett
2080
Petersburg
2280
Ericson
28
Loretto
ALBION MUNI (BVN)
AWOS-3 118.575
1806 L 37 122.9
OBJECTIONABLE
Newman
Grove
31
Spalding
junkyard
fairgrounds
Albion
VR1521
VR1520
abnd
Primrose
Boone
IR508
(Pvt)
GREELEY MUNI
2035 - 28
Cedar
Rapids
St
Edward
cemetery
Greeley
1890
2160
Belgrade
Scotia
2203
Brayton
elevator
IR518
abnd
Wolbach
Fullerton
AIR BATTLE

Fuel Up with Extra game sheets:

FOLD ALONG DOTTED LINE AND TEAR

FOLD ALONG DOTTED LINE AND TEAR

Call Sign: _____

MY AIRSPACE

KEY

FIGHTER
F F F F

BOMBER
B
B B B
B
B

ATTACK
A A
A A

STEALTH
S
S

TANKER
T
T T T
T

CIVILIAN
C

MY AIRSPACE grid

	A	B	C	D	E	F	G	H	I	J
	ALPHA	BRAVO	CHARLIE	DELTA	ECHO	FOXTROT	GOLF	HOTEL	INDIA	JULIETT
1										
2										
3										
4										
5										
6										
7										
8										
9										
10										

ALPHA BRAVO CHARLIE DELTA ECHO FOXTROT GOLF HOTEL INDIA JULIETT
A B C D E F G H I J

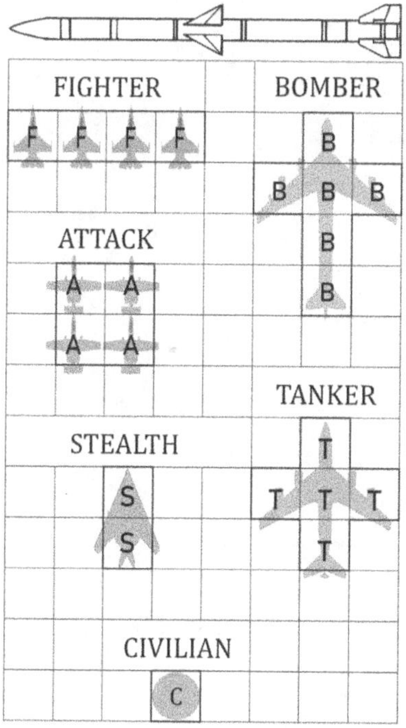

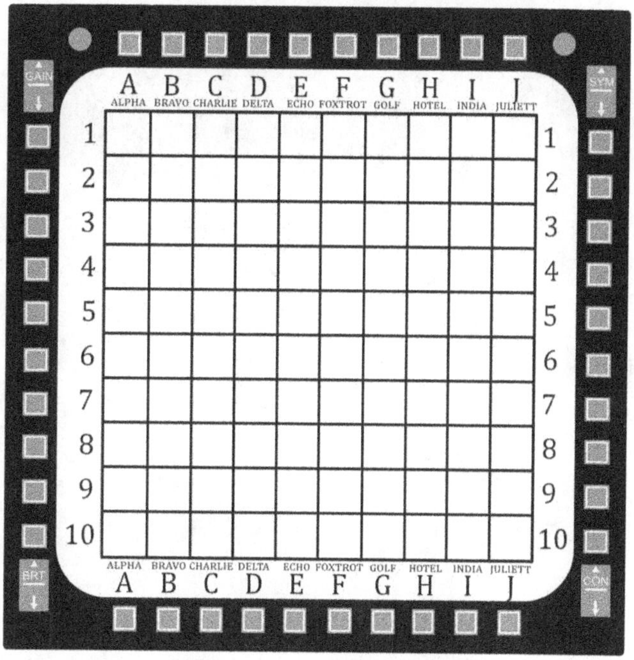

☒ HIT   ◯ MISS

Enemy Call Sign: _____

ENEMY AIRSPACE

KEY

FIGHTER
F F F F

BOMBER
B
B B B
B
B

ATTACK
A A
A A

STEALTH
S
S

TANKER
T
T T T
T

CIVILIAN
C

ENEMY AIRSPACE grid

	A	B	C	D	E	F	G	H	I	J
	ALPHA	BRAVO	CHARLIE	DELTA	ECHO	FOXTROT	GOLF	HOTEL	INDIA	JULIETT
1										
2										
3										
4										
5										
6										
7										
8										
9										
10										

ALPHA BRAVO CHARLIE DELTA ECHO FOXTROT GOLF HOTEL INDIA JULIETT
A B C D E F G H I J

☒ HIT   ◯ MISS

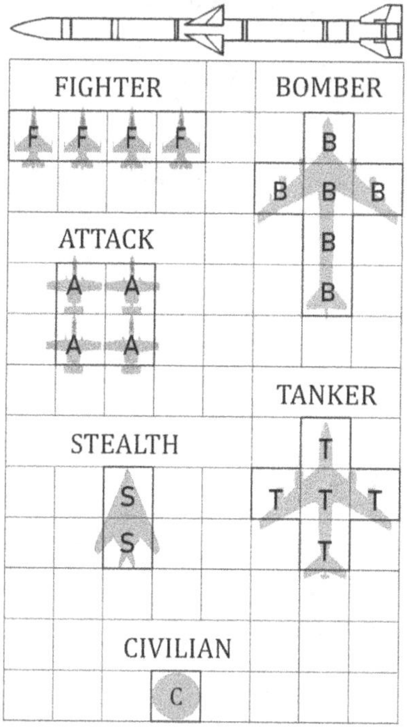

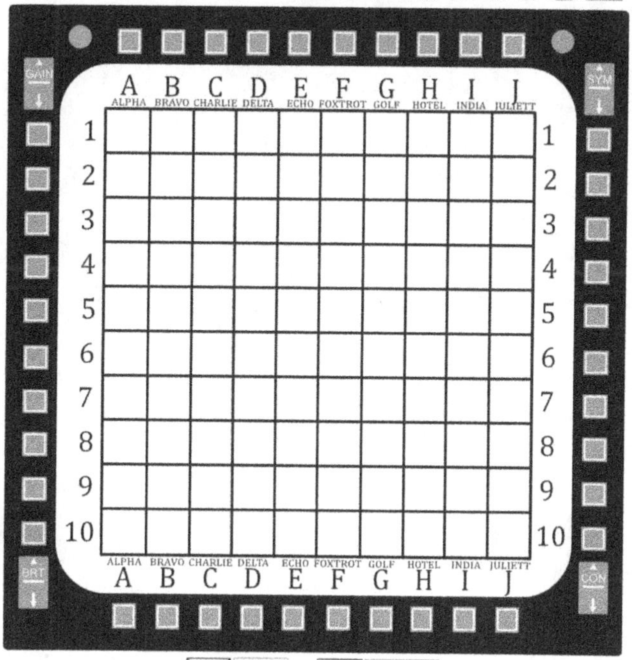

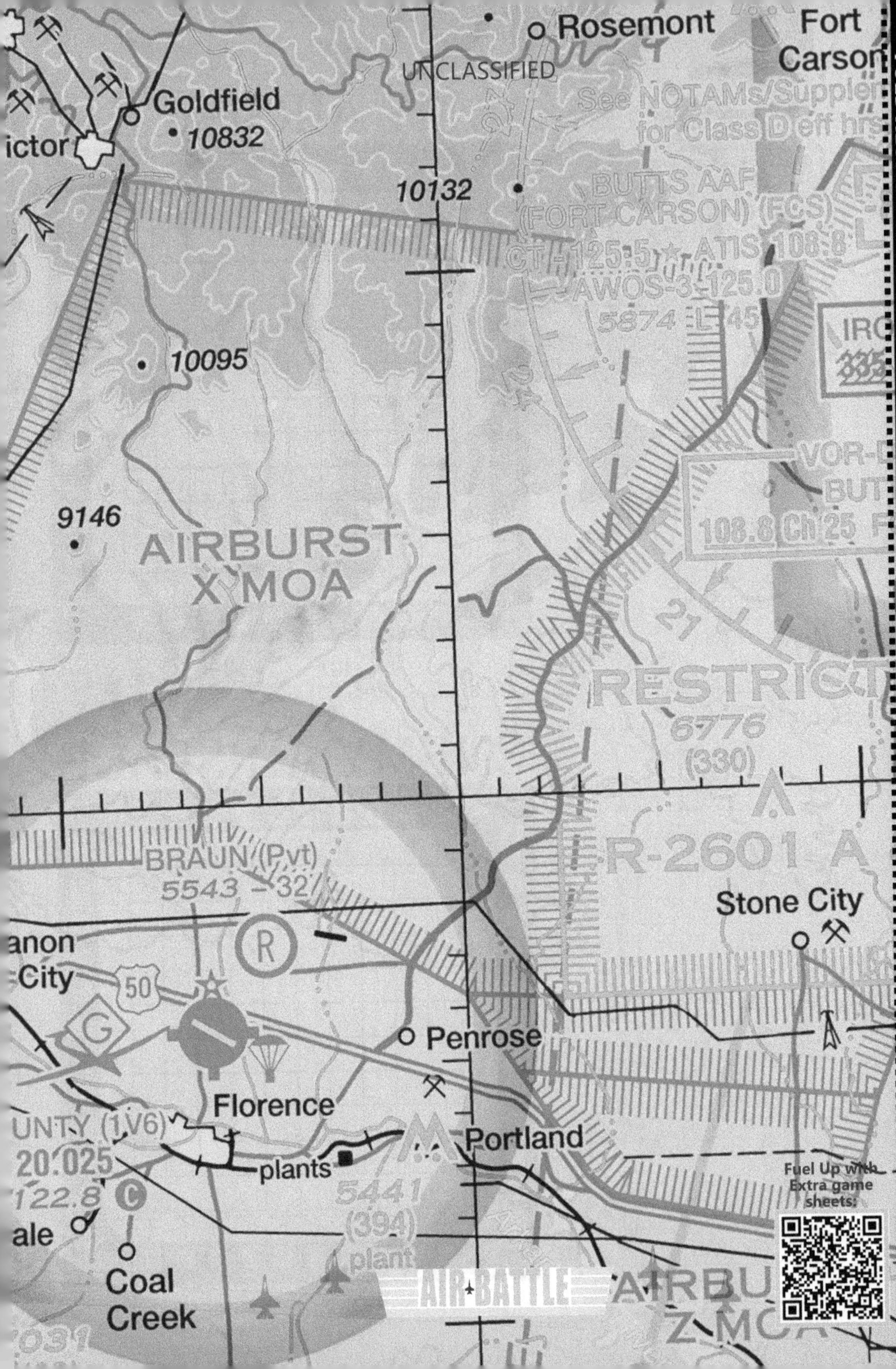
Rosemont
Fort Carson
UNCLASSIFIED
See NOTAMs/Supplement
for Class D eff hrs
Goldfield
10832
Victor
10132
BUTTS AAF
(FORT CARSON) (FCS)
CT-125.5 ATIS 108.8
AWOS-3 125.0
5874 L 45
IRG
10095
VOR-D
BUT
108.8 Ch 25
9146
AIRBURST X MOA
21
RESTRICTED
6776
(330)
R-2601 A
BRAUN (Pvt)
5543 - 32
Stone City
Canon City
50
G
R
Penrose
Florence
COUNTY (1V6)
120.025
122.8
C
plants
Portland
5441
(394)
plant
Fuel Up with Extra game sheets:
ale
Coal Creek
AIR BATTLE
AIRBURST X MOA

FOLD ALONG DOTTED LINE AND TEAR

FOLD ALONG DOTTED LINE AND TEAR

Call Sign: _____

KEY

MY AIRSPACE

FIGHTER
F F F F

BOMBER
B
B B B
B
B

ATTACK
A A
A A

STEALTH
S
S

TANKER
T
T T T
T

CIVILIAN
C

```
      A B C D E F G H I J
   ALPHA BRAVO CHARLIE DELTA ECHO FOXTROT GOLF HOTEL INDIA JULIETT
1                                          1
2                                          2
3                                          3
4                                          4
5                                          5
6                                          6
7                                          7
8                                          8
9                                          9
10                                         10
   ALPHA BRAVO CHARLIE DELTA ECHO FOXTROT GOLF HOTEL INDIA JULIETT
      A B C D E F G H I J
```

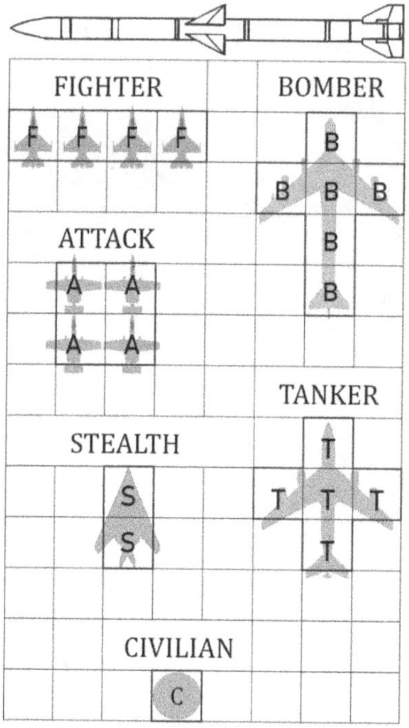

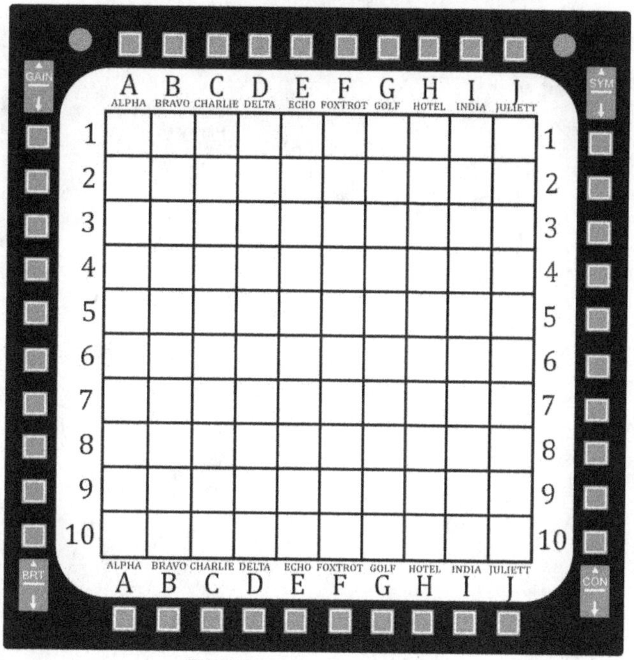

☒ HIT   ◯ MISS

Enemy Call Sign: _____

KEY

ENEMY AIRSPACE

FIGHTER
F F F F

BOMBER
B
B B B
B

ATTACK
A A
A A

STEALTH
S
S

TANKER
T
T T T
T

CIVILIAN
C

```
      A B C D E F G H I J
   ALPHA BRAVO CHARLIE DELTA ECHO FOXTROT GOLF HOTEL INDIA JULIETT
1                                          1
2                                          2
3                                          3
4                                          4
5                                          5
6                                          6
7                                          7
8                                          8
9                                          9
10                                         10
   ALPHA BRAVO CHARLIE DELTA ECHO FOXTROT GOLF HOTEL INDIA JULIETT
      A B C D E F G H I J
```

☒ HIT   ◯ MISS

FOLD ALONG DOTTED LINE AND TEAR

FOLD ALONG DOTTED LINE AND TEAR

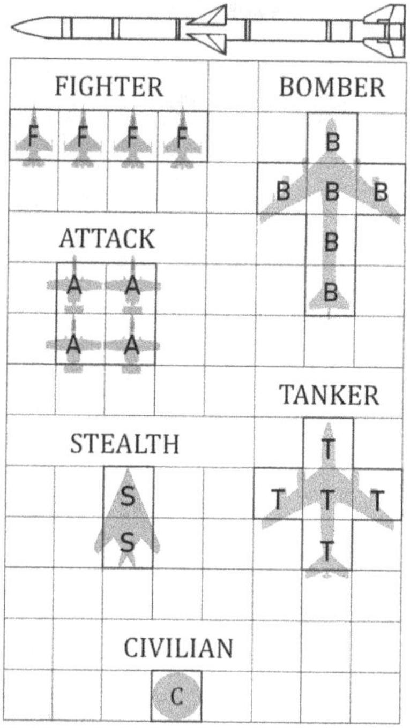

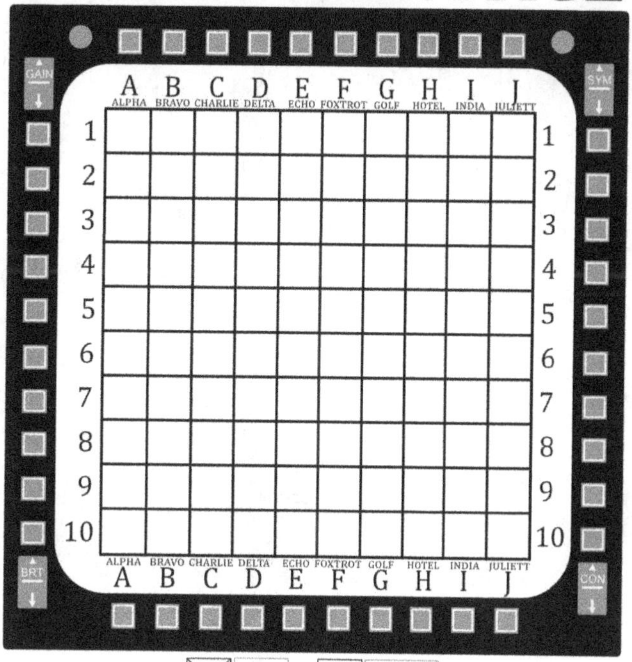

UNCLASSIFIED

Fuel Up with Extra game sheets:

AIR BATTLE

FOLD ALONG DOTTED LINE AND TEAR

FOLD ALONG DOTTED LINE AND TEAR

Call Sign: _____

KEY

MY AIRSPACE

FIGHTER

F F F F

BOMBER

B
B B B
B
B

ATTACK

A A
A A

STEALTH

S
S

TANKER

T
T T T
T

CIVILIAN

C

	A	B	C	D	E	F	G	H	I	J	
	ALPHA	BRAVO	CHARLIE	DELTA	ECHO	FOXTROT	GOLF	HOTEL	INDIA	JULIETT	
1											1
2											2
3											3
4											4
5											5
6											6
7											7
8											8
9											9
10											10
	ALPHA	BRAVO	CHARLIE	DELTA	ECHO	FOXTROT	GOLF	HOTEL	INDIA	JULIETT	
	A	B	C	D	E	F	G	H	I	J	

☒ HIT   ◯ MISS

Enemy Call Sign: _____

KEY

ENEMY AIRSPACE

FIGHTER

F F F F

BOMBER

B
B B B
B
B

ATTACK

A A
A A

STEALTH

S
S

TANKER

T
T T T
T

CIVILIAN

C

	A	B	C	D	E	F	G	H	I	J	
	ALPHA	BRAVO	CHARLIE	DELTA	ECHO	FOXTROT	GOLF	HOTEL	INDIA	JULIETT	
1											1
2											2
3											3
4											4
5											5
6											6
7											7
8											8
9											9
10											10
	ALPHA	BRAVO	CHARLIE	DELTA	ECHO	FOXTROT	GOLF	HOTEL	INDIA	JULIETT	
	A	B	C	D	E	F	G	H	I	J	

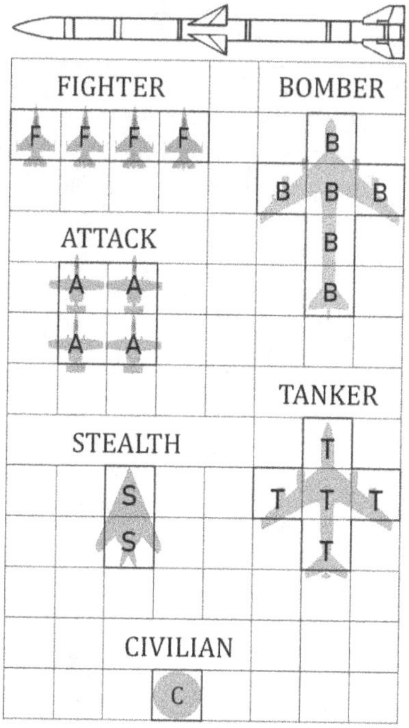

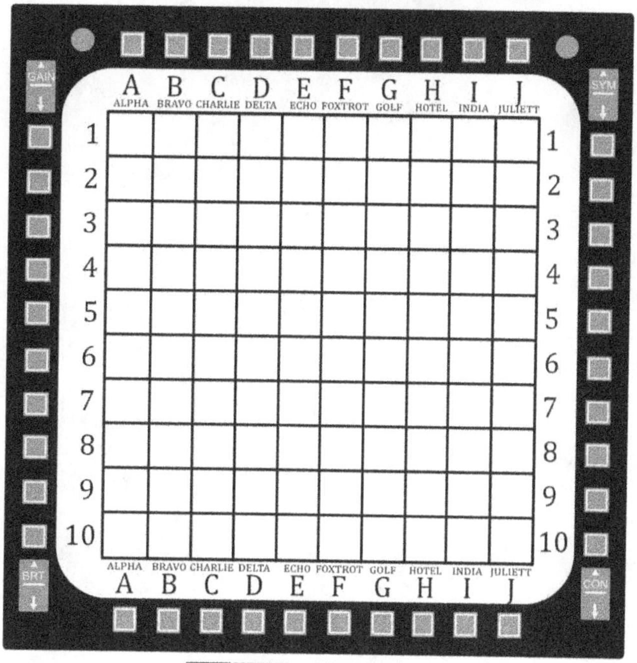

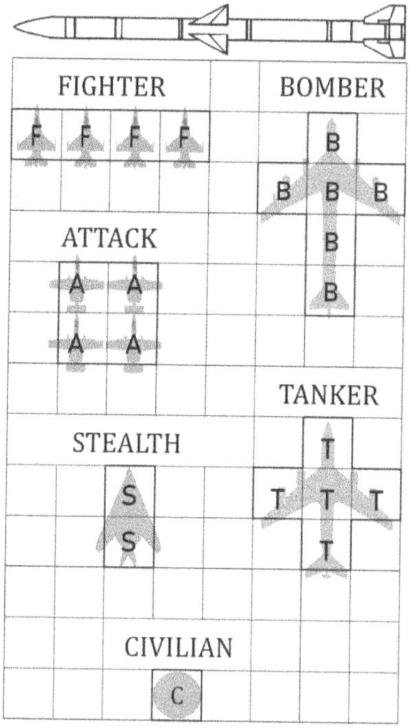

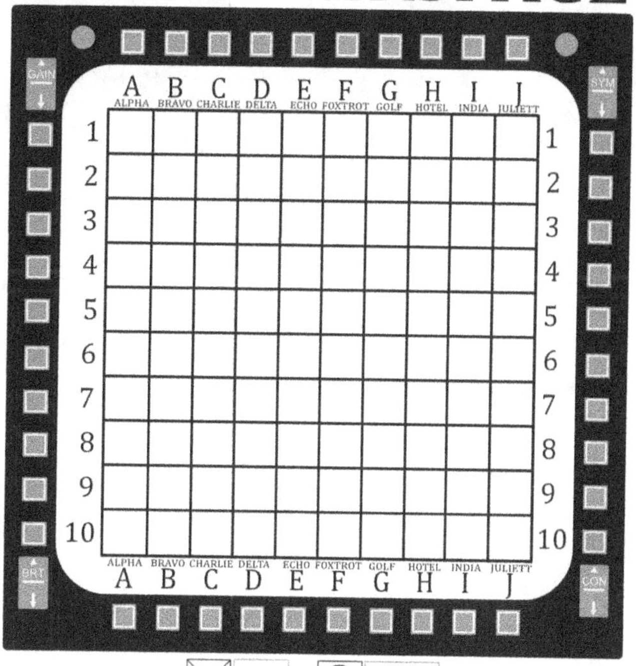

☒ HIT   ◯ MISS

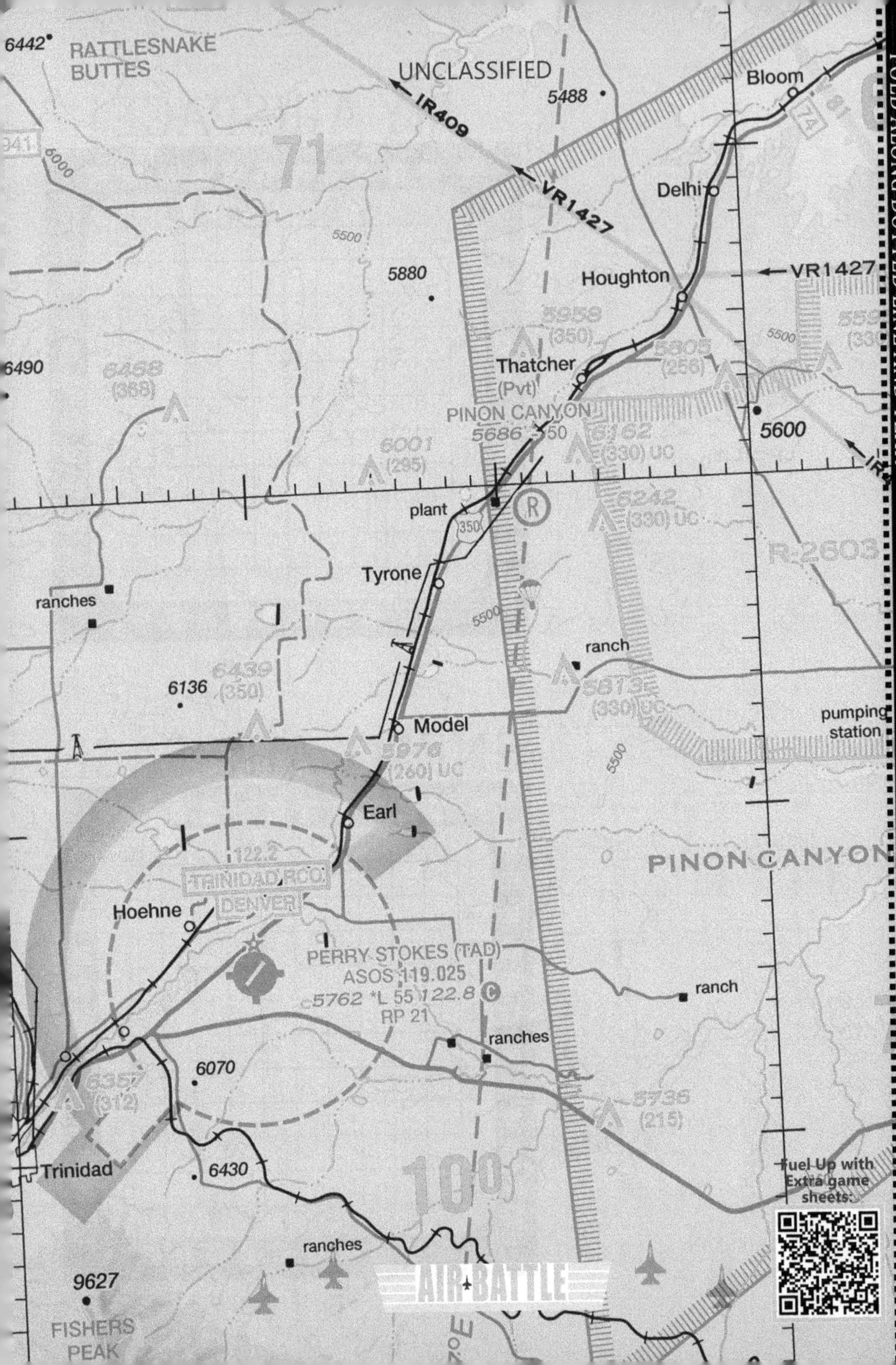
RATTLESNAKE BUTTES
6442
UNCLASSIFIED
IR409
VR1427
5488
Bloom
Delhi
Houghton
VR1427
5880
5500
6490
6458 (368)
5958 (350)
Thatcher (Pvt)
5805 (256)
PINON CANYON
5686
350
6162 (330) UC
5600
6001 (295)
plant
350
6242 (330) UC
R-2603
Tyrone
ranches
ranch
6136
6439 (350)
5813 (330) UC
Model
pumping station
5976 (260) UC
Earl
5500
PINON CANYON
122.2
TRINIDAD RCO
DENVER
Hoehne
PERRY STOKES (TAD)
ASOS 119.025
5762 *L 55 122.8 C
RP 21
ranch
ranches
6070
6357 (312)
5736 (215)
Trinidad
6430
ranches
9627
FISHERS PEAK
AIR BATTLE
Fuel Up with Extra game sheets:

FOLD ALONG DOTTED LINE AND TEAR

FOLD ALONG DOTTED LINE AND TEAR

Call Sign: _____

KEY

MY AIRSPACE

FIGHTER

F F F F

BOMBER

B
B B B
B
B

ATTACK

A A
A A

TANKER

T
T T T
T

STEALTH

S
S

CIVILIAN

C

```
      A   B   C   D   E   F   G   H   I   J
   ALPHA BRAVO CHARLIE DELTA ECHO FOXTROT GOLF HOTEL INDIA JULIETT
 1                                              1
 2                                              2
 3                                              3
 4                                              4
 5                                              5
 6                                              6
 7                                              7
 8                                              8
 9                                              9
10                                              10
   ALPHA BRAVO CHARLIE DELTA ECHO FOXTROT GOLF HOTEL INDIA JULIETT
      A   B   C   D   E   F   G   H   I   J
```

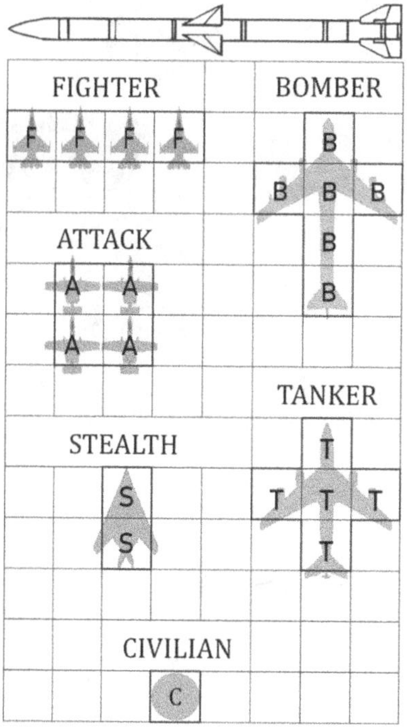

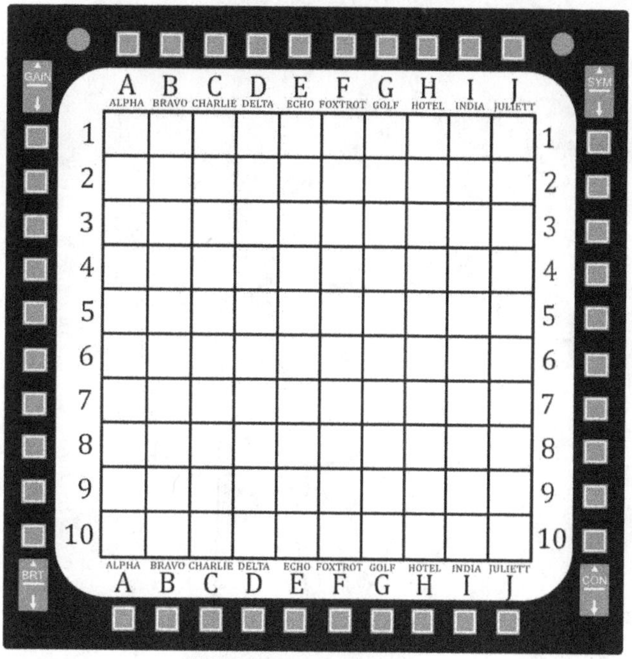

☒ HIT   ◯ MISS

Enemy Call Sign: _____

KEY

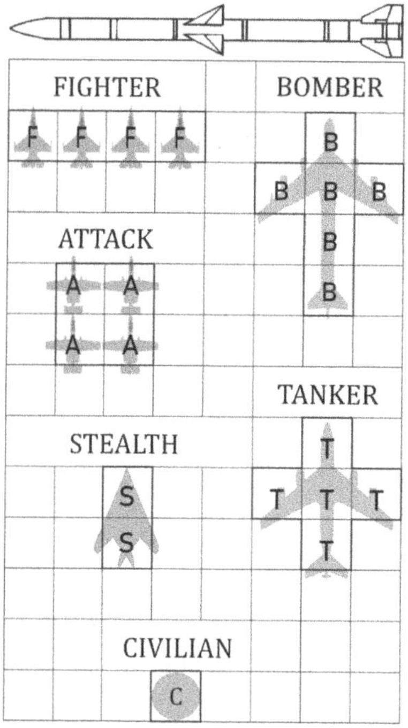

ENEMY AIRSPACE

FIGHTER

F F F F

BOMBER

B
B B B
B
B

ATTACK

A A
A A

TANKER

T
T T T
T

STEALTH

S
S

CIVILIAN

C

```
      A   B   C   D   E   F   G   H   I   J
   ALPHA BRAVO CHARLIE DELTA ECHO FOXTROT GOLF HOTEL INDIA JULIETT
 1                                              1
 2                                              2
 3                                              3
 4                                              4
 5                                              5
 6                                              6
 7                                              7
 8                                              8
 9                                              9
10                                              10
   ALPHA BRAVO CHARLIE DELTA ECHO FOXTROT GOLF HOTEL INDIA JULIETT
      A   B   C   D   E   F   G   H   I   J
```

☒ HIT   ◯ MISS

FOLD ALONG DOTTED LINE AND TEAR

FOLD ALONG DOTTED LINE AND TEAR

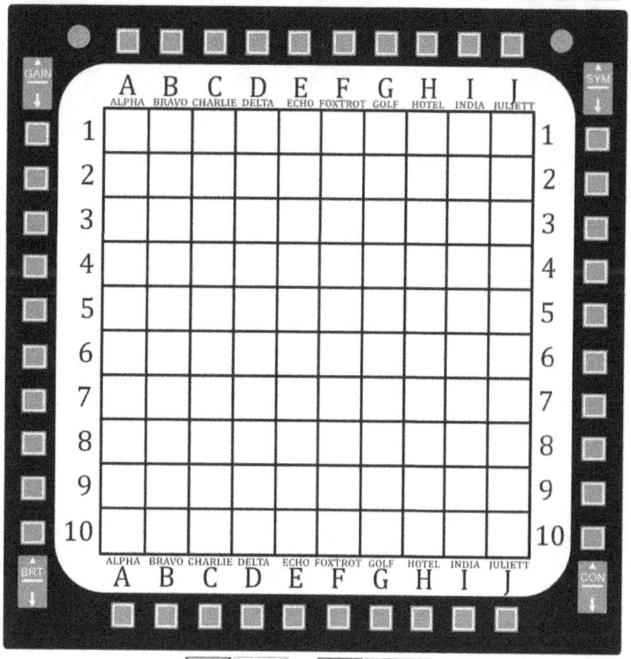

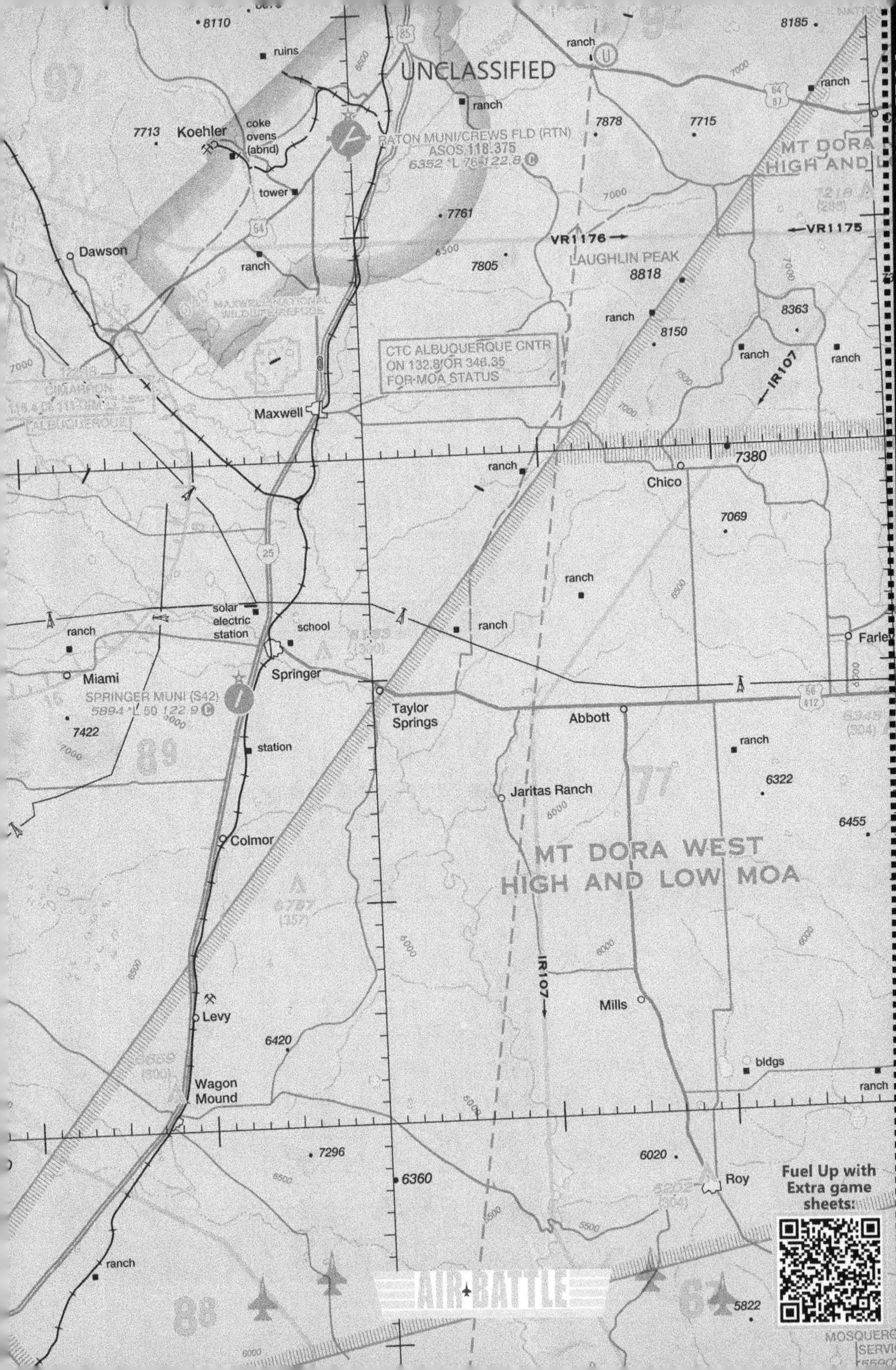
UNCLASSIFIED
8110
ruins
ranch
8185
Koehler
coke ovens (abnd)
7713
RATON MUNI/CREWS FLD (RTN)
ASOS 118.375
6352 *L 76 122.8
7878
7715
MT DORA
HIGH AND L
tower
7761
Dawson
ranch
VR1176
VR1175
LAUGHLIN PEAK
8818
7805
ranch
8150
8363
CTC ALBUQUERQUE CNTR
ON 132.8/OR 348.35
FOR MOA STATUS
IR107
Maxwell
7380
Chico
7069
solar electric station
school
Springer
Miami
SPRINGER MUNI (S42)
5894 *L 50 122.9
7422
station
Taylor Springs
Abbott
Farley
6322
6455
Jaritas Ranch
Colmor
MT DORA WEST
HIGH AND LOW MOA
Mills
Levy
6420
Wagon Mound
bldgs
7296
6020
6360
Roy
5822
AIR BATTLE
MOSQUERO

Fuel Up with
Extra game
sheets:

FOLD ALONG DOTTED LINE AND TEAR

FOLD ALONG DOTTED LINE AND TEAR

Call Sign: _____

KEY

MY AIRSPACE

FIGHTER	BOMBER
F F F F	B / B B B / B / B

ATTACK
A A / A A

STEALTH	TANKER
S / S	T / T T T / T

CIVILIAN

C

MY AIRSPACE

	A	B	C	D	E	F	G	H	I	J
1										
2										
3										
4										
5										
6										
7										
8										
9										
10										

ALPHA BRAVO CHARLIE DELTA ECHO FOXTROT GOLF HOTEL INDIA JULIETT

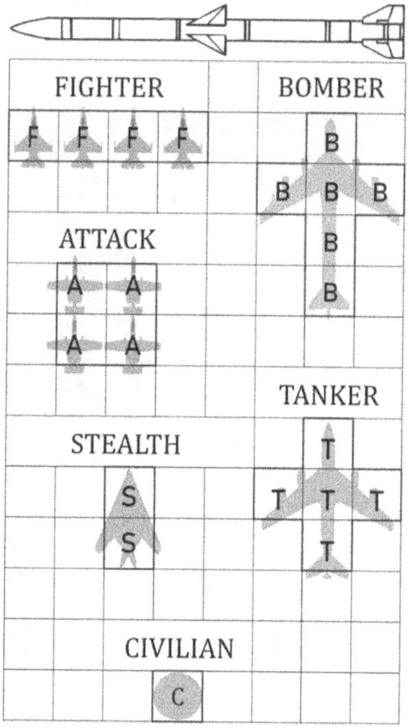

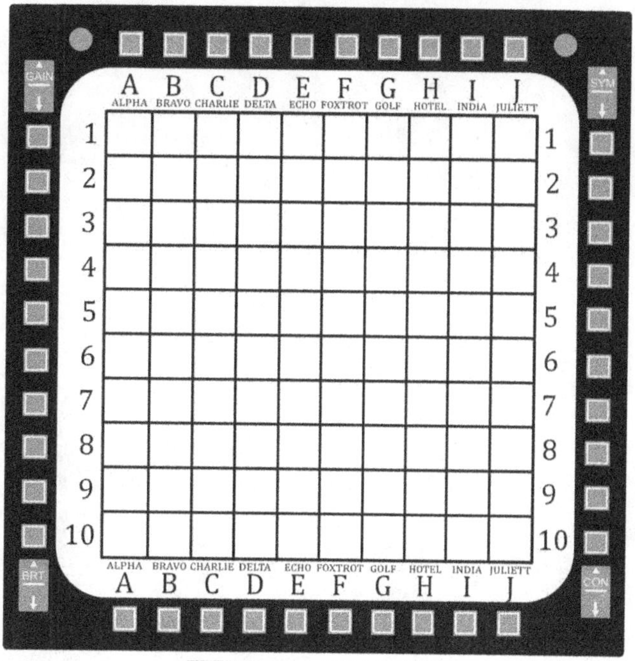

⊠ HIT   ◯ MISS

Enemy Call Sign: _____

KEY

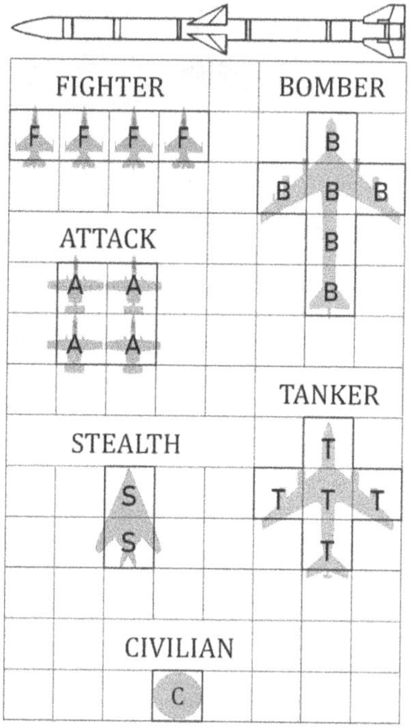

ENEMY AIRSPACE

FIGHTER	BOMBER
F F F F	B / B B B / B

ATTACK
A A / A A

STEALTH	TANKER
S / S	T / T T T / T

CIVILIAN

C

ENEMY AIRSPACE

	A	B	C	D	E	F	G	H	I	J
1										
2										
3										
4										
5										
6										
7										
8										
9										
10										

ALPHA BRAVO CHARLIE DELTA ECHO FOXTROT GOLF HOTEL INDIA JULIETT

⊠ HIT   ◯ MISS

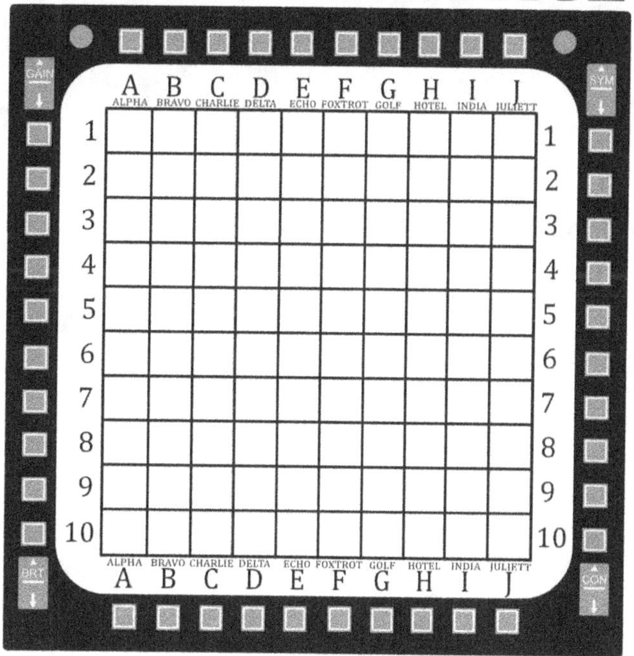

Ischua
2281
Belmont
2334
2401
2410
Cuba
Friendship
UNCLASSIFIED
Andover
Greenwood
Nile
WELLSVILLE MUNI/
TARANTINE FLD (ELZ)
ASOS 119.275
2125 *L 53 123.0
Hinsdale
W Clarksville
REISS GAME
FARM (Pvt)
1698 - 30
Wellsville
plant
2410
Rexville
2450
Stannards
Hallsport
Olean
2392
GIERMEK EXEC (8G3)
2397
Bolivar
Whitesville
Allegany
oil field
Troupsburg
Portville
FREEFALL OZ
1440 - 29
2515
oil
fields
Shongo
Little
Genesee
Alma
NEW YORK
PENNSYLVANIA
SWIFT AERO FLD
1990 - 16
microwave
tower
2342
Ceres
42°
2463
VR707
Mills
Harrison Valley
Eldred
Shinglehouse
2502
W Bingham
Westfield
29 DUKE MOA
34
Potter
Brook
Millport
2390
ADAMS (Pvt)
1780 - 29
GREELEY (Pvt)
2300 - 18
Ulysses
2610
2360
abnd
Rew
2500
Gold
HOOPES
FAMILY FARM
2373 - 23
Sabinsville
2570
2570
78°
refinery
SHARRETTS
2360 - 18
2460
UPMC COLE
1743
Port Allegany
2590
Ormsby
fairground
Coudersport
Sweden
Valley
West
Pike
2440
Gaines
2370
Roulette
RANCH-AERO (Pvt)
1575 - 25
Galeton
Watrous
Crosby
camp
2440
29
Hazel Hurst
2475
34
DUKE MOA
2420
Keating
Summit
2543
2489
Germania
2430
2408
Austin
Conrad
2250
2430
Costello
2320
CAMERON COUNTY
JUNIOR/SENIOR HIGH SCHOOL
2581
2341
VR704
Wharton
Emporium
2310
Cross
Fork
Truman
2190
2200
ST MARYS MUNI (OYM)
AWOS-3P 118.05
1934 *L 43 122.7
Cameron
pumping
station
2250
2369
VR707
plant
2230
2330
2360
Sterling
Run
stack
Gleasonton
2170
2310
1770
Driftwood
Hyner
Sinnemahoning
plant
Renovo
Benezett
2200
Westport
PONDER
1820
Weedville
2331
VR705
2342
2375
1670
substation
2284
plant
2250
2405
VR704-705-707
Orviston
2310
Karthaus
CLEARFIELD-LAWRENCE (FIG)
Monument

Fuel Up with Extra game sheets:

FOLD ALONG DOTTED LINE AND TEAR

FOLD ALONG DOTTED LINE AND TEAR

FOLD ALONG DOTTED LINE AND TEAR

Call Sign: ______________

AIR BATTLE

KEY

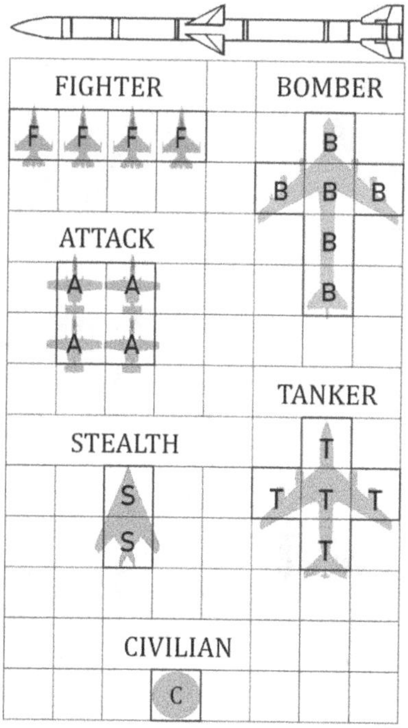

MY AIRSPACE

	A ALPHA	B BRAVO	C CHARLIE	D DELTA	E ECHO	F FOXTROT	G GOLF	H HOTEL	I INDIA	J JULIETT	
1											1
2											2
3											3
4											4
5											5
6											6
7											7
8											8
9											9
10											10
	ALPHA A	BRAVO B	CHARLIE C	DELTA D	ECHO E	FOXTROT F	GOLF G	HOTEL H	INDIA I	JULIETT J	

GAIN SYM BRT CON

☒ HIT ◯ MISS

FOLD ALONG DOTTED LINE AND TEAR

Enemy Call Sign: __________

KEY

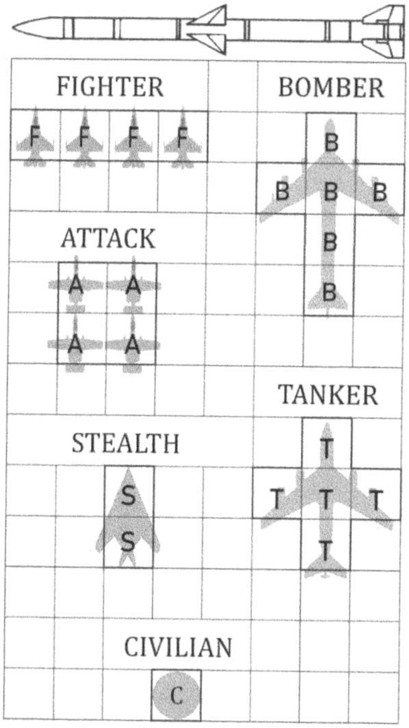

ENEMY AIRSPACE

	A ALPHA	B BRAVO	C CHARLIE	D DELTA	E ECHO	F FOXTROT	G GOLF	H HOTEL	I INDIA	J JULIETT	
1											1
2											2
3											3
4											4
5											5
6											6
7											7
8											8
9											9
10											10
	ALPHA A	BRAVO B	CHARLIE C	DELTA D	ECHO E	FOXTROT F	GOLF G	HOTEL H	INDIA I	JULIETT J	

GAIN SYM BRT CON

☒ HIT ◯ MISS

RONTO FIR CZYZ
CANADA
(ONTARIO)
UNCLASSIFIED
UNITED STATES
(NEW YORK)
MISTY 1 MOA
LAKE ONTARIO
RESTRICT
R-520
VOR-DME ROCHESTER
BUFFALO
CTC ROCHESTER APP 20 NM ON 119.55
ROCHESTER CLASS C
ROCHESTER
HILTON
BROCKPORT
SPENCERPORT
SPENCERPORT AIRPARK (D91)
WEBSTER
Union Hill
Morton
Gaines
Murray
Albion
Holley
Barre Center
LEDGEDALE (7G0)
CTC ROCHESTER APP WITHIN 20 NM ON 123.7 322.3
IROQUOIS NATIONAL WILDLIFE REFUGE
CHURCHVILLE
Bergen
GENESEE COUNTY (GVQ)
FREDERICK DOUGLASS/GREATER ROCHESTER INTL (ROC)
PITTSFORD
Scottsville
SKYVIEW (Pvt)
Honeoye Falls
BEDSON'S LAND BASE
CREEKSIDE
WEISS AIRFIELD
Le Roy
LE ROY (5G0)
CALEDONIA
BATAVIA
BUFFALO APP WITHIN
BETHANY AIRPARK (Pvt)
Lima
Avon
VOR-DME GENESEO
DARIEN
Alexander
Bethany
Pavilion
Bristol
Attica
Linden
Wyoming
Piffard
Livonia
GENESEO (D52)
LAKEVILLE (Pvt)
GENESEO
Honeoye Park
PERRY-WARSAW (01G)
Leicester
VARYSBURG
Warsaw
Perry
Conesus
Mount Morris
SEVEN GULLIES
Rock Glen
Sonyea
Groveland
Scottsburg
Webster Crossing
N Java
Silver Springs
Castile
Springwater
Gainesville
Nunda
Wayland
Fuel Up with Extra game sheets
AIR BATTLE

FOLD ALONG DOTTED LINE AND TEAR

FOLD ALONG DOTTED LINE AND TEAR

Call Sign: _____

KEY

FIGHTER
F F F F

BOMBER
B
B B B
B
B

ATTACK
A A
A A

STEALTH
S
S

TANKER
T
T T T
T

CIVILIAN
C

MY AIRSPACE

	A	B	C	D	E	F	G	H	I	J	
	ALPHA	BRAVO	CHARLIE	DELTA	ECHO	FOXTROT	GOLF	HOTEL	INDIA	JULIETT	
1											1
2											2
3											3
4											4
5											5
6											6
7											7
8											8
9											9
10											10

ALPHA BRAVO CHARLIE DELTA ECHO FOXTROT GOLF HOTEL INDIA JULIETT
A B C D E F G H I J

☒ HIT   ◯ MISS

Enemy Call Sign: _____

KEY

FIGHTER
F F F F

BOMBER
B
B B B
B
B

ATTACK
A A
A A

STEALTH
S
S

TANKER
T
T T T
T

CIVILIAN
C

ENEMY AIRSPACE

	A	B	C	D	E	F	G	H	I	J	
	ALPHA	BRAVO	CHARLIE	DELTA	ECHO	FOXTROT	GOLF	HOTEL	INDIA	JULIETT	
1											1
2											2
3											3
4											4
5											5
6											6
7											7
8											8
9											9
10											10

ALPHA BRAVO CHARLIE DELTA ECHO FOXTROT GOLF HOTEL INDIA JULIETT
A B C D E F G H I J

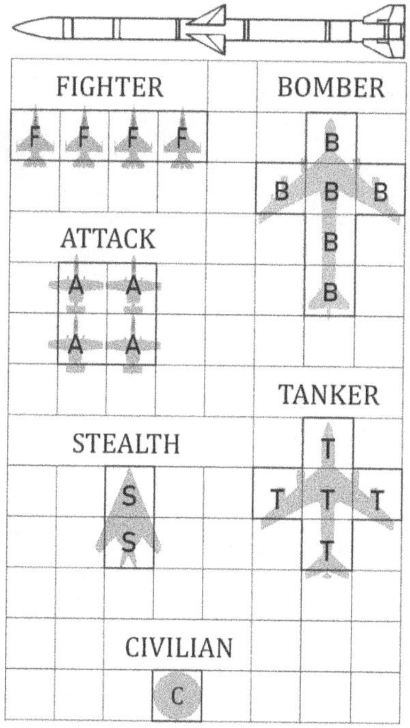

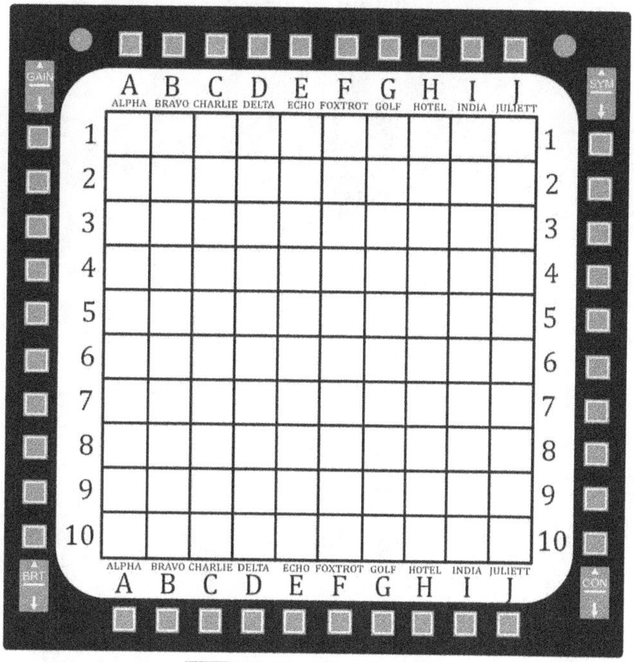

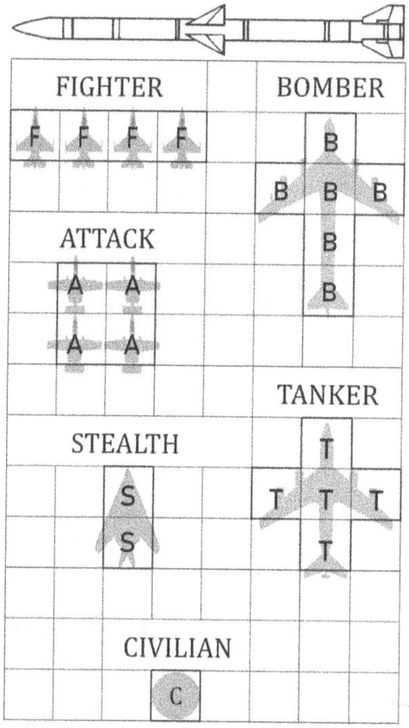

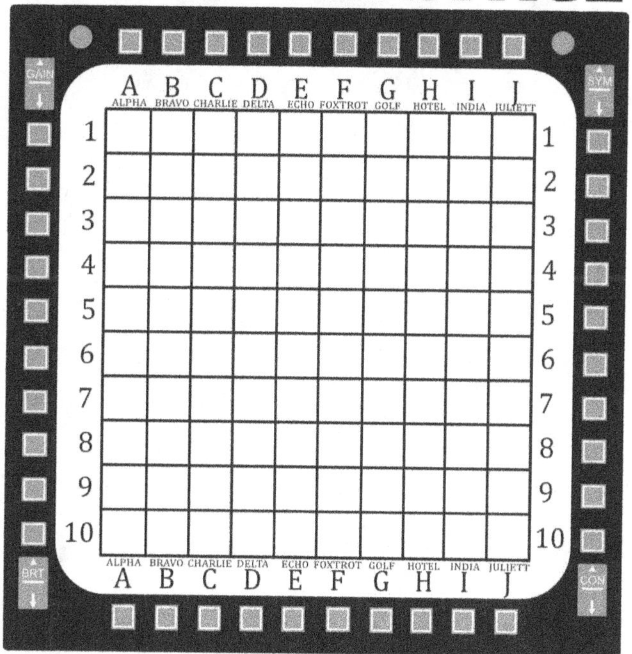

☒ HIT   ◯ MISS

UNCLASSIFIED
100
60
100
90
W SISTER ISLAND
NATIONAL WILDLIFE REFUGE
ADS-B OUT
West Sister Island
Scudder
Pelee Island
NORTH BASS ISLAND (3X5)
594 - 18 122.8 C
North Bass Island RP 19
MIDDLE BASS ISLAND (3T7)
579 - 18 122.8 C
RP 10
MIDDLE BASS-EAST POINT (3W9)
582 - 21 122.9 C
RP 27
Middle Bass Island
RATTLESNAKE ISLAND (Pvt)
586 - 15
R-5502B
EXCLUDES R-5502A
PUT IN BAY (3W2)
595 - 29
122.8 C
RP 3
Put-in-Bay
South Bass Island
OTTAWA NATIONAL WILDLIFE REFUGE
R-5502 A & B
Catawba Island
Moore Pt
Marblehead
Oak Harbor
Port Clinton
ERIE-OTTAWA INTL (PCW)
AWOS-3 118.775
590 *L 56 122.8 C
MAGRUDER MEML
580
BOGGY BOTTOMS
580 - 24
GIBBS FLD
580 - 22
SANDUSKY
ZIMMERMAN LANDING (Pvt)
607 - 26
MATHER FLD
640 - 34
Fremont
PROMEDICA MEML HOSPITAL
SANDUSKY COUNTY RGNL (S24)
AWOS-3P 119.575
665 *L 55 123.05 C
MISSLER-BELLEVUE
760 - 13
COLVIN
720 - 15
Clyde
Green Springs
BELLEVUE HOSPITAL
756
Old Fort
Monroeville
DOUGHERTY
OBJECTIONABLE
AIR BATTLE

Fuel Up with Extra game sheets:

FOLD ALONG DOTTED LINE AND TEAR

FOLD ALONG DOTTED LINE AND TEAR

Call Sign: _____

KEY

MY AIRSPACE

	FIGHTER				BOMBER	
F	F	F	F		B	
				B	B	B
ATTACK					B	
A		A			B	
A		A				
				TANKER		
STEALTH				T		
	S			T	T	T
	S				T	

CIVILIAN

C

MY AIRSPACE grid:

	A	B	C	D	E	F	G	H	I	J	
	ALPHA	BRAVO	CHARLIE	DELTA	ECHO	FOXTROT	GOLF	HOTEL	INDIA	JULIETT	
1											1
2											2
3											3
4											4
5											5
6											6
7											7
8											8
9											9
10											10
	ALPHA	BRAVO	CHARLIE	DELTA	ECHO	FOXTROT	GOLF	HOTEL	INDIA	JULIETT	
	A	B	C	D	E	F	G	H	I	J	

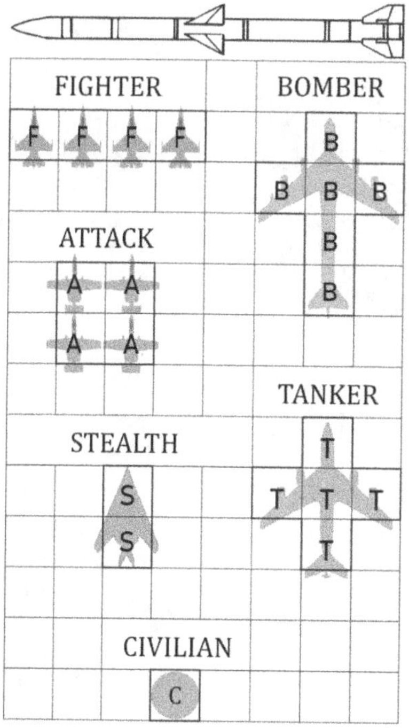

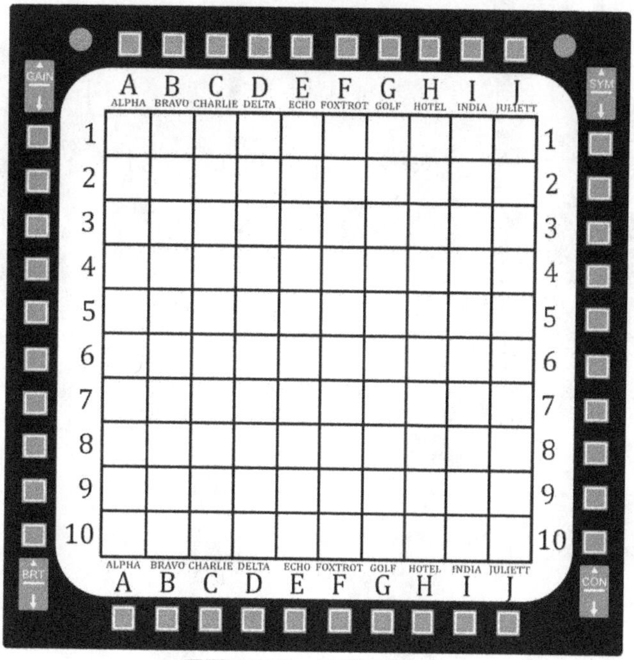

☒ HIT   ◯ MISS

Enemy Call Sign: _____

KEY

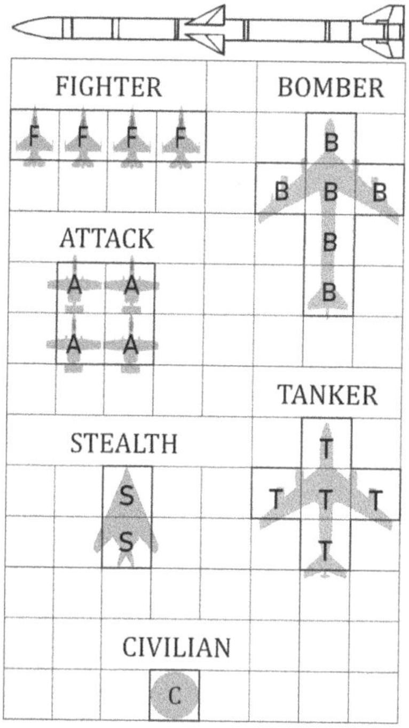

ENEMY AIRSPACE

	FIGHTER				BOMBER	
F	F	F	F		B	
				B	B	B
ATTACK					B	
A		A			B	
A		A				
				TANKER		
STEALTH				T		
	S			T	T	T
	S				T	

CIVILIAN

C

ENEMY AIRSPACE grid:

	A	B	C	D	E	F	G	H	I	J	
	ALPHA	BRAVO	CHARLIE	DELTA	ECHO	FOXTROT	GOLF	HOTEL	INDIA	JULIETT	
1											1
2											2
3											3
4											4
5											5
6											6
7											7
8											8
9											9
10											10
	ALPHA	BRAVO	CHARLIE	DELTA	ECHO	FOXTROT	GOLF	HOTEL	INDIA	JULIETT	
	A	B	C	D	E	F	G	H	I	J	

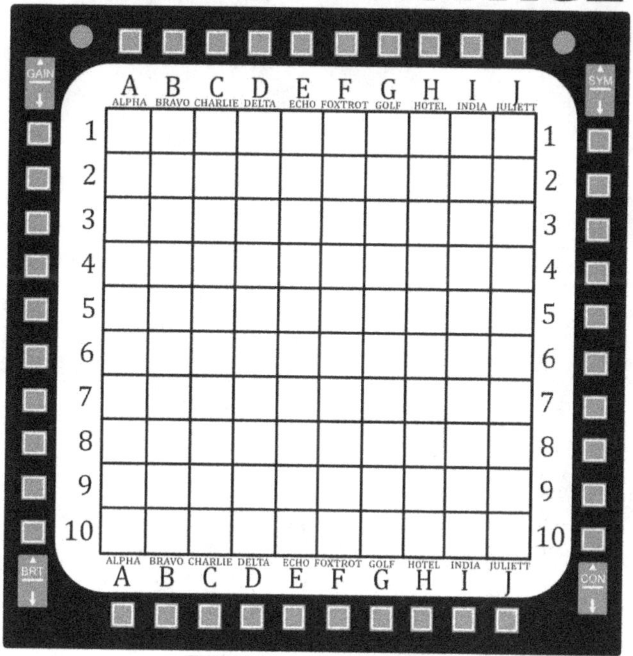

☒ HIT   ◯ MISS

FOLD ALONG DOTTED LINE AND TEAR

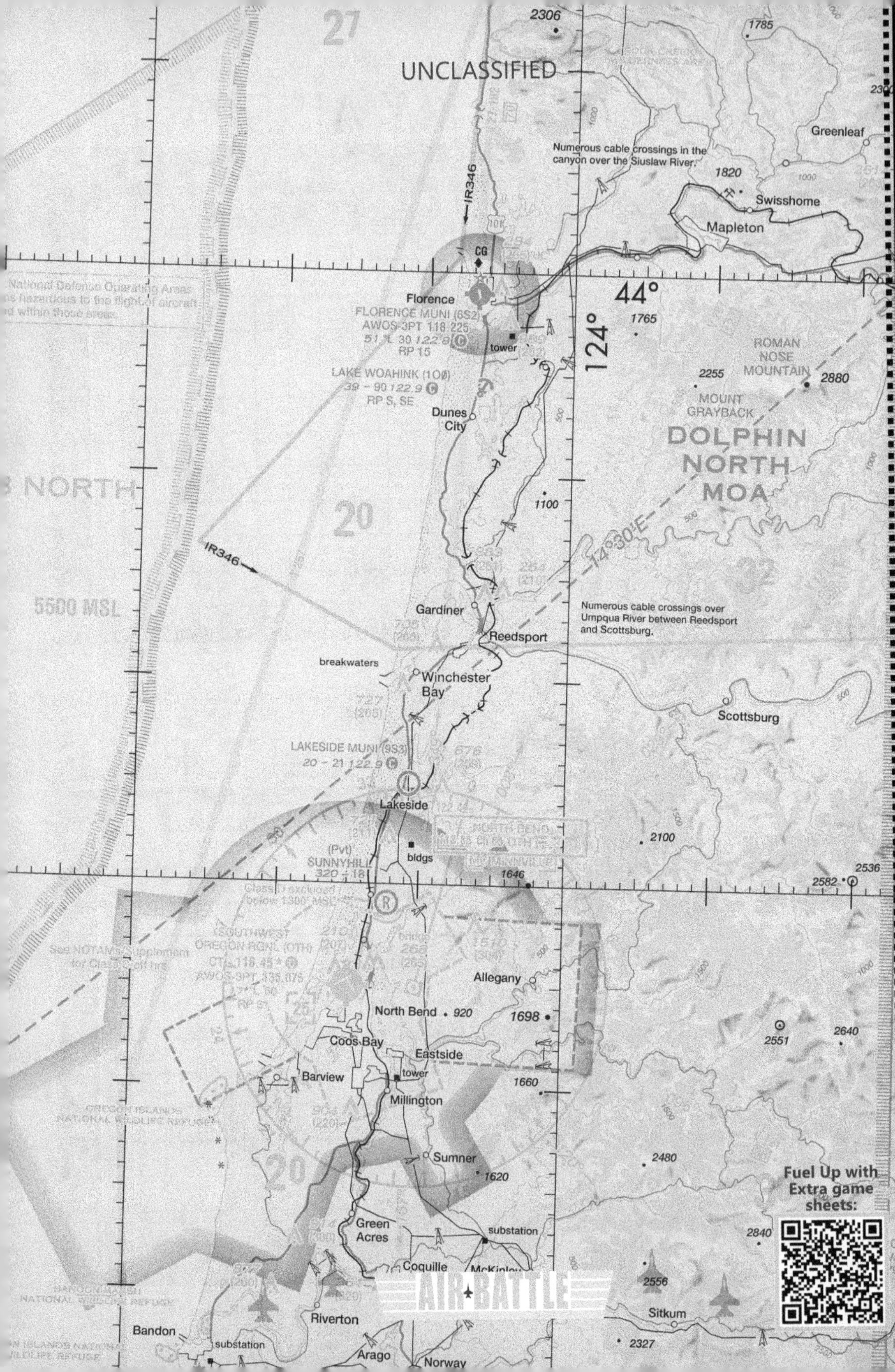
UNCLASSIFIED
2306
1785
Greenleaf
Numerous cable crossings in the canyon over the Siuslaw River.
1820
Swisshome
Mapleton
IR346
CG
Florence
FLORENCE MUNI (6S2)
AWOS-3PT 118.225
51 L 30 122.8
RP 15
tower
44°
124°
1765
LAKE WOAHINK (10G)
39 - 90 122.9
RP S, SE
ROMAN NOSE MOUNTAIN
2255
2880
MOUNT GRAYBACK
Dunes City
DOLPHIN NORTH MOA
NORTH
20
1100
14°30'E
IR346
5500 MSL
Gardiner
Numerous cable crossings over Umpqua River between Reedsport and Scottsburg.
Reedsport
breakwaters
Winchester Bay
Scottsburg
LAKESIDE MUNI (9S3)
20 - 21 122.9
Lakeside
NORTH BEND
2100
(Pvt) SUNNYHILL
320 - 18
bldgs
1646
2582
2536
Allegany
North Bend
920
1698
Coos Bay
Eastside
Barview
tower
Millington
1660
2551
2640
2480
Sumner
1620
Fuel Up with Extra game sheets:
Green Acres
substation
2840
Coquille
McKinley
AIR BATTLE
2556
Riverton
Sitkum
Bandon
substation
Arago
Norway
2327

FOLD ALONG DOTTED LINE AND TEAR

FOLD ALONG DOTTED LINE AND TEAR

Call Sign: _____

KEY

MY AIRSPACE

FIGHTER

F F F F

BOMBER

B
B B B
B
B

ATTACK

A A
A A

TANKER

T
T T T
T

STEALTH

S
S

CIVILIAN

C

MY AIRSPACE grid, columns A–J (ALPHA, BRAVO, CHARLIE, DELTA, ECHO, FOXTROT, GOLF, HOTEL, INDIA, JULIETT), rows 1–10.

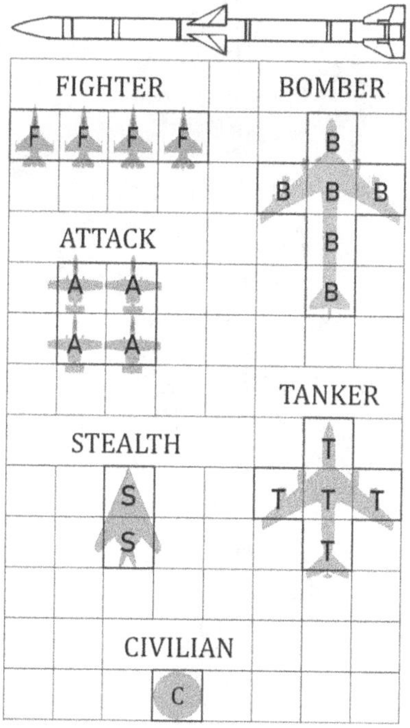

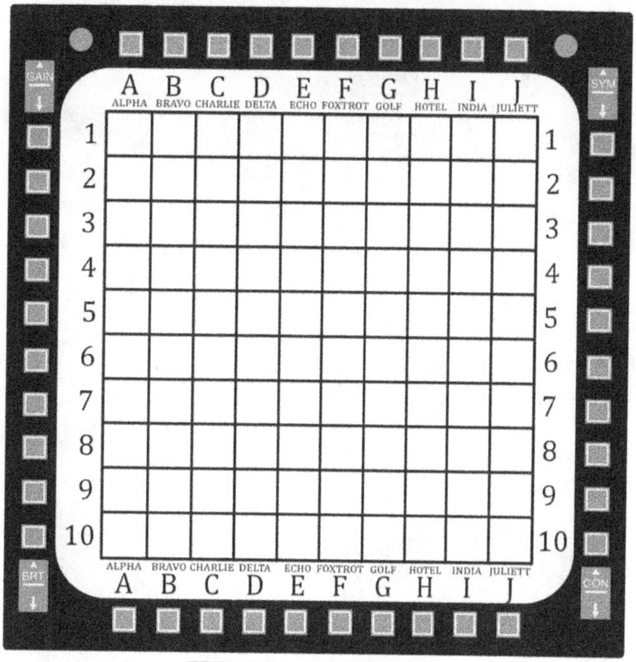

☒ HIT   ◯ MISS

Enemy Call Sign: _____

KEY

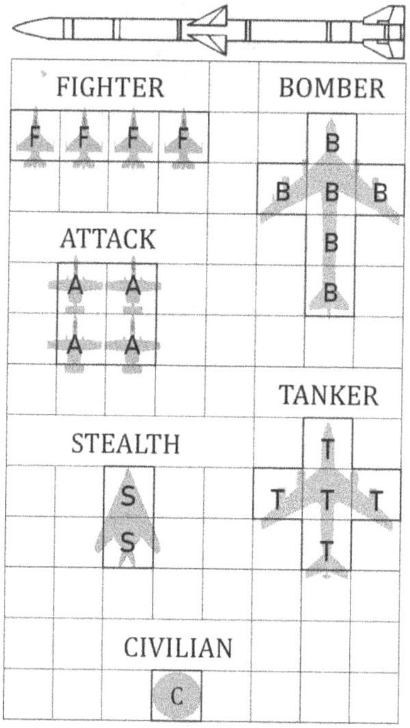

ENEMY AIRSPACE

FIGHTER

F F F F

BOMBER

B
B B B
B
B

ATTACK

A A
A A

TANKER

T
T T T
T

STEALTH

S
S

CIVILIAN

C

ENEMY AIRSPACE grid, columns A–J (ALPHA, BRAVO, CHARLIE, DELTA, ECHO, FOXTROT, GOLF, HOTEL, INDIA, JULIETT), rows 1–10.

☒ HIT   ◯ MISS

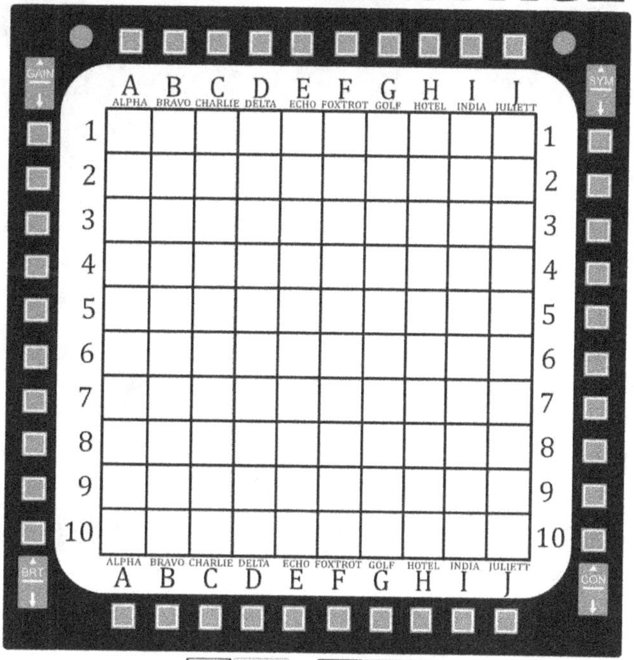

Nesika Beach

UNCLASSIFIED

3778

4126

4401

4560

towers

GOLD BEACH·MUNI (4S1)
AWOS-3PT 118.15
21 *L 32 122.8 Ⓒ
RP 16

Wedderburn

3512

Gold Beach

4220

4640

4320

Magnetic disturbance of as much as 6° exists at ground level between Cape Sebastian and Gold Beach

KALMIOPSIS
WILDERNESS AREA

5120

Cape Sebastian

2142

OREGON ISLANDS
NATIONAL WILDLIFE REFUGE

Pistol River

3240

Carpenterville

3432

W-93
NORTH

MOUNT
EMILY

DOLPHIN
NORTH
MOA

4680

4742

2925

KALMIOPSIS
WILDERNESS AREA

BROOKINGS (BOK)
AWOS-3PT 132.025
452 L 29 122.8 Ⓒ
RP 12

ILLINOIS
VALLEY (3S4)
1394 *L 48 122

OREGON ISLANDS
NATIONAL WILDLIFE
REFUGE

Harbor

4120

Brookings

OREGON   2707

CALIFORNIA   2680   124°   42°   3822

Smith
River   2440

2635

Fort
Dick   A 500

prison   Gasquet

JACK MC
NAMARA FLD (CEC)
ASOS 119.925
61 *L 50
122.8 Ⓒ

WARD FLD (909)
356 30 122.9

4157   5292

Crescent
City

330

235

DOLPHIN
SOUTH
MOA

3000

CASTLE ROCK
NATIONAL WILDLIFE
REFUGE

5360

30

bldgs

VORTAC
CRESCENT CITY
Ch 57 CEC

2360

ranches

OAKLAND

W-93
SOUTH

3650

4960

towers

Requa

RED
MTN   4253

Klamath
Glen

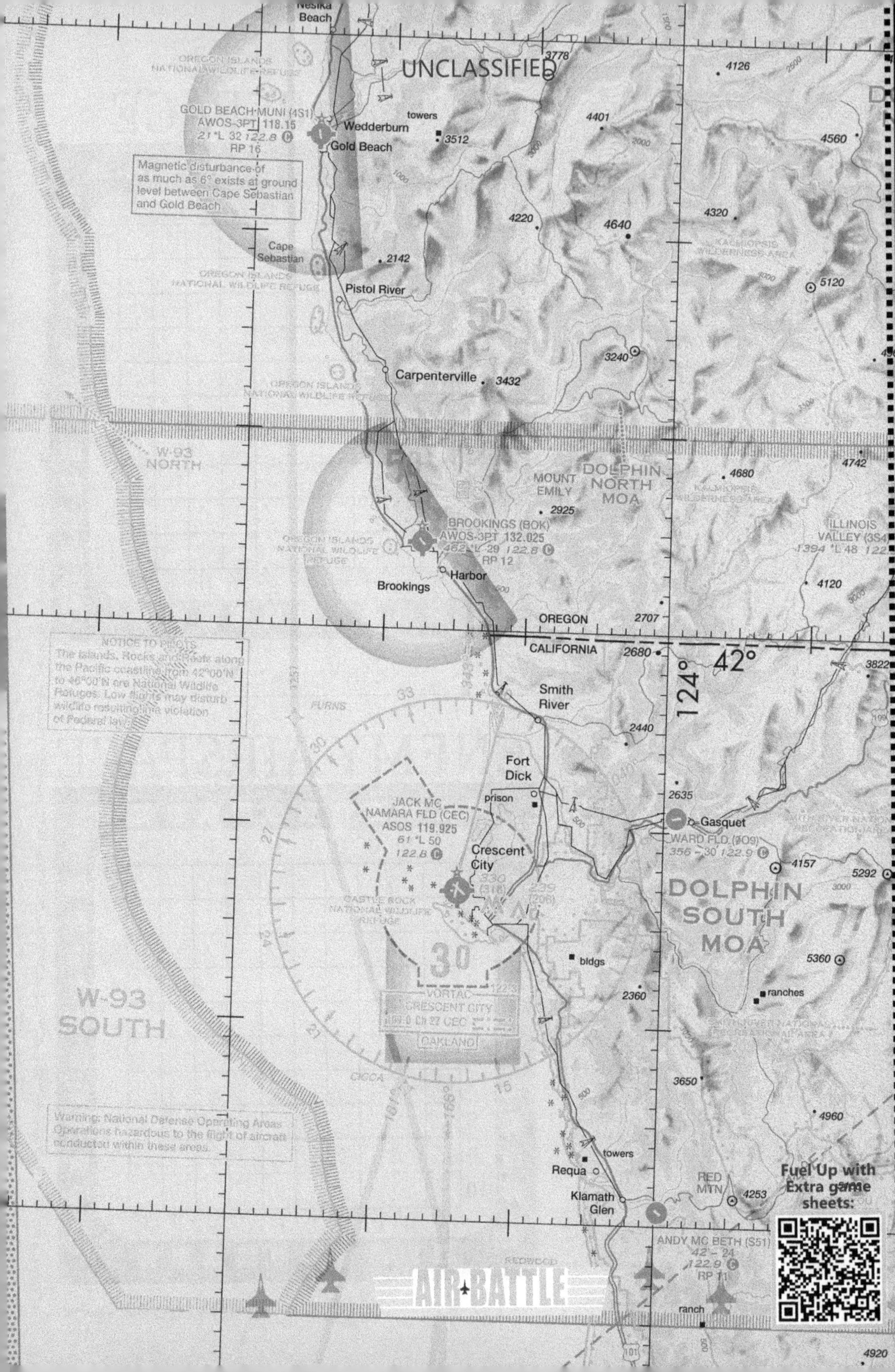

Fuel Up with Extra game sheets:

AIR BATTLE

REDWOOD

ANDY MC BETH (S51)
42 24
122.9
RP 11

ranch

4920

Call Sign: _____

KEY

FIGHTER
F F F F

BOMBER
B
B B B
B
B

ATTACK
A   A
A   A

STEALTH
S
S

TANKER
T
T T T
T

CIVILIAN
C

MY AIRSPACE

	A	B	C	D	E	F	G	H	I	J	
	ALPHA	BRAVO	CHARLIE	DELTA	ECHO	FOXTROT	GOLF	HOTEL	INDIA	JULIETT	
1											1
2											2
3											3
4											4
5											5
6											6
7											7
8											8
9											9
10											10
	ALPHA	BRAVO	CHARLIE	DELTA	ECHO	FOXTROT	GOLF	HOTEL	INDIA	JULIETT	
	A	B	C	D	E	F	G	H	I	J	

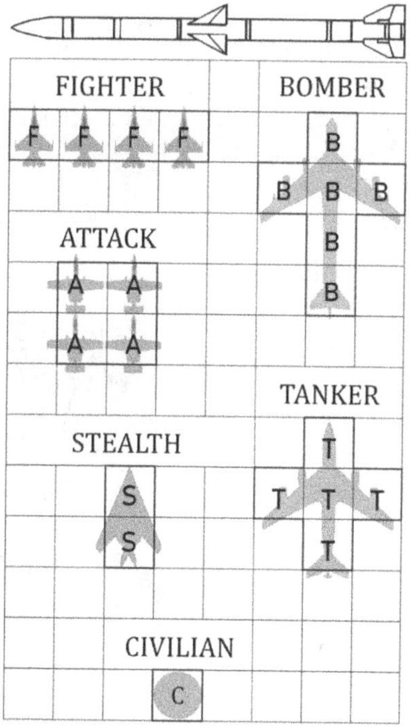

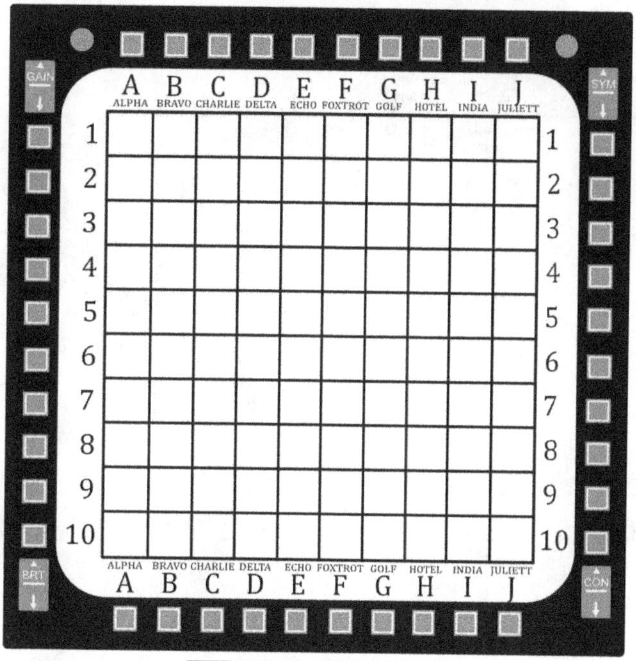

⊠ HIT   ◯ MISS

Enemy Call Sign: _____

KEY

FIGHTER
F F F F

BOMBER
B
B B B
B

ATTACK
A   A
A   A

STEALTH
S
S

TANKER
T
T T T
T

CIVILIAN
C

ENEMY AIRSPACE

	A	B	C	D	E	F	G	H	I	J	
	ALPHA	BRAVO	CHARLIE	DELTA	ECHO	FOXTROT	GOLF	HOTEL	INDIA	JULIETT	
1											1
2											2
3											3
4											4
5											5
6											6
7											7
8											8
9											9
10											10
	ALPHA	BRAVO	CHARLIE	DELTA	ECHO	FOXTROT	GOLF	HOTEL	INDIA	JULIETT	
	A	B	C	D	E	F	G	H	I	J	

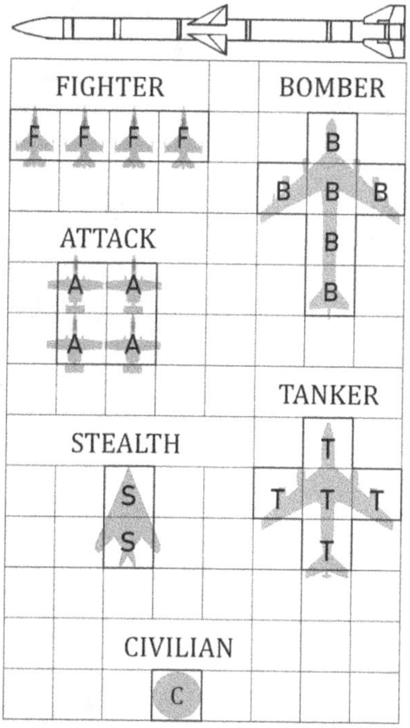

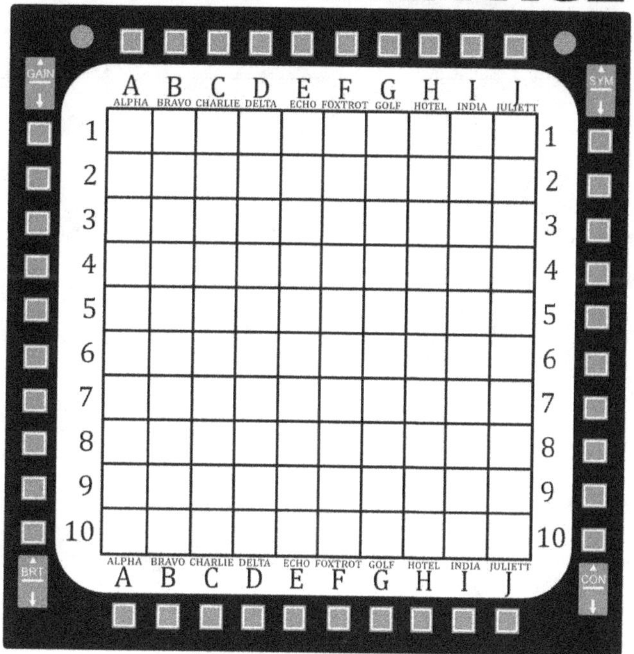

⊠ HIT   ◯ MISS

FOLD ALONG DOTTED LINE AND TEAR

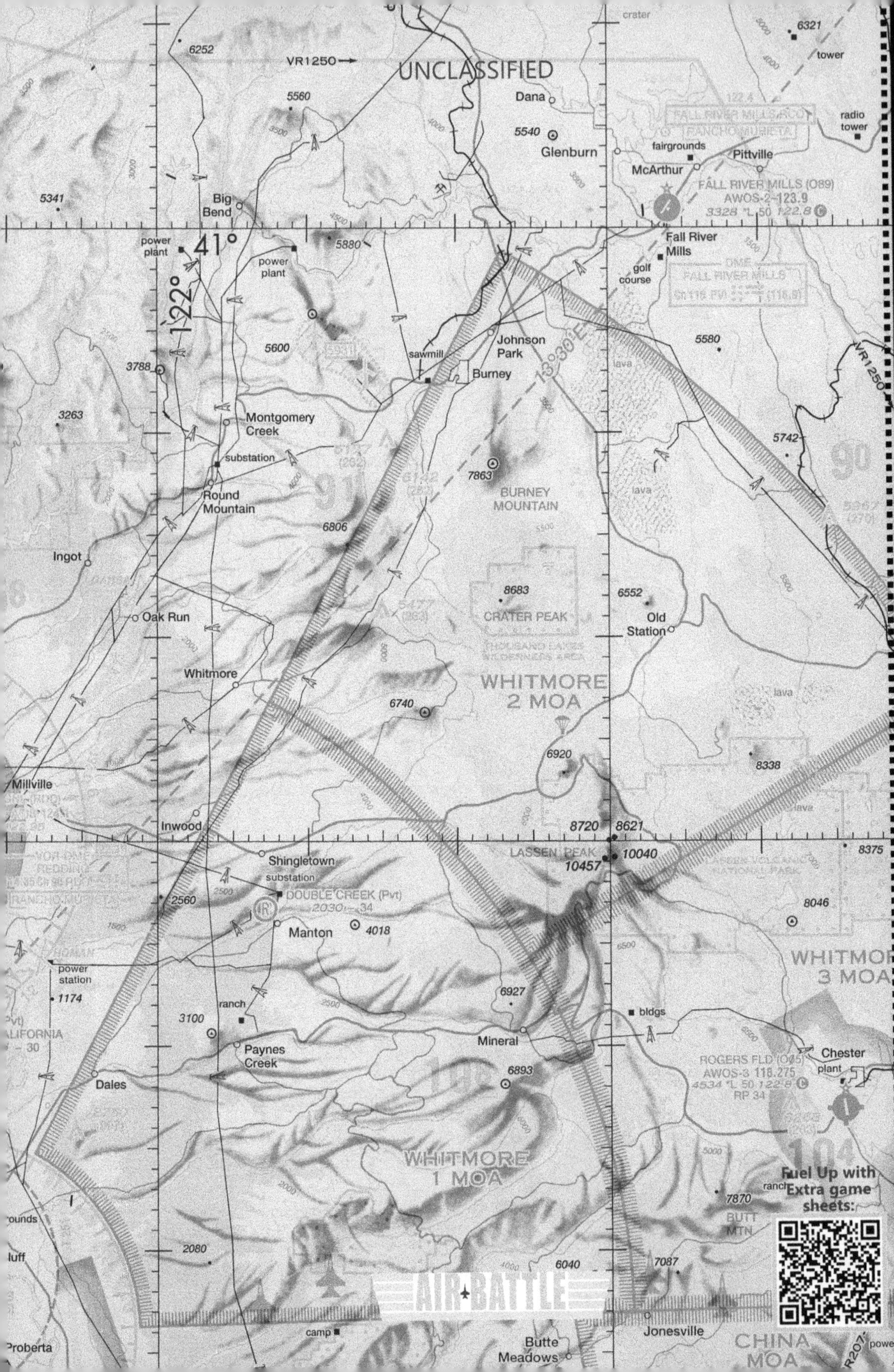
UNCLASSIFIED
VR1250
6252
5560
Dana
5540
Glenburn
crater
6321
tower
radio tower
122.4
fairgrounds
Pittville
McArthur
FALL RIVER MILLS (O89)
AWOS-2 123.9
3328 *L 50 122.8
5341
Big Bend
power plant
41°
122°
5880
Fall River Mills
golf course
FALL RIVER MILLS
5600
3788
sawmill
Johnson Park
Burney
13°30'E
5580
lava
3263
Montgomery Creek
substation
Round Mountain
7863
BURNEY MOUNTAIN
5742
6806
Ingot
8683
CRATER PEAK
6552
Old Station
Oak Run
Whitmore
WHITMORE 2 MOA
6740
6920
8338
Millville
Inwood
8720
8621
LASSEN PEAK
10457
10040
8375
Shingletown
substation
DOUBLE CREEK (Pvt)
2030 – 34
2560
Manton
4018
8046
power station
1174
WHITMORE 3 MOA
ranch
6927
3100
bldgs
Paynes Creek
Mineral
Chester
ROGERS FLD (O05)
AWOS-3 118.275
4534 *L 50 122.8
RP 34
plant
6893
Dales
WHITMORE 1 MOA
Fuel Up with Extra game sheets:
7870
ranch
BUTT MTN
2080
6040
7087
AIR BATTLE
camp
Butte Meadows
Jonesville
CHINA MOA
Proberta

FOLD ALONG DOTTED LINE AND TEAR

FOLD ALONG DOTTED LINE AND TEAR

Call Sign: _____

KEY

MY AIRSPACE

FIGHTER

BOMBER

ATTACK

TANKER

STEALTH

CIVILIAN

MY AIRSPACE

	A	B	C	D	E	F	G	H	I	J	
	ALPHA	BRAVO	CHARLIE	DELTA	ECHO	FOXTROT	GOLF	HOTEL	INDIA	JULIETT	
1											1
2											2
3											3
4											4
5											5
6											6
7											7
8											8
9											9
10											10
	ALPHA	BRAVO	CHARLIE	DELTA	ECHO	FOXTROT	GOLF	HOTEL	INDIA	JULIETT	
	A	B	C	D	E	F	G	H	I	J	

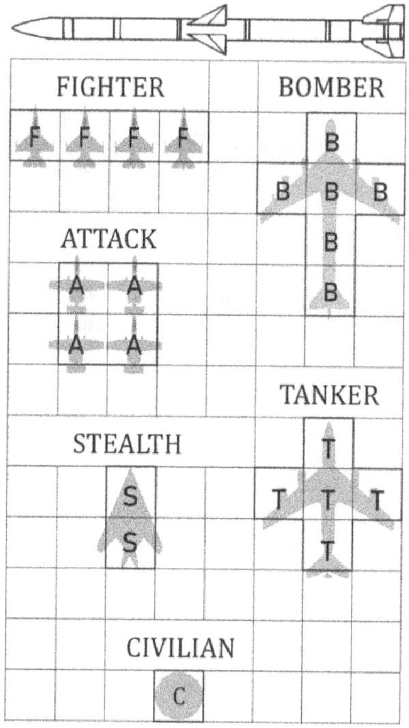

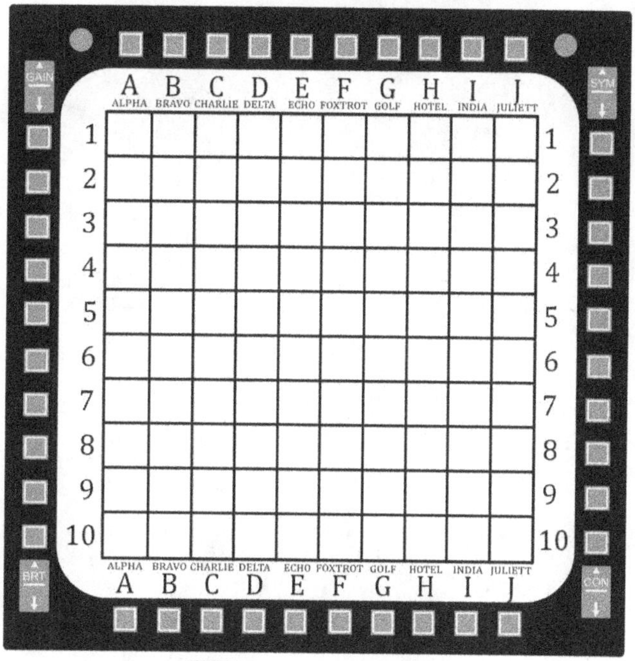

☒ HIT   ◯ MISS

Enemy Call Sign: _____

KEY

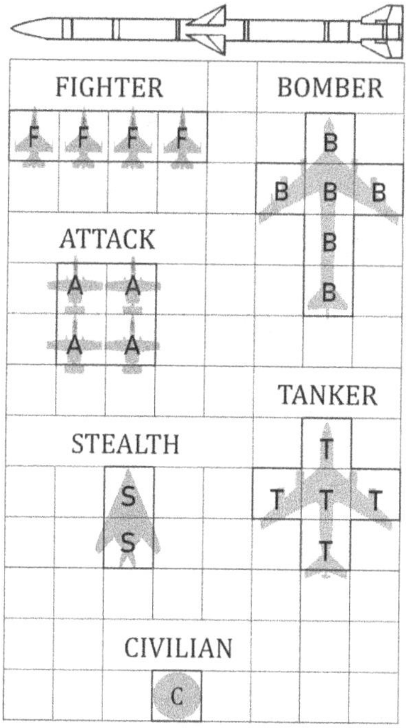

ENEMY AIRSPACE

FIGHTER

BOMBER

ATTACK

TANKER

STEALTH

CIVILIAN

ENEMY AIRSPACE

	A	B	C	D	E	F	G	H	I	J	
	ALPHA	BRAVO	CHARLIE	DELTA	ECHO	FOXTROT	GOLF	HOTEL	INDIA	JULIETT	
1											1
2											2
3											3
4											4
5											5
6											6
7											7
8											8
9											9
10											10
	ALPHA	BRAVO	CHARLIE	DELTA	ECHO	FOXTROT	GOLF	HOTEL	INDIA	JULIETT	
	A	B	C	D	E	F	G	H	I	J	

☒ HIT   ◯ MISS

FOLD ALONG DOTTED LINE AND TEAR

FOLD ALONG DOTTED LINE AND TEAR

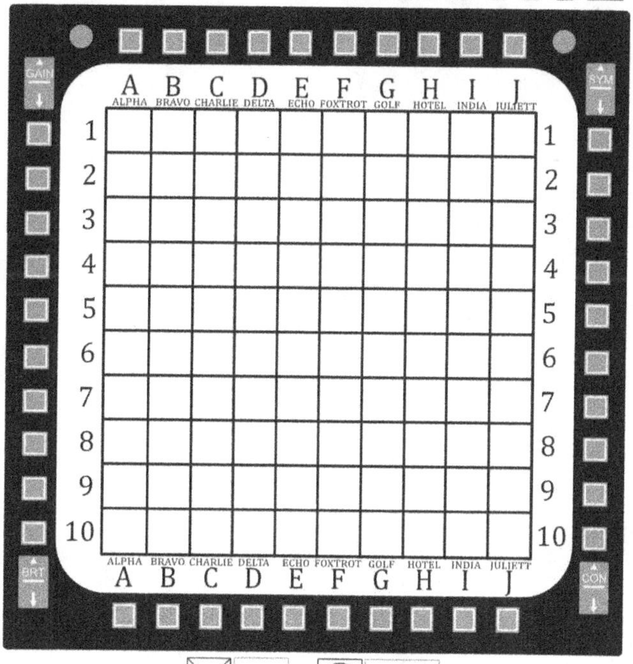

UNCLASSIFIED
KLAMATH FALLS
OLENE
Dairy
Bonanza
Lorella
SKY WAGON RANCH LLC (Pvt) 4150 - 32
(Pvt) NAIL SPRING RANCH 4249 - 25
(Pvt) ALLENS AIRSTRIP 4410 - 25
(Pvt) WILDERNESS 4540 - 25
HORSEFLY MOUNTAIN
BUTTE
GOOSE NORTH MOA
WORDEN
(Pvt) LONG RANCH 4080 - 19
Merrill
MALIN (4S7) 4053 - 28 122.9
MALIN
OREGON
CALIFORNIA
42°
121°
bldg
Tulelake
TULELAKE MUNI (O81) 4049 L 36 122.9 RP 30
TULE LAKE NATIONAL WILDLIFE REFUGE
CLEAR LAKE NATIONAL WILDLIFE REFUGE
GOOSE NORTH MOA
radar array
VR1251
VR1254
VR1261
VR1250
(Pvt) TRIPLE R RANCH 4380 - 23
BELL RANCH (Pvt) 4607 - 50
station
ROUND MOUNTAIN
ALTURAS MUNI (AAT) ASOS 124.175 4378 L 42 122.8 RP 13-21
Alturas
Canby
CALIFORNIA PINES (A24) 4389 - 41 122.9 RP 23
(Pvt) BATES FLD 4400 - 22
GOOSE SOUTH MOA
LIKELY (Pvt) 4420 - 19
Adin
ADIN (A26) 4234 - 28 122.9
SOUTHARD FLD (O55) 4163 L 30 122.9
Lookout
Day
Pondosa
Bieber
Nubieber
Dana
Glenburn
McArthur
Pittville
fairgrounds
FALL RIVER MILLS (O89) AWOS-2 123.9 3328 L 50 122.8
Fall River Mills
Johnson Park
Little Valley
13°30'E
AIR BATTLE
Fuel Up with Extra game sheets:

FOLD ALONG DOTTED LINE AND TEAR

FOLD ALONG DOTTED LINE AND TEAR

Call Sign: _____

KEY

MY AIRSPACE

FIGHTER
F F F F

BOMBER
B
B B B
B
B

ATTACK
A A
A A

TANKER
T
T T T
T

STEALTH
S
S

CIVILIAN
C

MY AIRSPACE

	A	B	C	D	E	F	G	H	I	J	
	ALPHA	BRAVO	CHARLIE	DELTA	ECHO	FOXTROT	GOLF	HOTEL	INDIA	JULIETT	
1											1
2											2
3											3
4											4
5											5
6											6
7											7
8											8
9											9
10											10

ALPHA BRAVO CHARLIE DELTA ECHO FOXTROT GOLF HOTEL INDIA JULIETT
A B C D E F G H I J

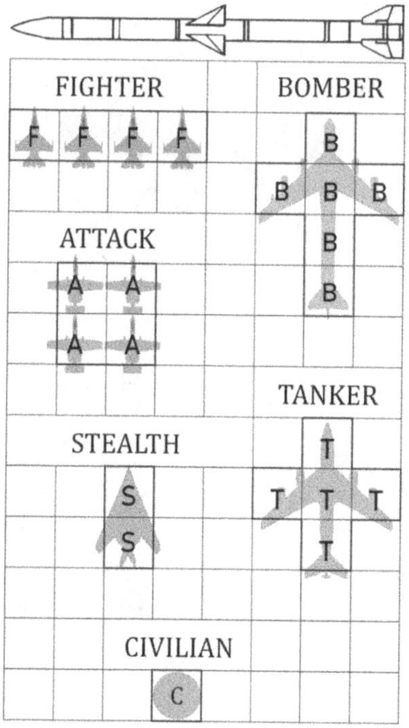

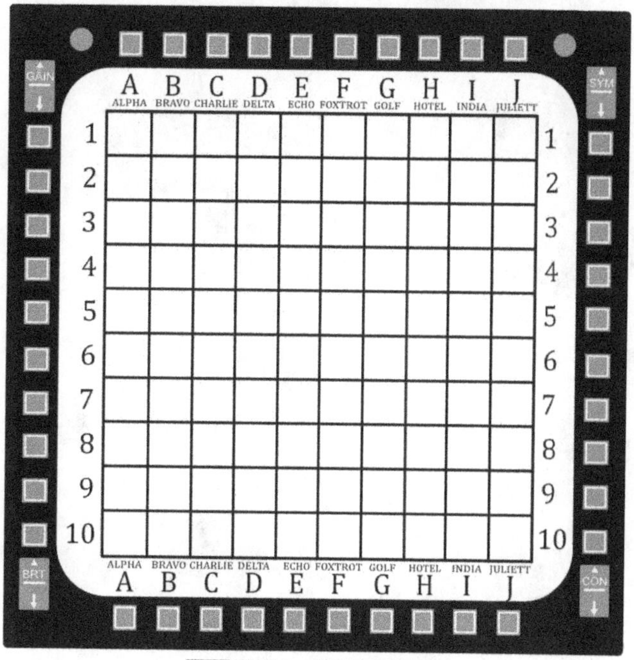

☒ HIT   ◯ MISS

Enemy Call Sign: _____

KEY

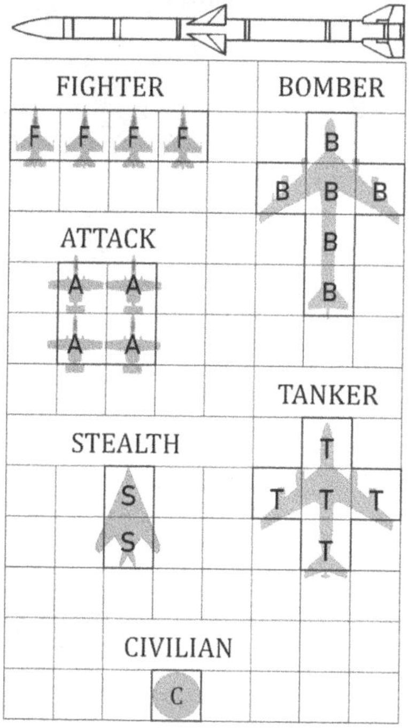

ENEMY AIRSPACE

FIGHTER
F F F F

BOMBER
B
B B B
B
B

ATTACK
A A
A A

TANKER
T
T T T
T

STEALTH
S
S

CIVILIAN
C

	A	B	C	D	E	F	G	H	I	J	
	ALPHA	BRAVO	CHARLIE	DELTA	ECHO	FOXTROT	GOLF	HOTEL	INDIA	JULIETT	
1											1
2											2
3											3
4											4
5											5
6											6
7											7
8											8
9											9
10											10

ALPHA BRAVO CHARLIE DELTA ECHO FOXTROT GOLF HOTEL INDIA JULIETT
A B C D E F G H I J

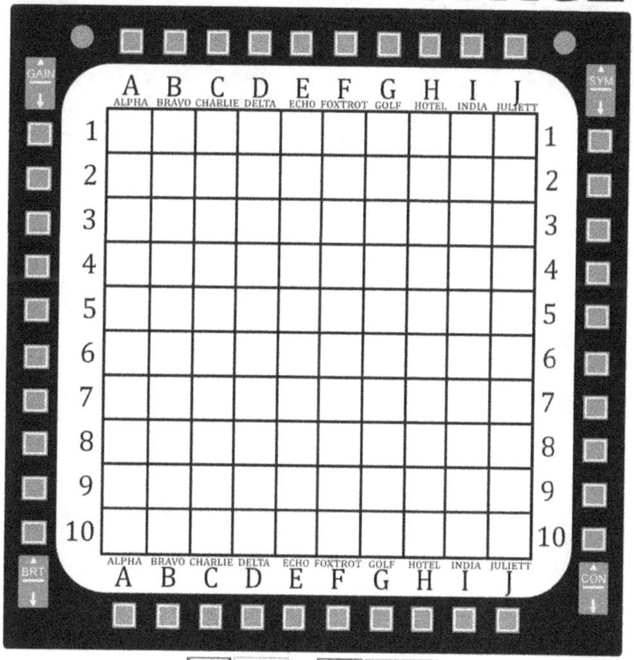

☒ HIT   ◯ MISS

FOLD ALONG DOTTED LINE AND TEAR

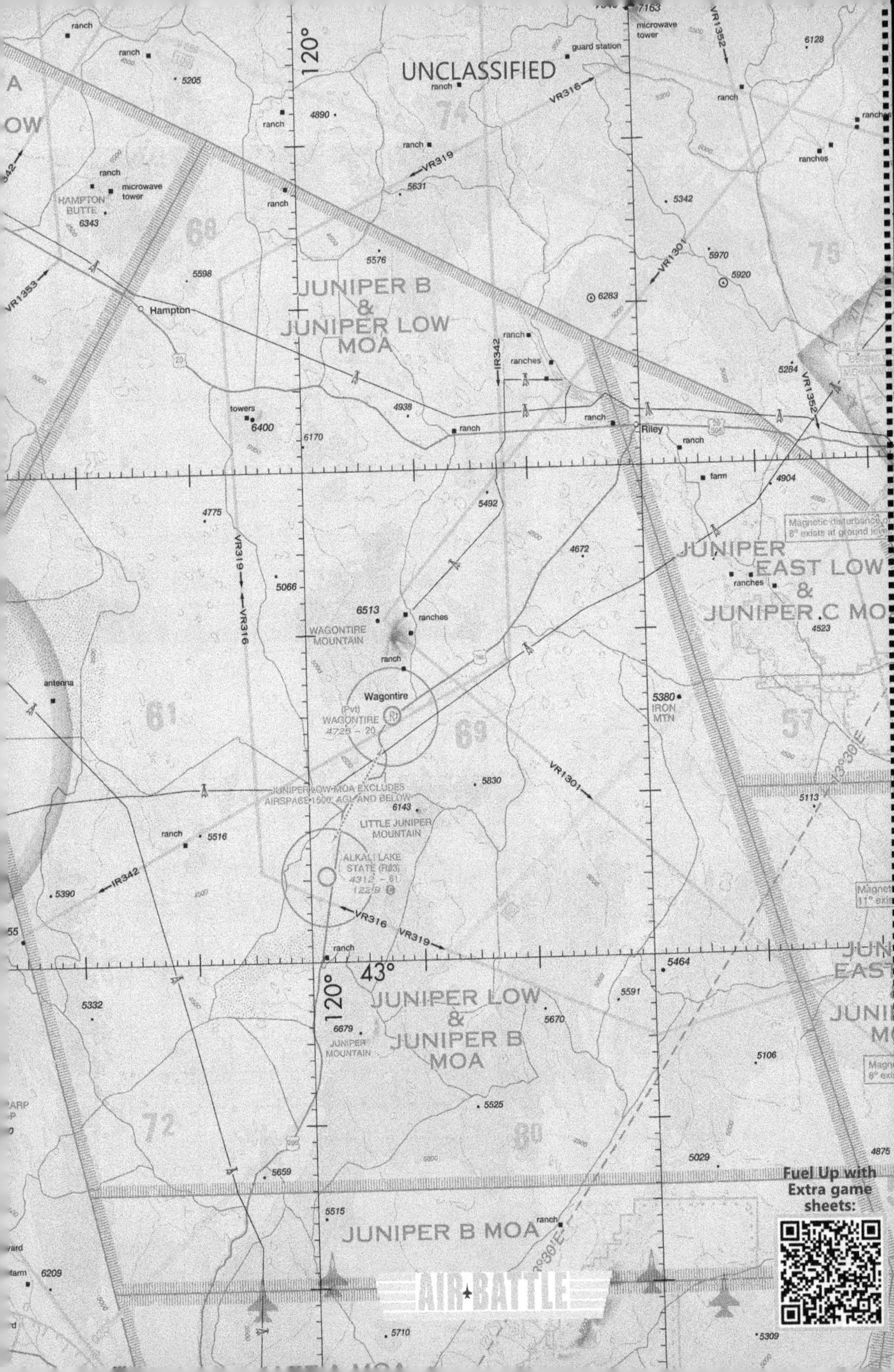
UNCLASSIFIED
120°
43°
JUNIPER B & JUNIPER LOW MOA
JUNIPER EAST LOW & JUNIPER C MOA
JUNIPER LOW & JUNIPER B MOA
JUNIPER B MOA
JUNIPER LOW MOA EXCLUDES AIRSPACE 1500' AGL AND BELOW
Magnetic disturbance of 8° exists at ground level
HAMPTON BUTTE
6343
Hampton
Riley
Wagontire
(Pvt) WAGONTIRE
4728 - 20
WAGONTIRE MOUNTAIN
LITTLE JUNIPER MOUNTAIN
ALKALI LAKE STATE (RB3)
4312 - 61
122.9
JUNIPER MOUNTAIN
5380 IRON MTN
VR316
VR319
VR1301
VR1352
VR1353
IR342
microwave tower
guard station
ranch
ranches
farm
towers
antenna
6400
6513
6679
7163
6128
5205
4890
5631
5342
5970
5920
6283
5598
5576
5284
4938
6170
4904
4775
5492
4672
5066
4523
5830
5113
6143
5516
5390
5464
5591
5332
5670
5106
5525
5029
4875
5659
5515
6209
5710
5309
AIR BATTLE

Fuel Up with Extra game sheets:

FOLD ALONG DOTTED LINE AND TEAR

FOLD ALONG DOTTED LINE AND TEAR

Call Sign: _____

KEY

FIGHTER
F F F F

ATTACK
A A
A A

STEALTH
S
S

BOMBER
B
B B B
B
B

TANKER
T
T T T
T

CIVILIAN
C

MY AIRSPACE

	A	B	C	D	E	F	G	H	I	J	
	ALPHA	BRAVO	CHARLIE	DELTA	ECHO	FOXTROT	GOLF	HOTEL	INDIA	JULIETT	
1											1
2											2
3											3
4											4
5											5
6											6
7											7
8											8
9											9
10											10
	ALPHA	BRAVO	CHARLIE	DELTA	ECHO	FOXTROT	GOLF	HOTEL	INDIA	JULIETT	
	A	B	C	D	E	F	G	H	I	J	

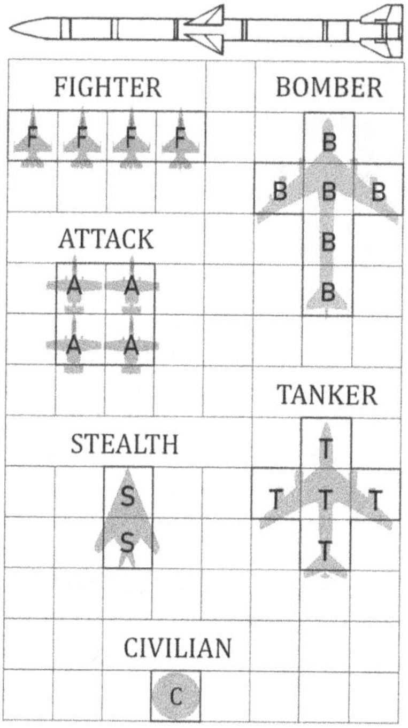

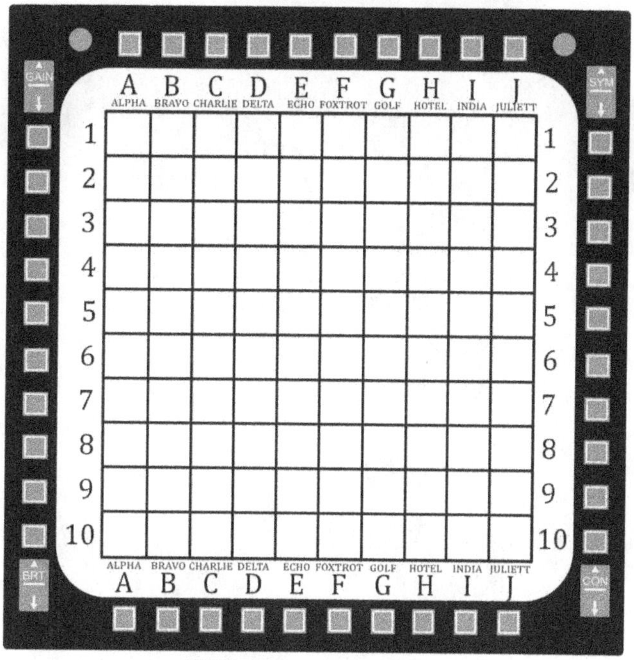

☒ HIT   ◯ MISS

Enemy Call Sign: _____

KEY

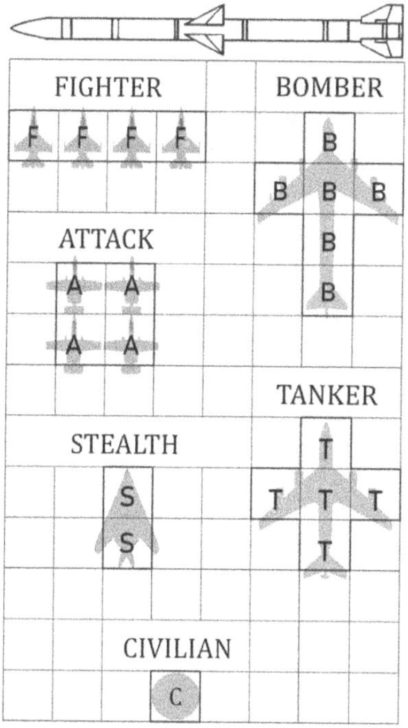

FIGHTER
F F F F

ATTACK
A A
A A

STEALTH
S
S

BOMBER
B
B B B
B
B

TANKER
T
T T T
T

CIVILIAN
C

ENEMY AIRSPACE

	A	B	C	D	E	F	G	H	I	J	
	ALPHA	BRAVO	CHARLIE	DELTA	ECHO	FOXTROT	GOLF	HOTEL	INDIA	JULIETT	
1											1
2											2
3											3
4											4
5											5
6											6
7											7
8											8
9											9
10											10
	ALPHA	BRAVO	CHARLIE	DELTA	ECHO	FOXTROT	GOLF	HOTEL	INDIA	JULIETT	
	A	B	C	D	E	F	G	H	I	J	

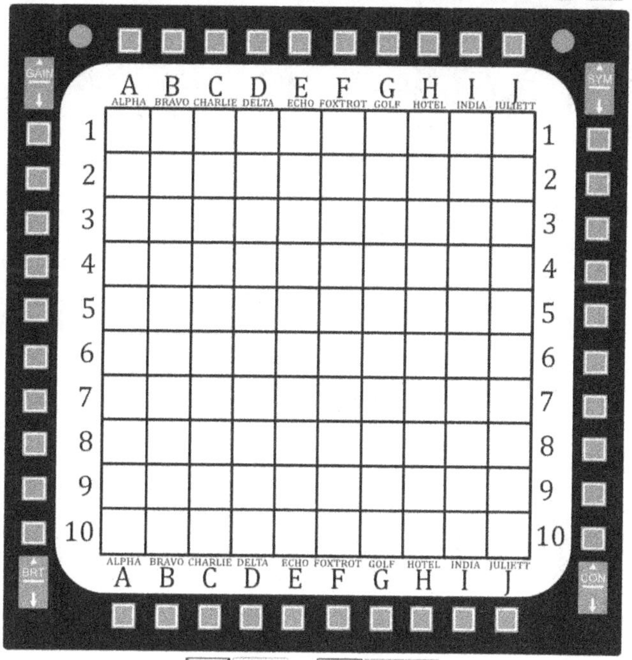

☒ HIT   ◯ MISS

FOLD ALONG DOTTED LINE AND TEAR

UNCLASSIFIED
JUNIPER B MOA
JUNIPER D
HART A MOA
HART B MOA
HART C
HART D MOA
HART E MOA
HART F MOA
HART MTN
BEATYS BUTTE
DRAKE PEAK
CRANE MOUNTAIN
BIDWELL MOUNTAIN
EAGLE PEAK
Valley Falls
Plush
Adel
New Pine Creek
Fort Bidwell
Lake City
Cedarville
Eagleville
microwave tower
OREGON
NEVADA
CALIFORNIA
42°
120°
119°
VR1353
VR1254
VR1251
IR300
IR313
(Pvt) ROARING SPRINGS
(Pvt) SOLDIER MEADOW 1
FORT BIDWELL (A26)
CEDARVILLE (O59)
AIR BATTLE

Fuel Up with Extra game sheets:

FOLD ALONG DOTTED LINE AND TEAR

FOLD ALONG DOTTED LINE AND TEAR

Call Sign: _____

KEY

FIGHTER

BOMBER

ATTACK

TANKER

STEALTH

CIVILIAN

MY AIRSPACE

	A	B	C	D	E	F	G	H	I	J	
	ALPHA	BRAVO	CHARLIE	DELTA	ECHO	FOXTROT	GOLF	HOTEL	INDIA	JULIETT	
1											1
2											2
3											3
4											4
5											5
6											6
7											7
8											8
9											9
10											10

ALPHA BRAVO CHARLIE DELTA ECHO FOXTROT GOLF HOTEL INDIA JULIETT

A B C D E F G H I J

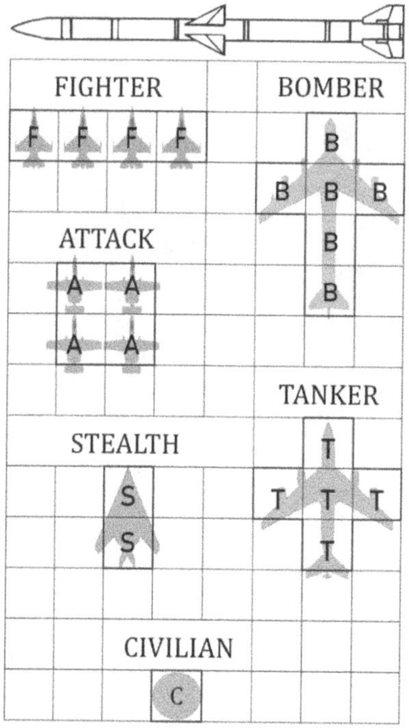

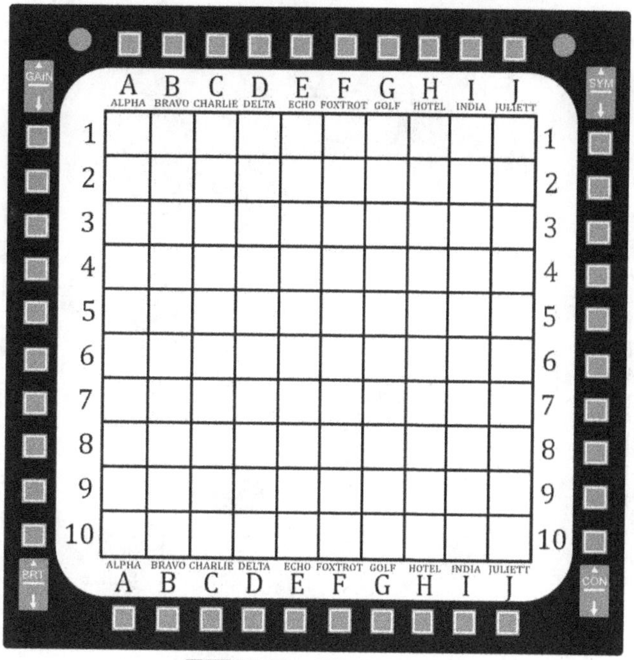

⊠ HIT   ◯ MISS

Enemy Call Sign: _____

KEY

FIGHTER

BOMBER

ATTACK

TANKER

STEALTH

CIVILIAN

ENEMY AIRSPACE

	A	B	C	D	E	F	G	H	I	J	
	ALPHA	BRAVO	CHARLIE	DELTA	ECHO	FOXTROT	GOLF	HOTEL	INDIA	JULIETT	
1											1
2											2
3											3
4											4
5											5
6											6
7											7
8											8
9											9
10											10

ALPHA BRAVO CHARLIE DELTA ECHO FOXTROT GOLF HOTEL INDIA JULIETT

A B C D E F G H I J

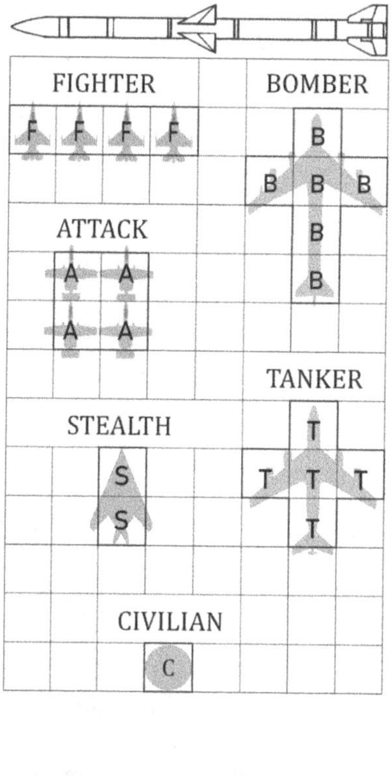

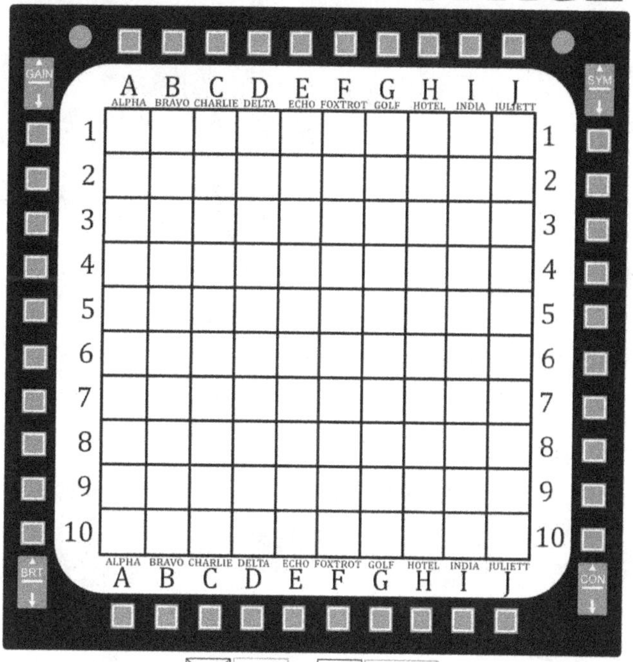

⊠ HIT   ◯ MISS

FOLD ALONG DOTTED LINE AND TEAR

UNCLASSIFIED
MTN
8182
microwave tower
7240
ranch
41°
120°
8533
7719
6476
IR313
ranch
ranches
ranch
7635
GRANITE PEAK
9000
6832
RENO MOA
76
94
BLACK ROCK CITY (Pvt)
3908 - 60
6130
VR1251
VR1254-1261
ranches
ranch
Gerlach
ranch
3859
farm
farm
6591
7115
Empire
(Pvt)
EMPIRE
3990 - 38
6092
DESERT
CREEK
SMOKE
7420
CALIFORNIA
NEVADA
6849
PAH RUM PEAK
7608
13°E
ranch
radio tower
6271
KUMIVA PEAK
8237
6221
bldgs
86
IR207
90
5877
7114
5494
TOHAKUM PEAK
8160
VR202
VR1251-1254-1261
VR202
7574
6584
Fuel Up with Extra game sheets:

FOLD ALONG DOTTED LINE AND TEAR

FOLD ALONG DOTTED LINE AND TEAR

FOLD ALONG DOTTED LINE AND TEAR

Call Sign: ____________

AIR BATTLE

MY AIRSPACE

KEY

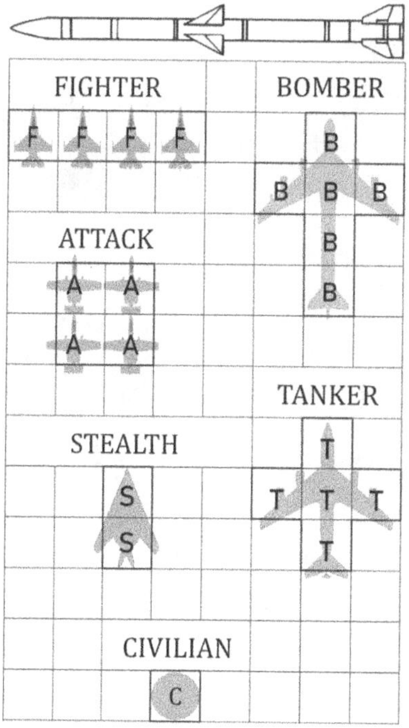

FIGHTER
F F F F
BOMBER
B
B B B
B
B
ATTACK
A A
A A
TANKER
T
T T T
T
STEALTH
S
S
CIVILIAN
C

GAIN SYM

	A ALPHA	B BRAVO	C CHARLIE	D DELTA	E ECHO	F FOXTROT	G GOLF	H HOTEL	I INDIA	J JULIETT	
1											1
2											2
3											3
4											4
5											5
6											6
7											7
8											8
9											9
10											10
	ALPHA A	BRAVO B	CHARLIE C	DELTA D	ECHO E	FOXTROT F	GOLF G	HOTEL H	INDIA I	JULIETT J	

BRT CON

☒ HIT ◯ MISS

Enemy Call Sign: ________

ENEMY AIRSPACE

KEY

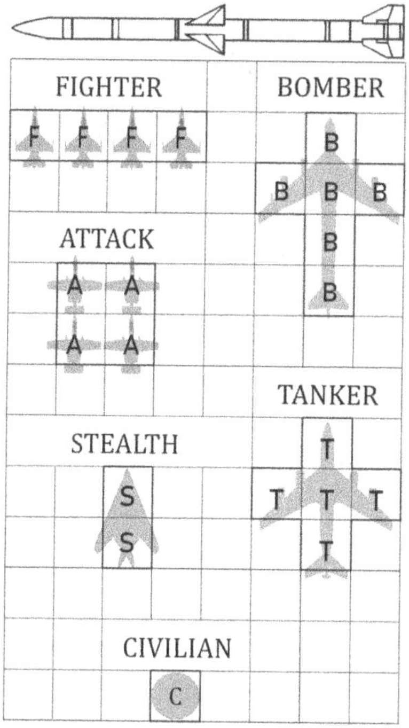

FIGHTER
F F F F
BOMBER
B
B B B
B
B
ATTACK
A A
A A
TANKER
T
T T T
T
STEALTH
S
S
CIVILIAN
C

GAIN SYM

	A ALPHA	B BRAVO	C CHARLIE	D DELTA	E ECHO	F FOXTROT	G GOLF	H HOTEL	I INDIA	J JULIETT	
1											1
2											2
3											3
4											4
5											5
6											6
7											7
8											8
9											9
10											10
	ALPHA A	BRAVO B	CHARLIE C	DELTA D	ECHO E	FOXTROT F	GOLF G	HOTEL H	INDIA I	JULIETT J	

BRT CON

☒ HIT ◯ MISS

FOLD ALONG DOTTED LINE AND TEAR

UNCLASSIFIED
OWYHEE RESERVOIR STATE (28U)
2620 - 18 122.9
(Pvt) CROWLEY RANCH AIRSTRIP
4128 - 25
Venator
VR1302
IR304
IR300
VR319
VR316
MAHOGANY MOUNTAIN
SADDLE A MOA
SADDLE B MOA
(Pvt) BLACK BULL SPRING
4114 - 14
SADDLE BUTTE
5286
IR313
43°
118°
(Pvt) SKINNER RANCH
4273 - 22
Danner
Arock
Rome
(Pvt) ROME SERVICE
3387 - 29
VR1301
ROME STATE (REO)
4053 - 80 122.9
MST
-7 (+6DT) = UTC
PST
-8 (+7DT) = UTC
VR389
VR391
IR303
VR1352
BLUE MOUNTAIN PASS
5294
(Pvt) WHITEHORSE RANCH
4447 - 32
MOA REAL TIME INFORMATION
CTC COWBOY 134.1 OR
208-828-4804
PARADISE NO
MOA
Magnetic disturbance of as much as 14° exists at ground level
AIR BATTLE
MC DERMITT STATE (26U)
Fuel Up with
Extra game
sheets:

FOLD ALONG DOTTED LINE AND TEAR

FOLD ALONG DOTTED LINE AND TEAR

Call Sign: _____

KEY

FIGHTER	BOMBER
F F F F	B / B B B / B / B

ATTACK	
A A / A A	TANKER

STEALTH	T / T T T / T
S S	

CIVILIAN	
C	

AIR BATTLE

MY AIRSPACE

	A	B	C	D	E	F	G	H	I	J	
	ALPHA	BRAVO	CHARLIE	DELTA	ECHO	FOXTROT	GOLF	HOTEL	INDIA	JULIETT	
1											1
2											2
3											3
4											4
5											5
6											6
7											7
8											8
9											9
10											10
	A	B	C	D	E	F	G	H	I	J	

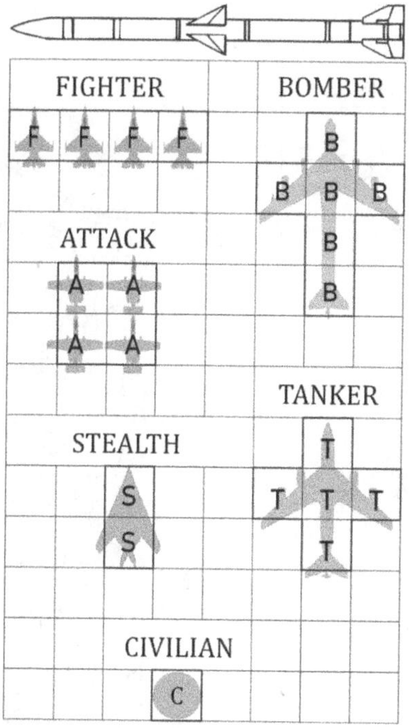

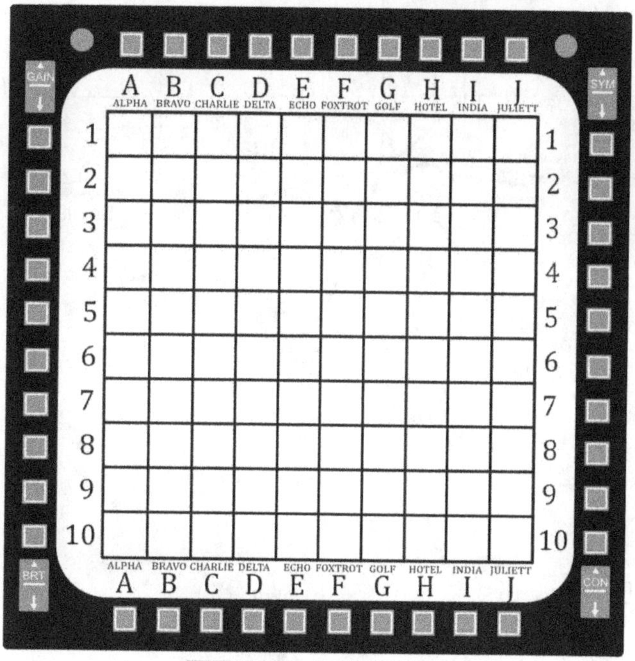

☒ HIT   ◯ MISS

Enemy Call Sign: _____

KEY

FIGHTER	BOMBER
F F F F	B / B B B / B

ATTACK	
A A / A A	TANKER

STEALTH	T / T T T / T
S S	

CIVILIAN	
C	

ENEMY AIRSPACE

	A	B	C	D	E	F	G	H	I	J	
	ALPHA	BRAVO	CHARLIE	DELTA	ECHO	FOXTROT	GOLF	HOTEL	INDIA	JULIETT	
1											1
2											2
3											3
4											4
5											5
6											6
7											7
8											8
9											9
10											10
	A	B	C	D	E	F	G	H	I	J	

☒ HIT   ◯ MISS

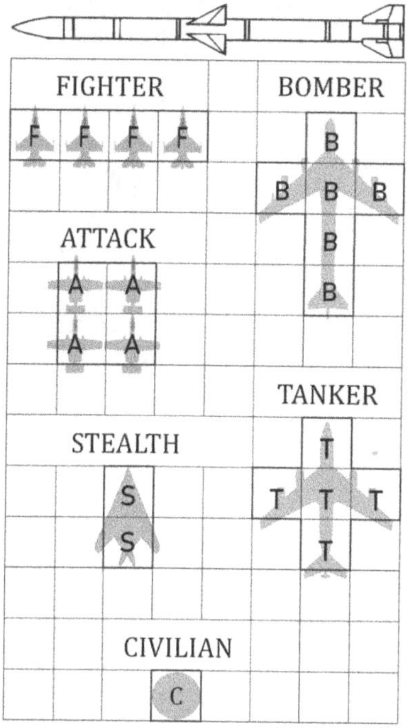

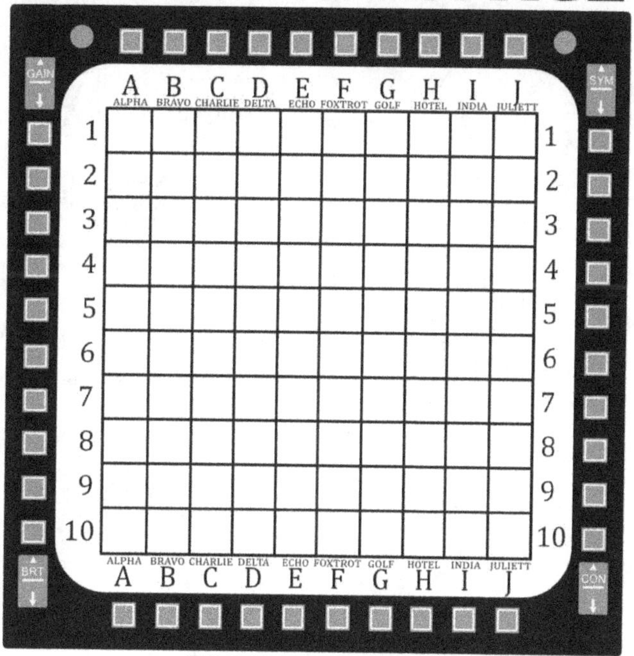

Pineview
Vienna
Tippettville
UNCLASSIFIED
CONEY
CRISP COUNTY-CORDELE (CKF)
AWOS-3PT 119.325
310 *L 50
123.05
RP 24, 28
Ross
32°
air museum
Cordele
Seville
Pitts
Rochelle
MUSTANG MOA
Warwick
Arabi
THUD MOA
Rebecca
VR100
Dakota
RICHTER AIRPARK (Pvt)
357 - 47 122.95
Abba
Ashburn
TURNER COUNTY (75J)
389 *L 50 122.7
CRYSTAL LAKE AIRPARK (Pvt)
327 - 30
Doles
Sycamore
Irwinville
Coverdale
MUSTANG MOA
Mystic
Shingler
MUSTANG LOW MOA
Chula
IR19
Sylvester
Poulan
Gorday
Ty Ty
Tifton
HENRY TIFT MYERS (TMA)
AWOS-3PT
355 *L 65
122.3
OAK RIDGE PLANTATION (Pvt)
350 - 34 122.8
Doerun
Omega
AIR BATTLE
Fuel Up with Extra game sheets:

FOLD ALONG DOTTED LINE AND TEAR

FOLD ALONG DOTTED LINE AND TEAR

Call Sign: _____

KEY

MY AIRSPACE

FIGHTER

BOMBER
B
B B B
B
B

ATTACK
A A
A A

TANKER
T
T T T
T

STEALTH
S
S

CIVILIAN
C

	A ALPHA	B BRAVO	C CHARLIE	D DELTA	E ECHO	F FOXTROT	G GOLF	H HOTEL	I INDIA	J JULIETT	
1											1
2											2
3											3
4											4
5											5
6											6
7											7
8											8
9											9
10											10

ALPHA BRAVO CHARLIE DELTA ECHO FOXTROT GOLF HOTEL INDIA JULIETT
A B C D E F G H I J

☒ HIT   ◯ MISS

Enemy Call Sign: _____

KEY

ENEMY AIRSPACE

FIGHTER

BOMBER
B
B B B
B
B

ATTACK
A A
A A

TANKER
T
T T T
T

STEALTH
S
S

CIVILIAN
C

	A ALPHA	B BRAVO	C CHARLIE	D DELTA	E ECHO	F FOXTROT	G GOLF	H HOTEL	I INDIA	J JULIETT	
1											1
2											2
3											3
4											4
5											5
6											6
7											7
8											8
9											9
10											10

ALPHA BRAVO CHARLIE DELTA ECHO FOXTROT GOLF HOTEL INDIA JULIETT
A B C D E F G H I J

☒ HIT   ◯ MISS

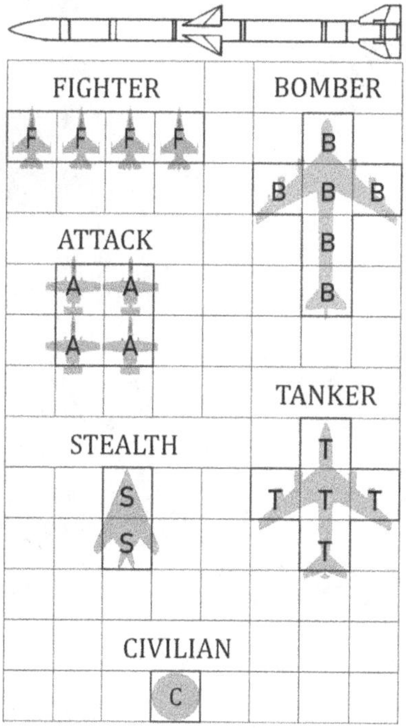

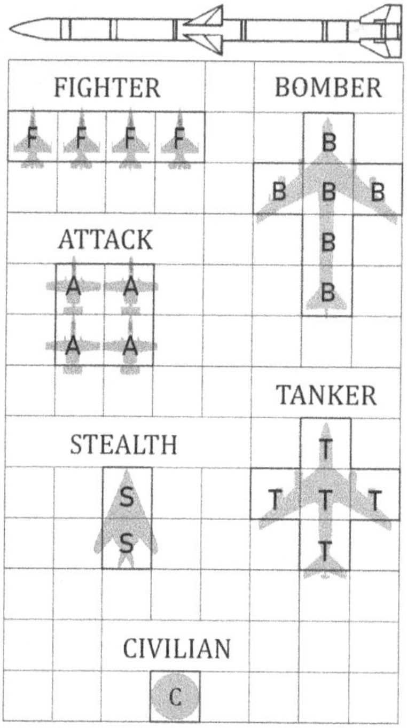

Willacoochee
VR1001
VR1066
VR1002-1003
UNCLASSIFIED
Pearson
Axson
sawmill
HAWG NORTH MOA
VR1004
BERRIEN COUNTY (4J2)
OBJECTIONABLE
HAWG NORTH MOA
MOA EXCLUDES AIRSPACE BELOW 500 AGL
MOODY 2 NORTH MOA
R-3008C EXCLUDES AIRSPACE BELOW 1500 AGL
MOA EXCLUDES AIRSPACE BELOW 1500 AGL
Cogdell
Ray City
Lakeland
HOMERVILLE (HOE)
AWOS-3 118.725
Homerville
sawmill
MOODY AFB (VAD)
GRAND BAY MOA,
HAWG SOUTH MOA
Du Pont
31°
Stockton
Bemiss
Naylor
CHRISTIANS FOLLY
83°
radome
MOODY 2 SOUTH MOA
HAWG SOUTH MOA
GRAND BAY MOA
HAWG SOUTH MOA
Howell
Mayday
Haylow
Thelma
VALDOSTA
ALYSSAS ANIMAL SANCTUARY AIR PARK
VALDOSTA RGNL (VLD)
IR16
Lake Park
Statenville
HAWG SOUTH MOA
Needmore
Jennings
BIRD FLD (Pvt)
AIR BATTLE
GEORGIA
FLORIDA
Bakers Mill

Fuel Up with Extra game sheets:

FOLD ALONG DOTTED LINE AND TEAR

FOLD ALONG DOTTED LINE AND TEAR

Call Sign: _____

KEY

 AIR BATTLE

MY AIRSPACE

FIGHTER	BOMBER
F F F F	B / B B B / B / B

| ATTACK | |
| A A / A A | |

| STEALTH | TANKER |
| S / S | T / T T T / T |

| CIVILIAN | |
| C | |

MY AIRSPACE GRID

GAIN — SYM

	A	B	C	D	E	F	G	H	I	J	
	ALPHA	BRAVO	CHARLIE	DELTA	ECHO	FOXTROT	GOLF	HOTEL	INDIA	JULIETT	
1											1
2											2
3											3
4											4
5											5
6											6
7											7
8											8
9											9
10											10

ALPHA BRAVO CHARLIE DELTA ECHO FOXTROT GOLF HOTEL INDIA JULIETT
A B C D E F G H I J

BRT — CON

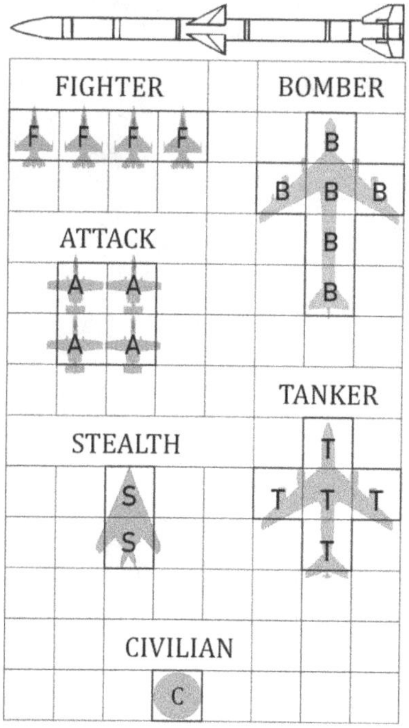

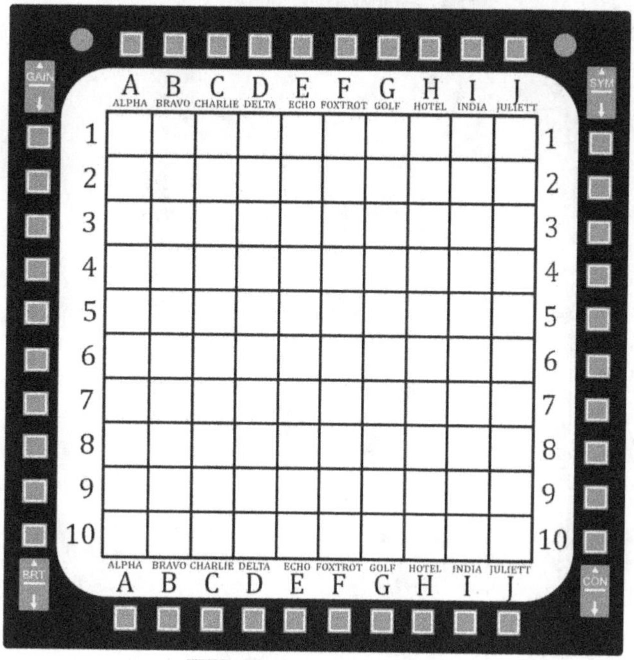

☒ HIT   ◯ MISS

Enemy Call Sign: _____

KEY

ENEMY AIRSPACE

FIGHTER	BOMBER
F F F F	B / B B B / B / B

| ATTACK | |
| A A / A A | |

| STEALTH | TANKER |
| S / S | T / T T T / T |

| CIVILIAN | |
| C | |

ENEMY AIRSPACE GRID

GAIN — SYM

	A	B	C	D	E	F	G	H	I	J	
	ALPHA	BRAVO	CHARLIE	DELTA	ECHO	FOXTROT	GOLF	HOTEL	INDIA	JULIETT	
1											1
2											2
3											3
4											4
5											5
6											6
7											7
8											8
9											9
10											10

ALPHA BRAVO CHARLIE DELTA ECHO FOXTROT GOLF HOTEL INDIA JULIETT
A B C D E F G H I J

BRT — CON

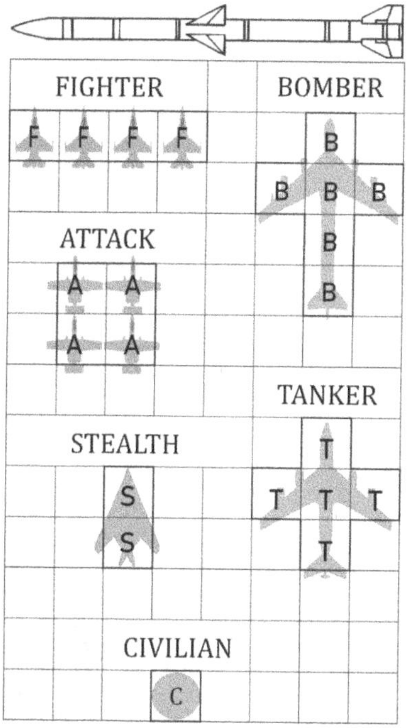

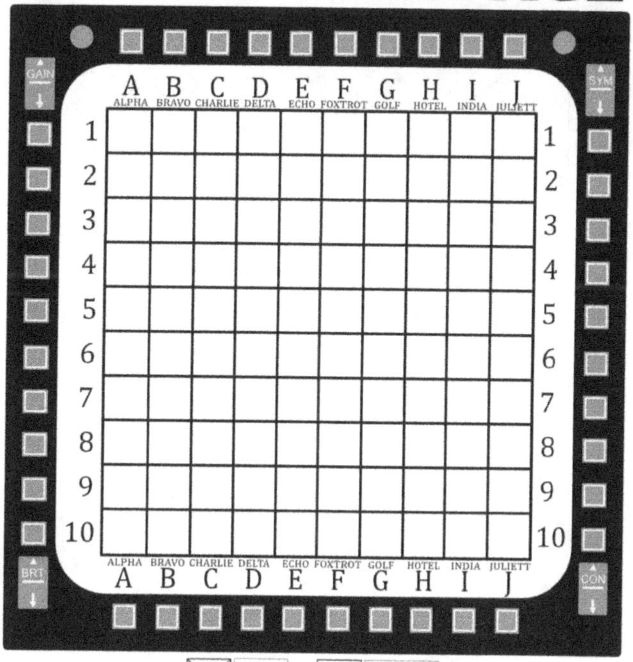

☒ HIT   ◯ MISS

FOLD ALONG DOTTED LINE AND TEAR

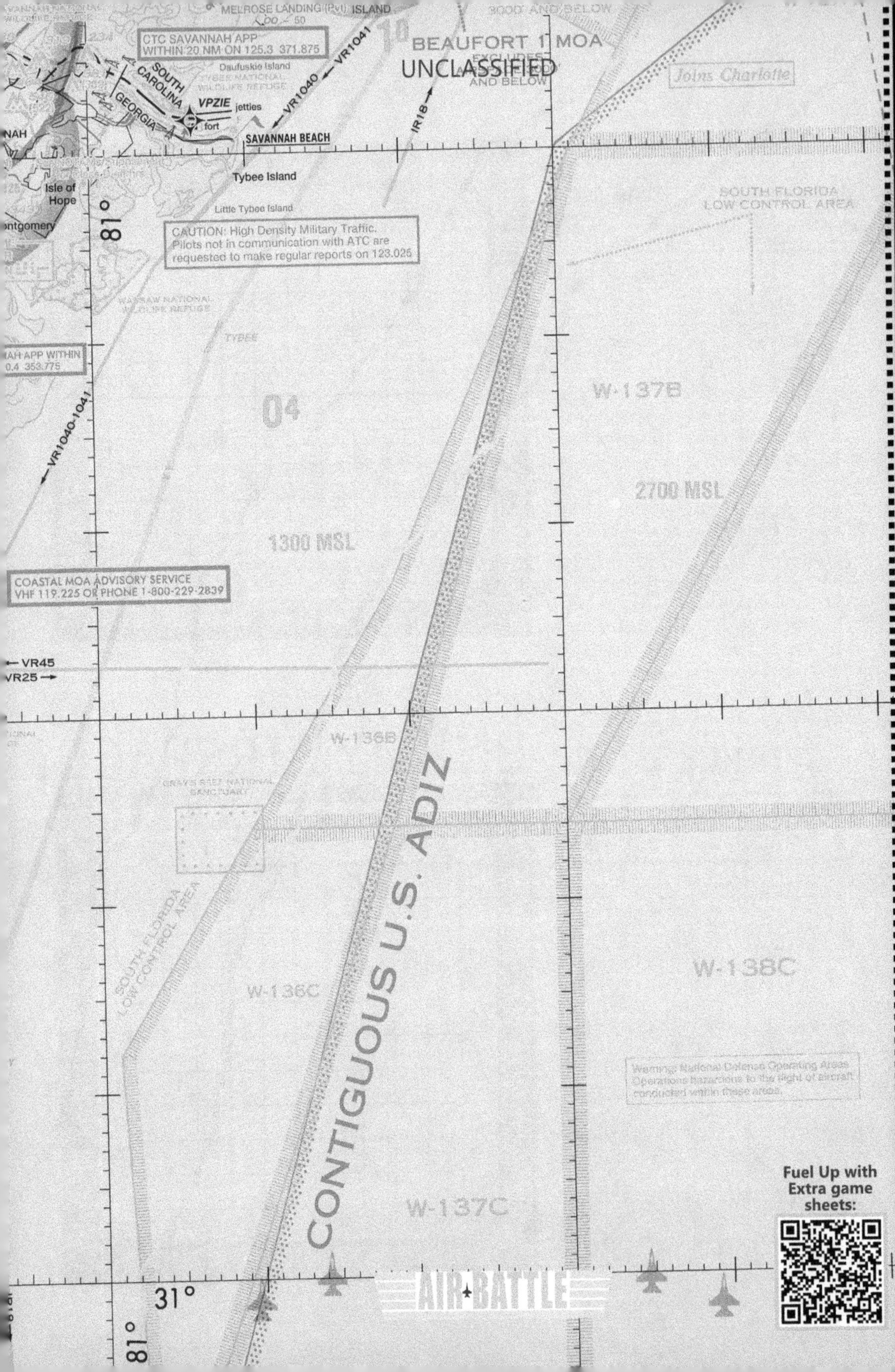
UNCLASSIFIED
MELROSE LANDING (Pvt) ISLAND
3000 AND BELOW
BEAUFORT 1 MOA
EXCLUDES
AND BELOW
Joins Charlotte
CTC SAVANNAH APP
WITHIN 20 NM ON 125.3 371.875
Daufuskie Island
SOUTH CAROLINA
GEORGIA
VPZIE
jetties
fort
VR1040
VR1041
IR18
SAVANNAH BEACH
Tybee Island
Little Tybee Island
Isle of Hope
81°
CAUTION: High Density Military Traffic.
Pilots not in communication with ATC are
requested to make regular reports on 123.025
SOUTH FLORIDA
LOW CONTROL AREA
TYBEE
04
W-137B
2700 MSL
1300 MSL
VR1040-1041
COASTAL MOA ADVISORY SERVICE
VHF 119.225 OR PHONE 1-800-229-2839
VR45
VR25
W-136B
CONTIGUOUS U.S. ADIZ
W-136C
W-138C
W-137C
Warning: National Defense Operating Areas
Operations hazardous to the flight of aircraft
conducted within these areas.
31°
81°
AIR BATTLE

Fuel Up with
Extra game
sheets:

FOLD ALONG DOTTED LINE AND TEAR

FOLD ALONG DOTTED LINE AND TEAR

Call Sign: _____

KEY

FIGHTER

F F F F

BOMBER

B
B B B
B
B

ATTACK

A A
A A

STEALTH

S
S

TANKER

T
T T T
T

CIVILIAN

C

MY AIRSPACE

	A	B	C	D	E	F	G	H	I	J	
	ALPHA	BRAVO	CHARLIE	DELTA	ECHO	FOXTROT	GOLF	HOTEL	INDIA	JULIETT	
1											1
2											2
3											3
4											4
5											5
6											6
7											7
8											8
9											9
10											10

ALPHA BRAVO CHARLIE DELTA ECHO FOXTROT GOLF HOTEL INDIA JULIETT
A B C D E F G H I J

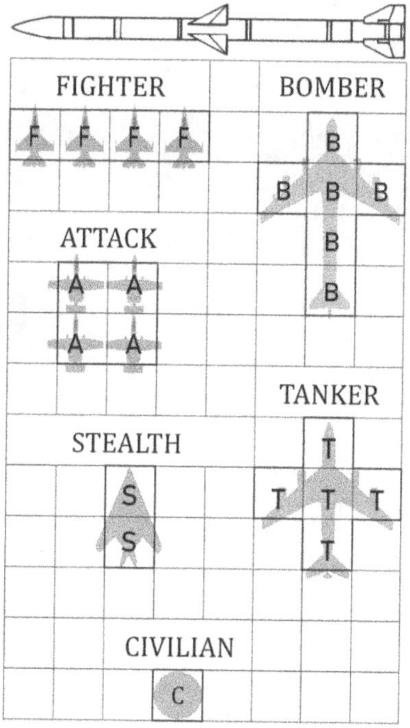

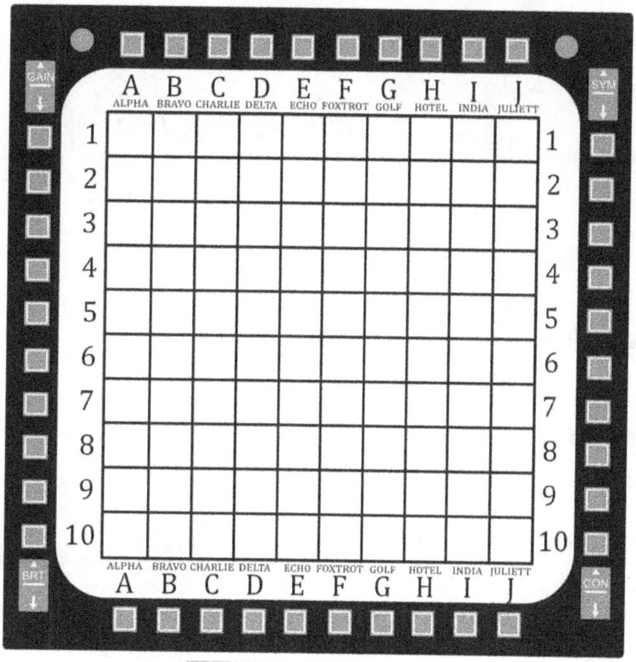

☒ HIT   ◯ MISS

Enemy Call Sign: _____

KEY

FIGHTER

F F F F

BOMBER

B
B B B
B

ATTACK

A A
A A

STEALTH

S
S

TANKER

T
T T T
T

CIVILIAN

C

ENEMY AIRSPACE

	A	B	C	D	E	F	G	H	I	J	
	ALPHA	BRAVO	CHARLIE	DELTA	ECHO	FOXTROT	GOLF	HOTEL	INDIA	JULIETT	
1											1
2											2
3											3
4											4
5											5
6											6
7											7
8											8
9											9
10											10

ALPHA BRAVO CHARLIE DELTA ECHO FOXTROT GOLF HOTEL INDIA JULIETT
A B C D E F G H I J

☒ HIT   ◯ MISS

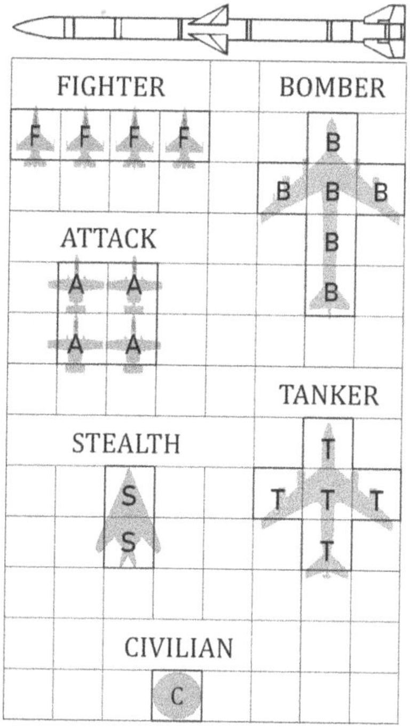

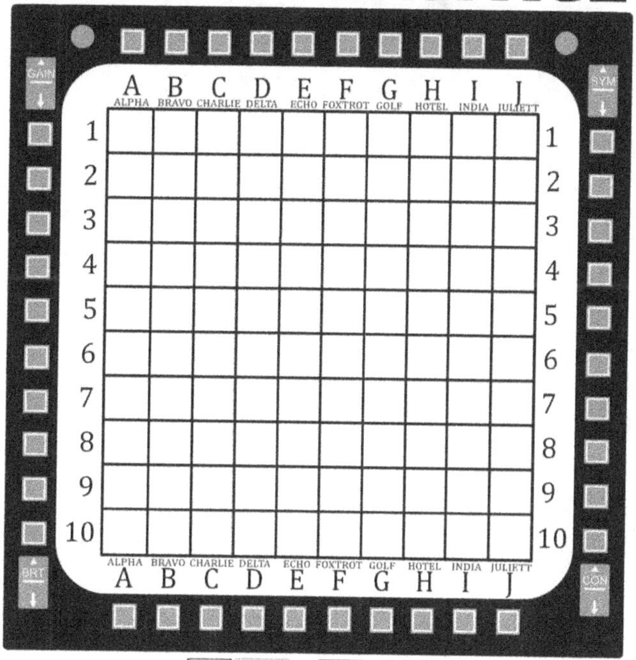

UNCLASSIFIED
OAK RIDGE (Pvt)
72 – 30
street pattern
Satsuma
POMONA LANDING (Pvt)
50 – 27
Espanola
VR1009
R-2906
Welaka
THUNDERBIRD AIR PARK (Pvt)
67 – 29 122.8
LITTLE LAKE GEORGE WILDERNESS
(Pvt)
JIM FINLAY FARM
40 – 24
Crescent City
SKINNERS WHOLESALE NURSERY (Pvt)
20 – 34
2 MOA EXCLUDES
SPACE WITHIN R-2906
907 B WHEN ACTIVE
MOA
(Pvt)
MOUNT ROYAL
60 – 30
00 – 24
VPJM
EAGLES NEST AERODROME (Pvt)
63 – 32
43 – 33
Georgetown
MORNINGWOOD (Pvt)
40 – 40
VR1040
VR1041
A-293
CAUTION: High volume of flight training surface to 4000' MSL
R-2907 B & C
Salt Springs
R-2907A
PALATKA 1 MOA EXCLUDES THE AIRSPACE WITHIN R-2907 A & B AND R-2910 A & D WHEN ACTIVE
68
grove
LAKE DISSTON
PIERSON MUNI (2J8)
63 – 26 122.9
RP 23
JUNIPER PRAIRIE WILDERNESS
VR1039
180
R-2910 D & E
LAFAYETTE
R-2910 A
Astor Park
LAKE WOODRUFF NATIONAL WILDLIFE REFUGE
17
star
marina
ALEXANDER SPRINGS WILDERNESS
VR1009
SAND LAKES AIRPARK (Pvt)
100 – 25
USFS
75
(Emerg only)
DELAND MUNI-SIDNEY H TAYLOR FLD
AWOS-3 119.575
De Land
79 L 60 123.075
BILLIES BAY WILDERNESS
awaha
DEEP WOODS RANCH (Pvt)
45 – 28
VPDF
Starkes Ferry
rsdale
Altoona
R-2910 B
(Pvt)
LOVE FLD
80 – 37
ROCKIN G RANCH (Pvt)
67 – 41
(Pvt)
BRADSHAW
55 – 21
Fuel Up with Extra game sheets:
Umatilla
See NOTAMs/Supplement for Class D/E (sfc) eff hrs
R-2910 C
water
AIR BATTLE
Cassia
ORLANDO
(Pvt)
FLYING H
80 – 26
Eustis
MID-FLORIDA (X55)
167 *L 32 122.8

FOLD ALONG DOTTED LINE AND TEAR

FOLD ALONG DOTTED LINE AND TEAR

Call Sign: _____

KEY

FIGHTER
F F F F

BOMBER
B
B B B
B
B

ATTACK
A A
A A

TANKER
T
T T T
T

STEALTH
S
S

CIVILIAN
C

MY AIRSPACE

	A ALPHA	B BRAVO	C CHARLIE	D DELTA	E ECHO	F FOXTROT	G GOLF	H HOTEL	I INDIA	J JULIETT	
1											1
2											2
3											3
4											4
5											5
6											6
7											7
8											8
9											9
10											10

A ALPHA B BRAVO C CHARLIE D DELTA E ECHO F FOXTROT G GOLF H HOTEL I INDIA J JULIETT
A B C D E F G H I J

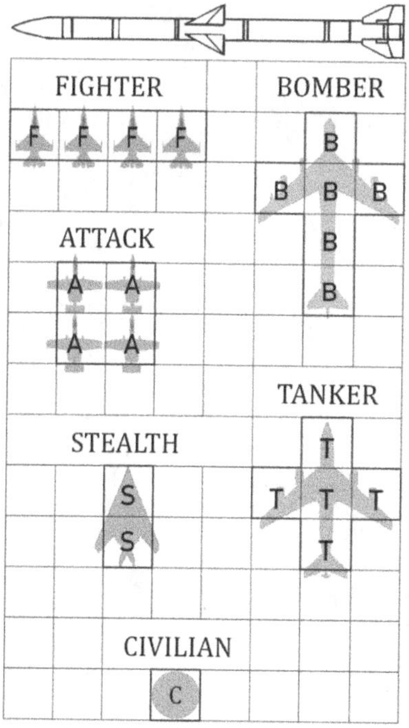

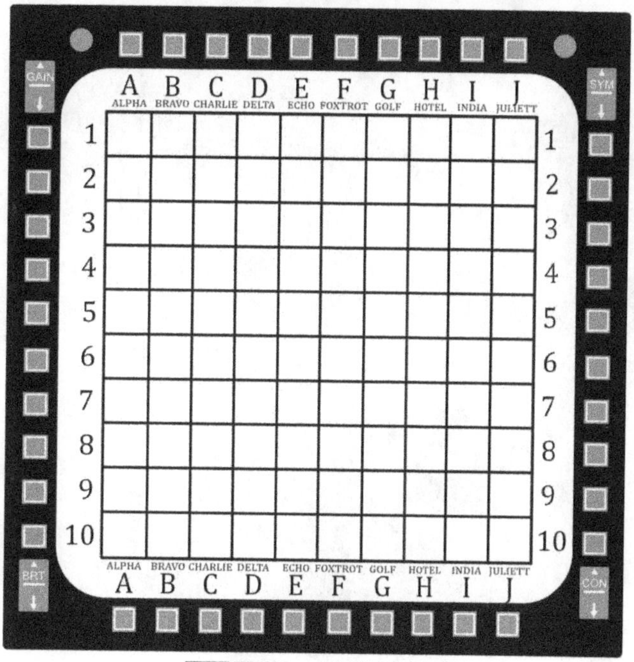

⊠ HIT   ◯ MISS

Enemy Call Sign: _____

KEY

FIGHTER
F F F F

BOMBER
B
B B B
B

ATTACK
A A
A A

TANKER
T
T T T
T

STEALTH
S
S

CIVILIAN
C

ENEMY AIRSPACE

	A ALPHA	B BRAVO	C CHARLIE	D DELTA	E ECHO	F FOXTROT	G GOLF	H HOTEL	I INDIA	J JULIETT	
1											1
2											2
3											3
4											4
5											5
6											6
7											7
8											8
9											9
10											10

ALPHA BRAVO CHARLIE DELTA ECHO FOXTROT GOLF HOTEL INDIA JULIETT
A B C D E F G H I J

⊠ HIT   ◯ MISS

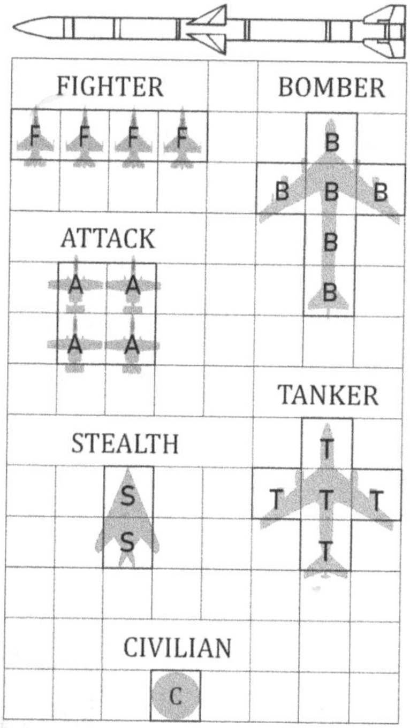

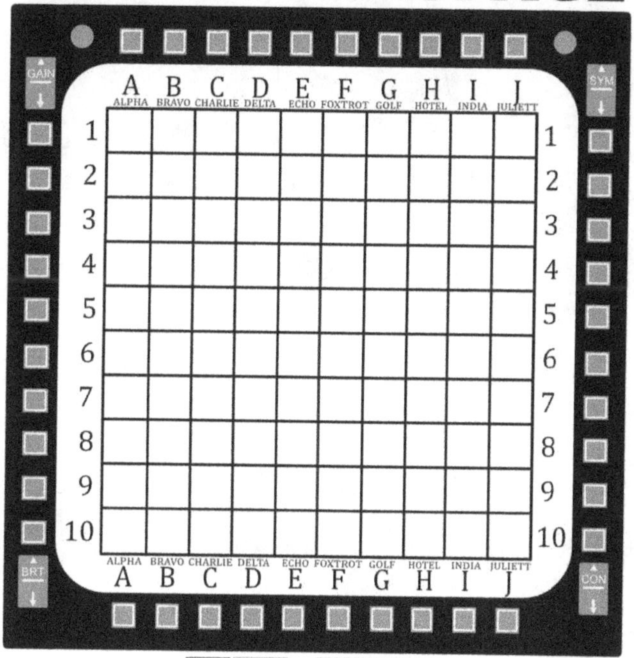

UNCLASSIFIED
CAUTION: High volume of flight training surface to 4000' MSL
EXAMPLES OF CLASS C ALTITUDES
T — Ceiling is to but not including floor of CLASS B
30 — Floor in hundreds of feet MSL
SOUTH FLORIDA LOW CONTROL AREA
V3, V437 and V533 excluded within R-2934 R-2935
R-2934
Shiloh
MERRITT ISLAND NATIONAL WILDLIFE REFUGE
SPACE FLORIDA LAUNCH AND LANDING FACILITY (TTS)
See NOTAMs/Supplement for Class D eff hrs
Class D excluded when R-2932 & R-2934 are active
KENNEDY SPAC
FAR 91.143 SPACE
ACTIVE: INTERMITTE
Listed under Melb
(Launch minus 3
(Recovery minus 3
ALTITUDES: Surface
CONTACT FSS 1-80
TITUSVILLE
MERRITT IS
R-2932
R-2933
DARKER TINT IS FAR 91.143 AREA
CAPE CANAVERAL SPACE FORCE STATION SKID STRIP (XMR)
CT - 118.625* 143.15*
ASOS 118.325
10 *L 100
CT 118.9*
ATIS 120.625
VPCNY
CAUTION: If R-2933, 2934 or 2935 are activ
or 4978 may contain flying rockets or falling
Warning Areas if briefed that R-2933, 2934
Cape Canaveral
Contact Miami RADIO for Class D eff hrs
EXCLUDES AIRSPACE BELOW 1200' AGL
MERRITT ISLAND (COI)
AWOS-3PT 119.025
06 *L 36 122.975
Cocoa Beach
1300 M
ROCKLEDGE
GEZIK (Pvt)
See NOTAMs/Supplement for Class D/E (sfc) eff hrs
AIR BATTLE

FOLD ALONG DOTTED LINE AND TEAR

Fuel Up with Extra game sheets:

FOLD ALONG DOTTED LINE AND TEAR

Call Sign: _____

KEY

MY AIRSPACE

FIGHTER
F F F F

BOMBER
B
B B B
B
B

ATTACK
A A
A A

STEALTH
S
S

TANKER
T
T T T
T

CIVILIAN
C

MY AIRSPACE grid

	A	B	C	D	E	F	G	H	I	J
ALPHA	BRAVO	CHARLIE	DELTA	ECHO	FOXTROT	GOLF	HOTEL	INDIA	JULIETT

1 2 3 4 5 6 7 8 9 10

A B C D E F G H I J
ALPHA BRAVO CHARLIE DELTA ECHO FOXTROT GOLF HOTEL INDIA JULIETT

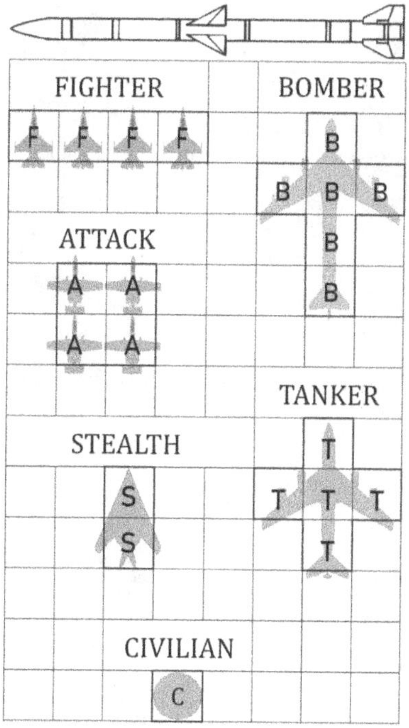

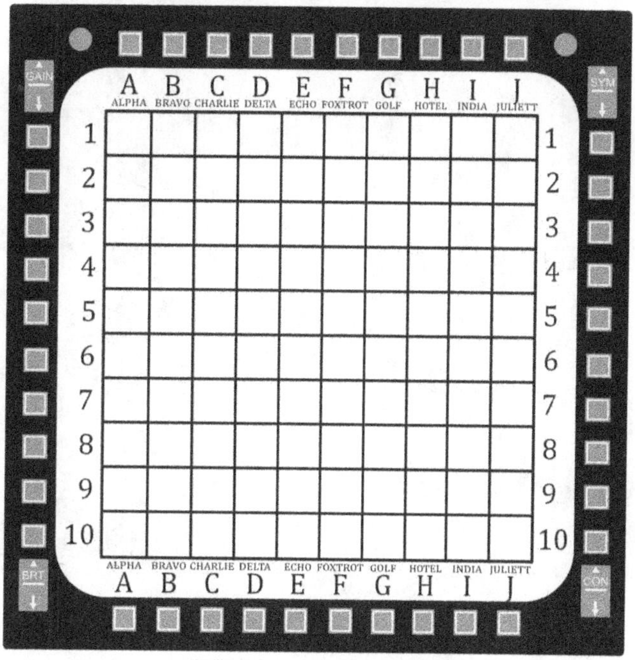

☒ HIT   ○ MISS

Enemy Call Sign: _____

KEY

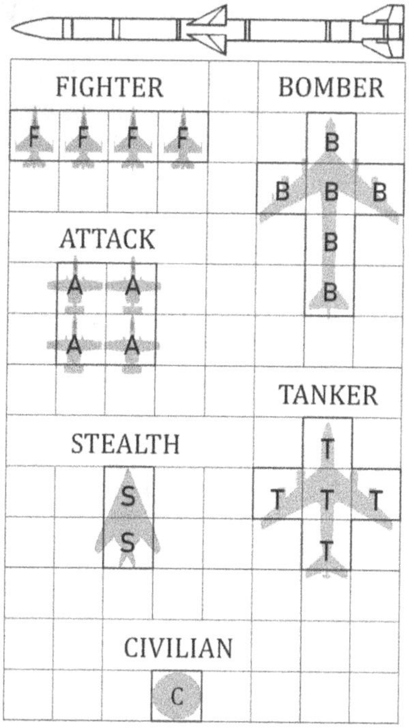

ENEMY AIRSPACE

FIGHTER
F F F F

BOMBER
B
B B B
B
B

ATTACK
A A
A A

STEALTH
S
S

TANKER
T
T T T
T

CIVILIAN
C

ENEMY AIRSPACE grid

A B C D E F G H I J
ALPHA BRAVO CHARLIE DELTA ECHO FOXTROT GOLF HOTEL INDIA JULIETT

1 2 3 4 5 6 7 8 9 10

A B C D E F G H I J
ALPHA BRAVO CHARLIE DELTA ECHO FOXTROT GOLF HOTEL INDIA JULIETT

☒ HIT   ○ MISS

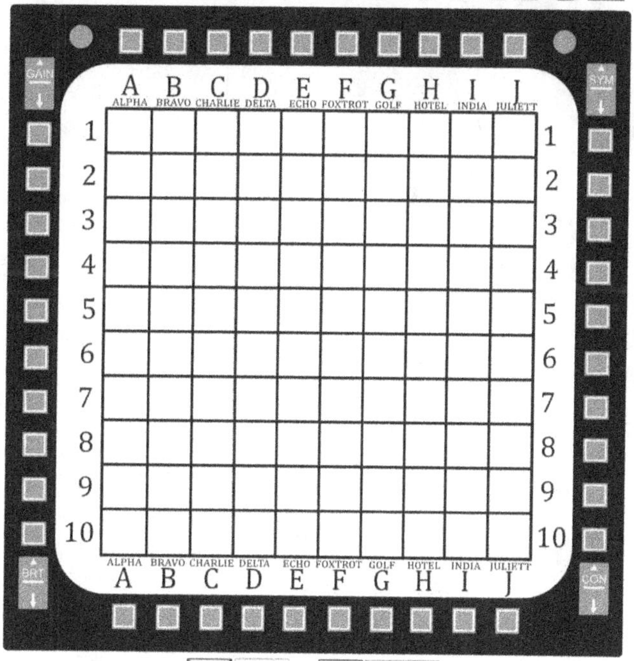

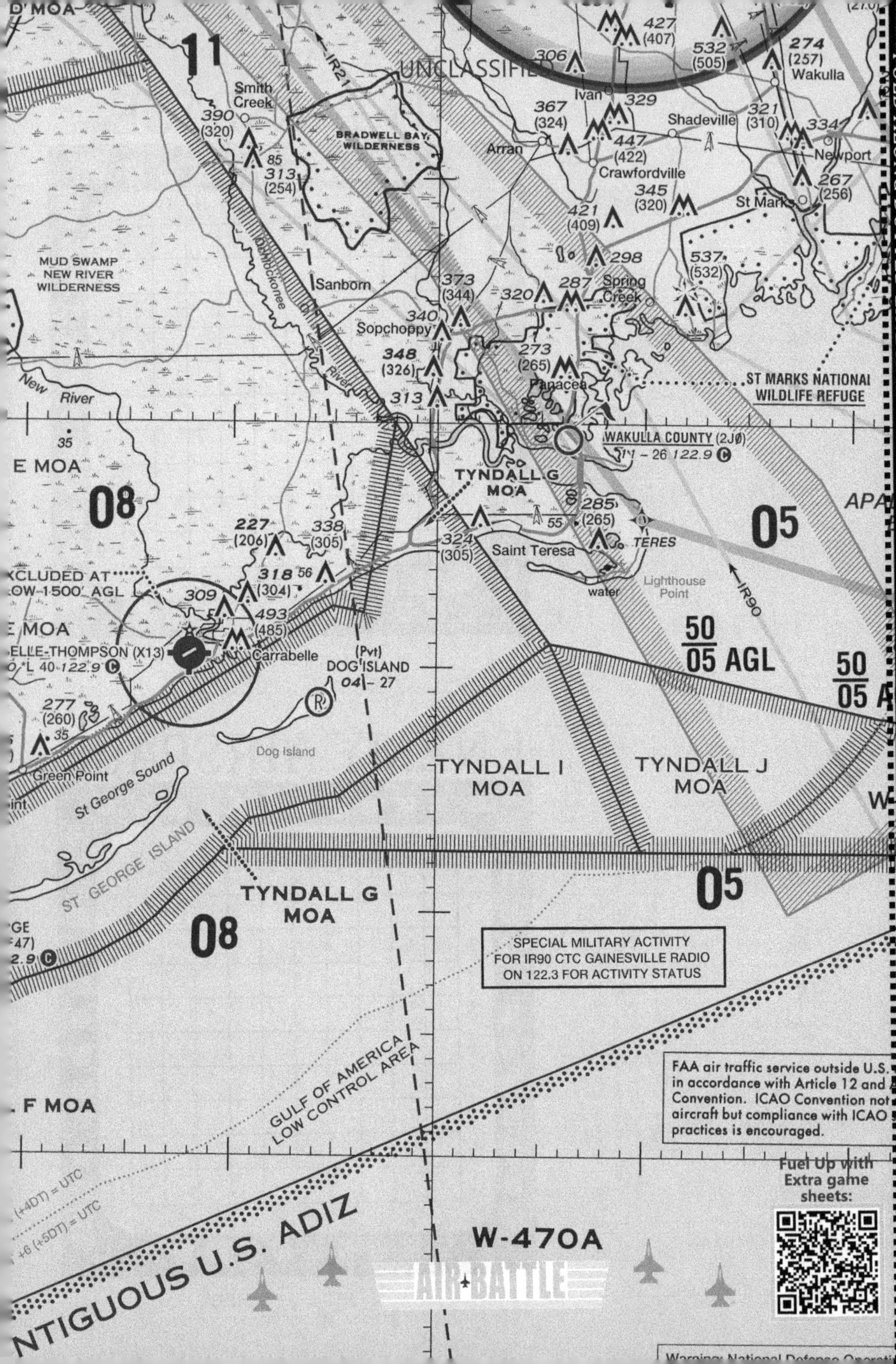

UNCLASSIFIED
Smith Creek
BRADWELL BAY WILDERNESS
MUD SWAMP NEW RIVER WILDERNESS
Sanborn
Sopchoppy
New River
Ochlockonee River
Arran
Ivan
Crawfordville
Shadeville
Wakulla
Newport
St Marks
Spring Creek
Panacea
ST MARKS NATIONAL WILDLIFE REFUGE
WAKULLA COUNTY (2J0)
11 - 26 122.9
TYNDALL G MOA
Saint Teresa
TERES
Lighthouse Point
water
IR90
IR21
50
05 AGL
E MOA
EXCLUDED AT
LOW 1500' AGL
ELLE-THOMPSON (X13)
L 40 122.9
Carrabelle
(Pvt)
DOG ISLAND
04 - 27
Dog Island
Green Point
St George Sound
ST GEORGE ISLAND
TYNDALL I MOA
TYNDALL J MOA
TYNDALL G MOA
SPECIAL MILITARY ACTIVITY
FOR IR90 CTC GAINESVILLE RADIO
ON 122.3 FOR ACTIVITY STATUS
F MOA
GULF OF AMERICA
LOW CONTROL AREA
FAA air traffic service outside U.S.
in accordance with Article 12 and
Convention. ICAO Convention not
aircraft but compliance with ICAO
practices is encouraged.
NTIGUOUS U.S. ADIZ
W-470A
AIR BATTLE
Fuel Up with
Extra game
sheets:

FOLD ALONG DOTTED LINE AND TEAR

FOLD ALONG DOTTED LINE AND TEAR

AIR BATTLE

Call Sign: ______________

KEY

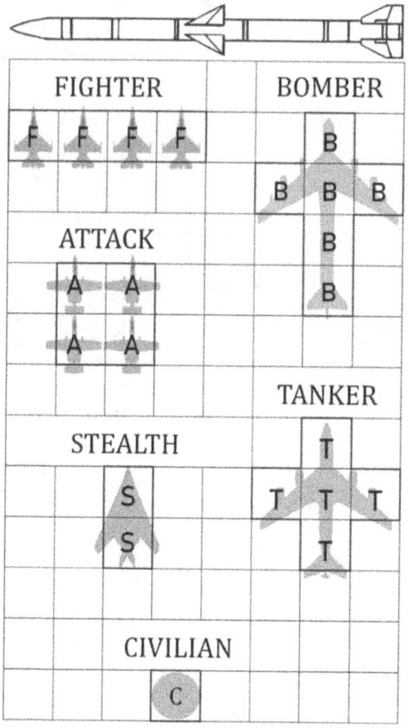

MY AIRSPACE

	A ALPHA	B BRAVO	C CHARLIE	D DELTA	E ECHO	F FOXTROT	G GOLF	H HOTEL	I INDIA	J JULIETT	
1											1
2											2
3											3
4											4
5											5
6											6
7											7
8											8
9											9
10											10
	ALPHA A	BRAVO B	CHARLIE C	DELTA D	ECHO E	FOXTROT F	GOLF G	HOTEL H	INDIA I	JULIETT J	

GAIN SYM BRT CON

☒ HIT ◯ MISS

Enemy Call Sign: __________

KEY

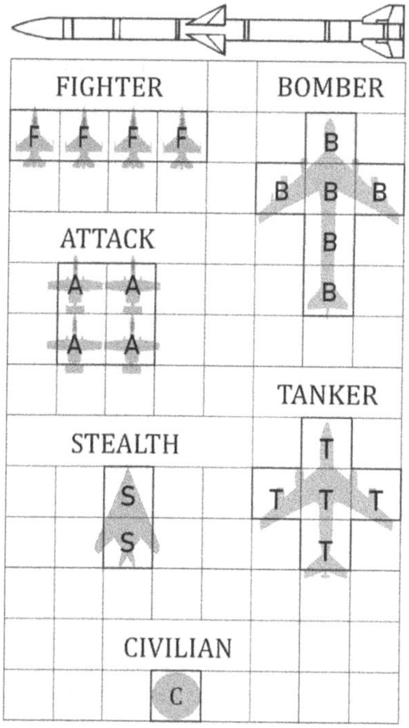

ENEMY AIRSPACE

	A ALPHA	B BRAVO	C CHARLIE	D DELTA	E ECHO	F FOXTROT	G GOLF	H HOTEL	I INDIA	J JULIETT	
1											1
2											2
3											3
4											4
5											5
6											6
7											7
8											8
9											9
10											10
	ALPHA A	BRAVO B	CHARLIE C	DELTA D	ECHO E	FOXTROT F	GOLF G	HOTEL H	INDIA I	JULIETT J	

GAIN SYM BRT CON

☒ HIT ◯ MISS

FOLD ALONG DOTTED LINE AND TEAR

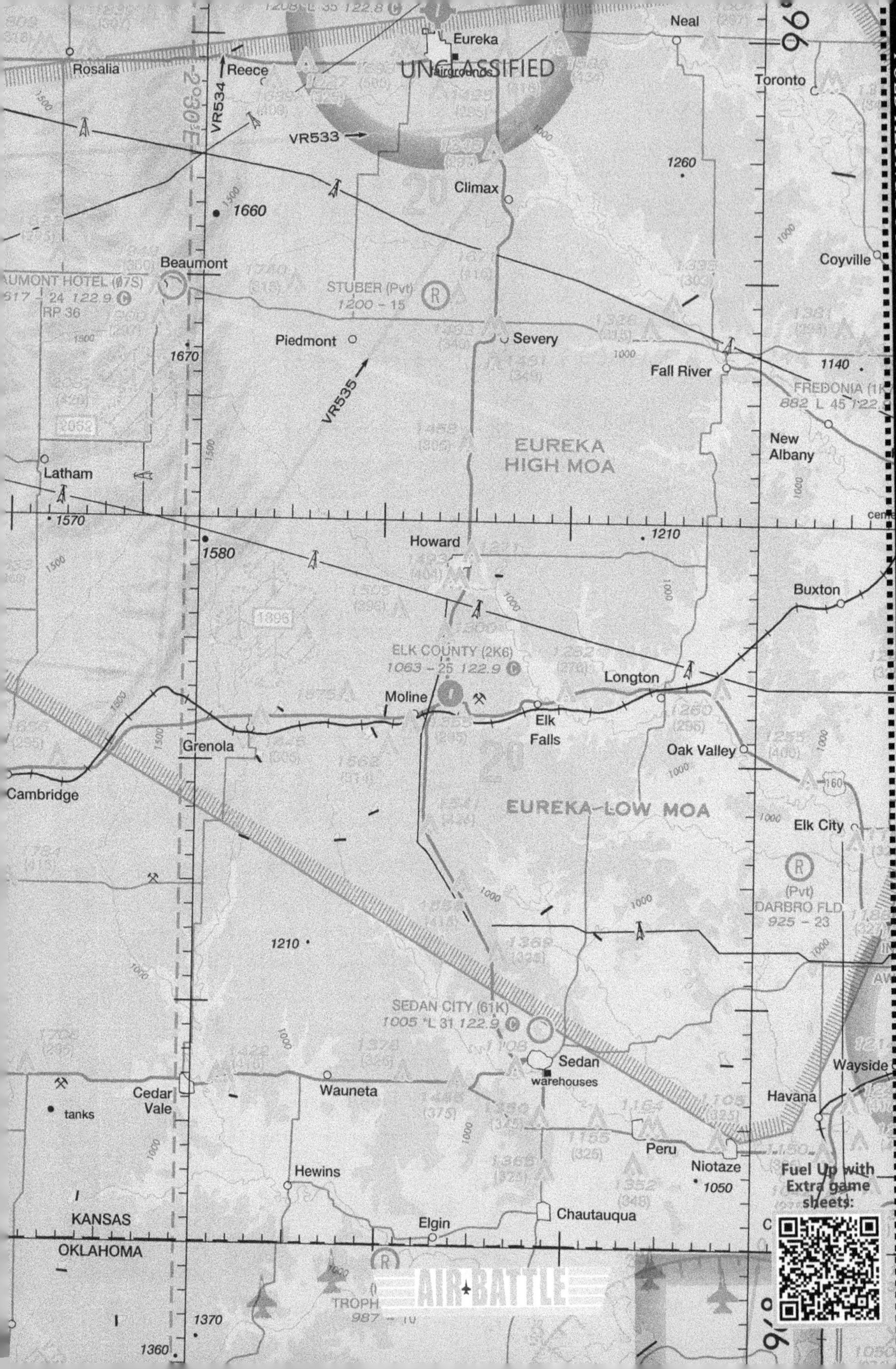
UNCLASSIFIED
Eureka
Neal
Rosalia
Reece
VR534
VR533
VR535
Toronto
1260
Climax
1660
Coyville
Beaumont
BEAUMONT HOTEL (07S)
STUBER (Pvt)
1200 - 15
Piedmont
Severy
1670
Fall River
1140
FREDONIA
EUREKA
HIGH MOA
New
Albany
Latham
1570
1210
1580
Howard
Buxton
ELK COUNTY (2K6)
1063 - 25 122.9
Longton
Moline
Elk
Falls
Grenola
Oak Valley
Cambridge
EUREKA LOW MOA
Elk City
(Pvt)
DARBRO FLD
925 - 23
1210
SEDAN CITY (61K)
1005 *L 31 122.9
Sedan
warehouses
Wayside
Cedar
Vale
Wauneta
tanks
Havana
Peru
Niotaze
1050
Hewins
Chautauqua
Elgin
KANSAS
OKLAHOMA
AIR BATTLE
TROPH
1370
1360
Fuel Up with
Extra game
sheets:

FOLD ALONG DOTTED LINE AND TEAR

FOLD ALONG DOTTED LINE AND TEAR

FOLD ALONG DOTTED LINE AND TEAR

Call Sign: ________________

AIR BATTLE

KEY

FIGHTER
F F F F
BOMBER
B
B B B
B
B
ATTACK
A A
A A
STEALTH
S
S
TANKER
T
T T T
T
CIVILIAN
C

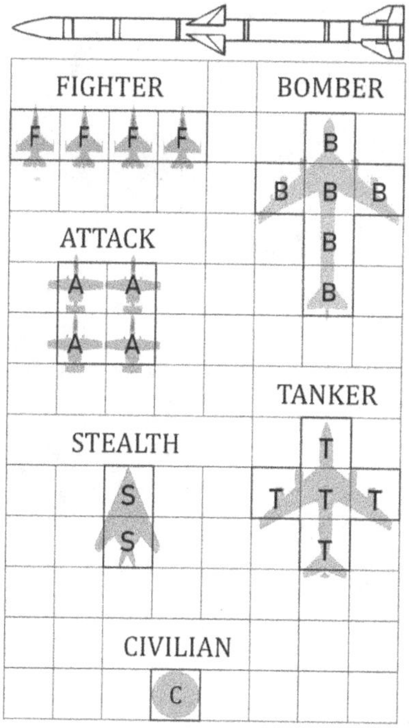

MY AIRSPACE

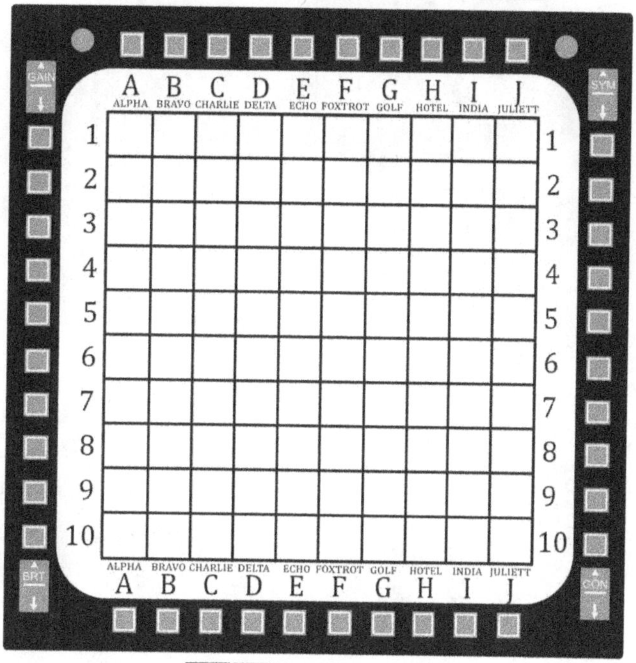

HIT MISS

Enemy Call Sign: __________

KEY

FIGHTER
F F F F
BOMBER
B
B B B
B
B
ATTACK
A A
A A
STEALTH
S
S
TANKER
T
T T T
T
CIVILIAN
C

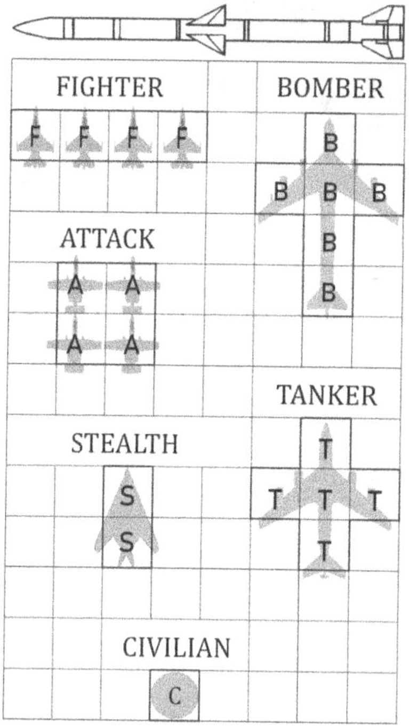

ENEMY AIRSPACE

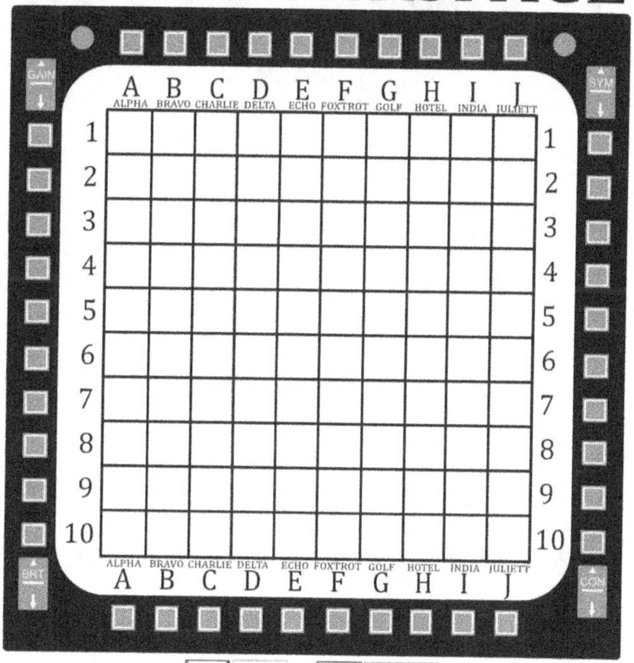

HIT MISS

FOLD ALONG DOTTED LINE AND TEAR

93°

UNCLASSIFIED

TRUMAN
A MOA

TRUMAN
B MOA

TRUMAN
C MOA

TRUMAN C MOA EXCLUDES
AIRSPACE BELOW 1500 AGL

Up with
Extra game
sheets.

AIR BATTLE

38

Call Sign: _____

KEY

FIGHTER
F F F F

BOMBER
B
B B B
B
B

ATTACK
A A
A A

STEALTH
S
S

TANKER
T
T T T
T

CIVILIAN
C

MY AIRSPACE

	A	B	C	D	E	F	G	H	I	J	
	ALPHA	BRAVO	CHARLIE	DELTA	ECHO	FOXTROT	GOLF	HOTEL	INDIA	JULIETT	
1											1
2											2
3											3
4											4
5											5
6											6
7											7
8											8
9											9
10											10

ALPHA BRAVO CHARLIE DELTA ECHO FOXTROT GOLF HOTEL INDIA JULIETT
A B C D E F G H I J

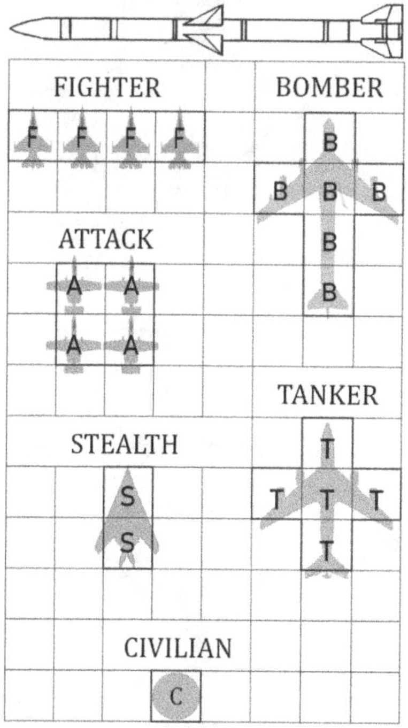

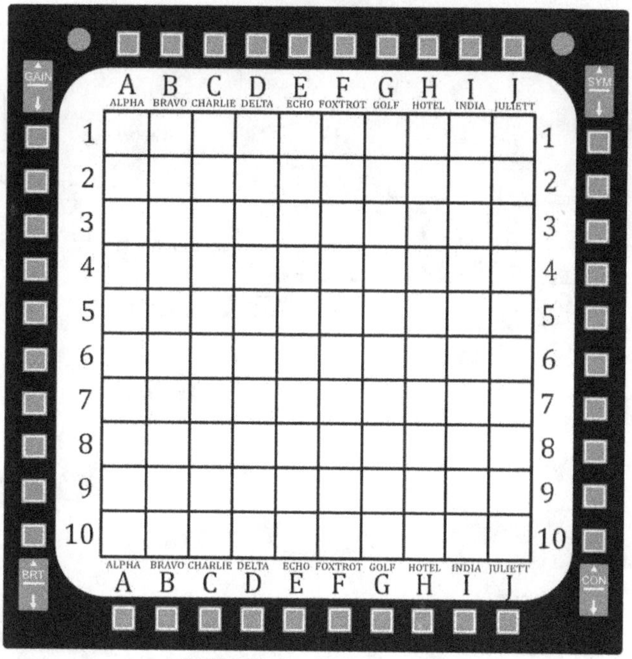

☒ HIT   ◯ MISS

Enemy Call Sign: _____

KEY

FIGHTER
F F F F

BOMBER
B
B B B
B
B

ATTACK
A A
A A

STEALTH
S
S

TANKER
T
T T T
T

CIVILIAN
C

ENEMY AIRSPACE

	A	B	C	D	E	F	G	H	I	J	
	ALPHA	BRAVO	CHARLIE	DELTA	ECHO	FOXTROT	GOLF	HOTEL	INDIA	JULIETT	
1											1
2											2
3											3
4											4
5											5
6											6
7											7
8											8
9											9
10											10

ALPHA BRAVO CHARLIE DELTA ECHO FOXTROT GOLF HOTEL INDIA JULIETT
A B C D E F G H I J

☒ HIT   ◯ MISS

FOLD ALONG DOTTED LINE AND TEAR

FOLD ALONG DOTTED LINE AND TEAR

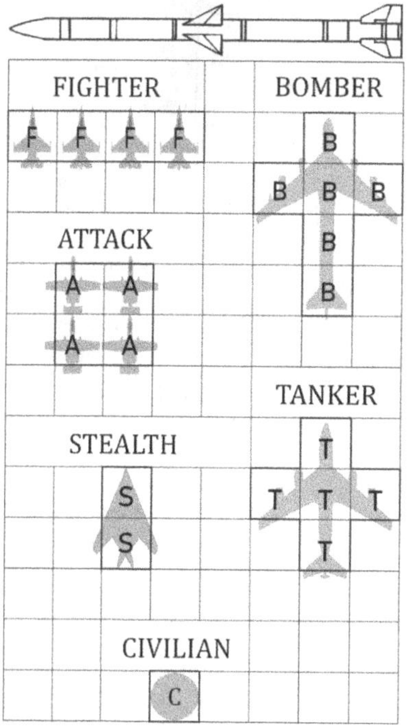

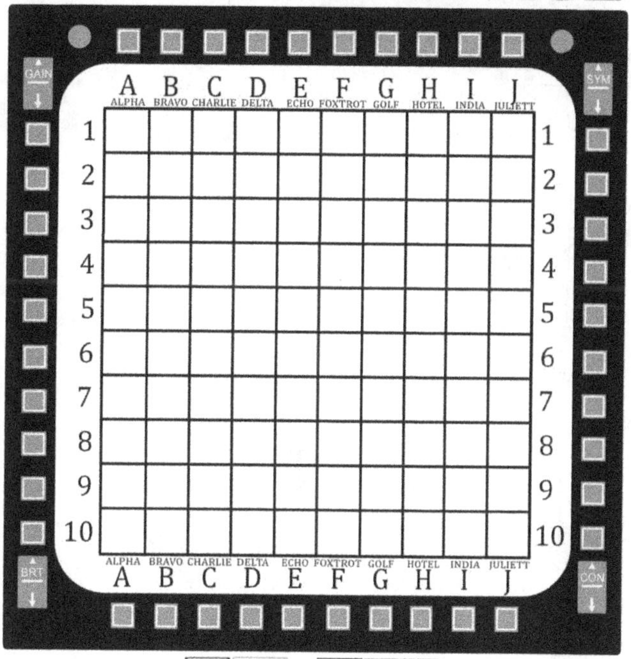

HOWARD EAST MOA
UNCLASSIFIED
Camden
Rushville
prison
La Praire
Golden
(Pvt)
HERREN
654 – 15
SCHUY-RUSH (5K4)
665 L 35 123.0
Bader
HOWARD EAST MOA
Frederick
MOUNT STERLING (163)
AWOS-3PT 118.325
734 L 59 122.8
PRUITT A MOA
Ripley
Beardstown
820
Timewell
Mt Sterling
fairgrounds
40°
Bluff Springs
Cooperstown
GREATER BEARDSTOWN (K06)
465 L 40 122.9
VIRGINIA
prison
Hersman
PRUITT A MOA EXCLUDES AIRSPACE 1500 AGL & BELOW
91°
Kellerville
KROHE (Pvt)
450 – 25
MEREDOSIA NATIONAL WILDLIFE REFUGE
(Pvt)
KINSEY
455 – 26
Versailles
Arenzville
Arcadia
Supplement
PRUITT A MOA
Meredosia
Fishhook
Chambersburg
stack & tower
JACKSONVILLE MUNI (IJX)
AWOS-3PT 120.525
624 L 50 122.8
Kingston
850
Beverly
13
Perry
elevator
Naples
Chapin
Bluffs
JACKSONVILLE
Baylis
New Salem
Griggsville
Lynnville
Barry
PITTSFIELD PENSTONE (PPQ)
AWOS-3PT 118.525
710 L 40 122.8
Winchester
18
El Dara
New Canton
Detroit
Pittsfield
PRUITT A MOA EXCLUDES AIRSPACE 1500 AGL & BELOW
Alsey
Milton
Glasgow
Manchester
YATES
616
Rockport
Summer Hill
Atlas
(Pvt)
HARTWELL RANCH
427 – 32
Patterson
Roodhouse
Pearl
MARK TWAIN NATIONAL WILDLIFE REFUGE
Pleasant Hill
Nebo
Hillview
White Hall
PRUITT B MOA
Louisiana
plant
Wrights
Berdan
stack
elevators
Clarksville
(Pvt)
HERRENS BESS HOLLOW AIRFIELD
580 – 19
ferry
Carrollton
CLARENCE CANNON NATIONAL WILDLIFE REFUGE
AIR BATTLE
Paynesville
Annada
Michael
TAC

Fuel Up with Extra game sheets:

FOLD ALONG DOTTED LINE AND TEAR

FOLD ALONG DOTTED LINE AND TEAR

Call Sign: _____

KEY

MY AIRSPACE

FIGHTER
F F F F

BOMBER
B
B B B
B
B

ATTACK
A A
A A

TANKER
T
T T T
T

STEALTH
S
S

CIVILIAN
C

MY AIRSPACE grid:

	A ALPHA	B BRAVO	C CHARLIE	D DELTA	E ECHO	F FOXTROT	G GOLF	H HOTEL	I INDIA	J JULIETT	
1											1
2											2
3											3
4											4
5											5
6											6
7											7
8											8
9											9
10											10

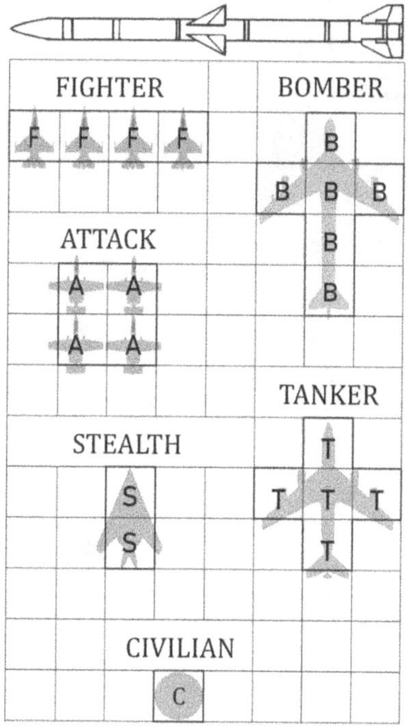

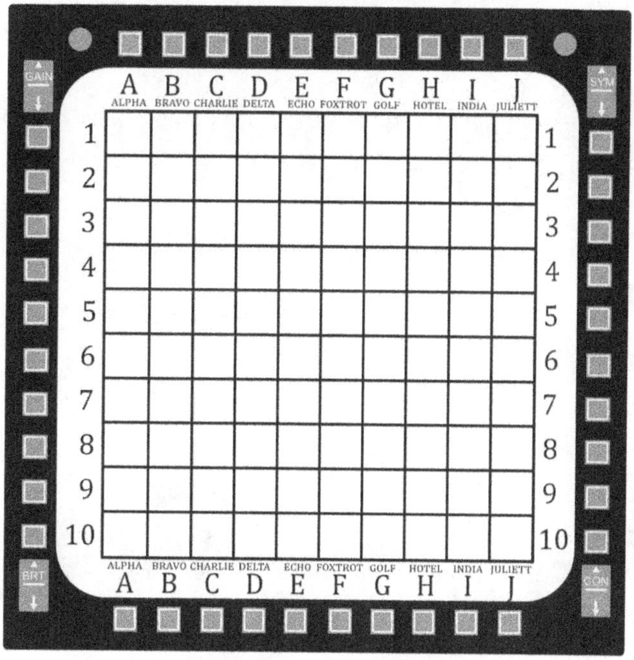

☒ HIT   ◯ MISS

Enemy Call Sign: _____

KEY

ENEMY AIRSPACE

FIGHTER
F F F F

BOMBER
B
B B B
B
B

ATTACK
A A
A A

TANKER
T
T T T
T

STEALTH
S
S

CIVILIAN
C

ENEMY AIRSPACE grid:

	A ALPHA	B BRAVO	C CHARLIE	D DELTA	E ECHO	F FOXTROT	G GOLF	H HOTEL	I INDIA	J JULIETT	
1											1
2											2
3											3
4											4
5											5
6											6
7											7
8											8
9											9
10											10

☒ HIT   ◯ MISS

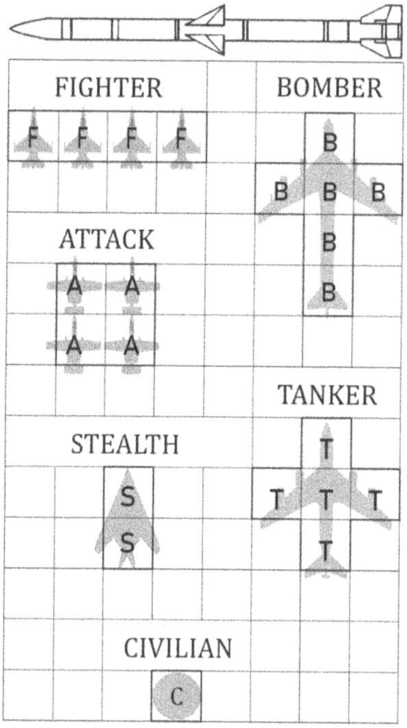

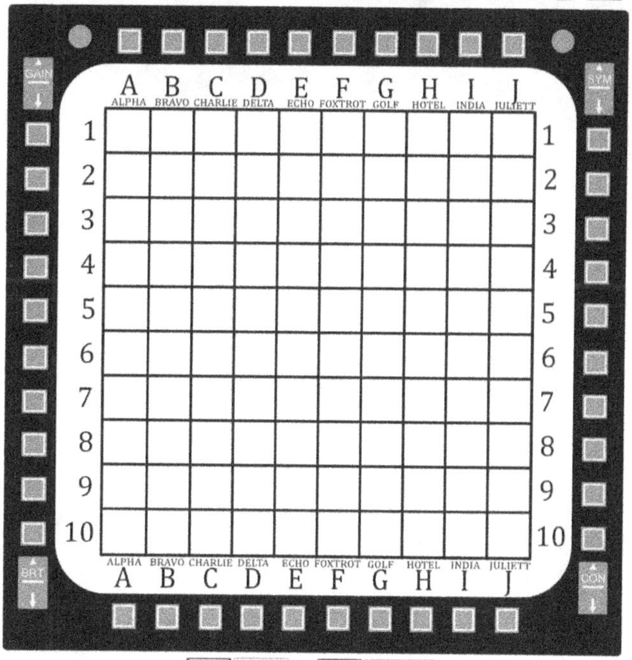

FOR MOA ADVISORIES CTC ZKC ON 128.35
UNCLASSIFIED
Edgar Springs
Lenox
VPWRO
Salem
SALEM MEML (K33)
1241 *L 30 122.9 C
BAKER FARM (Pvt)
1362 - 23
Boss
Bixby
plant
SALEM MOA
LINDBERGH A MOA
Bunker
Reynolds
Corridon
Rector
LINDBERGH A MOA
IR592
Raymondville
camp
Round Spring
CARR CREEK
835 - 45
Hartshorn
VPGXY
Summersville
Eminence
Alley Spring
1348
BOLLINGER-CRASS MEML (MO5)
652 - 28 122.9 C
Winona
Birch Tree
Van Buren
Fremont
Mountain View
MOUNTAIN VIEW (MNF)
1182 *L 50 122.8 C
Hutton Valley
LINDBERGH B MOA
FOR MOA ADVISORIES CTC ZKC ON 128.35
WEST PLAINS RGNL (UNO)
ASOS 123.825
1228 *L 51 122.8 C
Eastwood
Pomona
Peace Valley
Thomasville
LINDBERGH C MOA
West Plains
Alton
Many Springs
Brandsville
AIR BATTLE

Fuel Up with Extra game sheets:

FOLD ALONG DOTTED LINE AND TEAR

FOLD ALONG DOTTED LINE AND TEAR

Call Sign: _____

KEY

FIGHTER
F F F F

BOMBER
B
B B B
B
B

ATTACK
A   A
A   A

STEALTH
S
S

TANKER
T
T T T
T

CIVILIAN
C

MY AIRSPACE

	A	B	C	D	E	F	G	H	I	J	
	ALPHA	BRAVO	CHARLIE	DELTA	ECHO	FOXTROT	GOLF	HOTEL	INDIA	JULIETT	
1											1
2											2
3											3
4											4
5											5
6											6
7											7
8											8
9											9
10											10
	ALPHA	BRAVO	CHARLIE	DELTA	ECHO	FOXTROT	GOLF	HOTEL	INDIA	JULIETT	
	A	B	C	D	E	F	G	H	I	J	

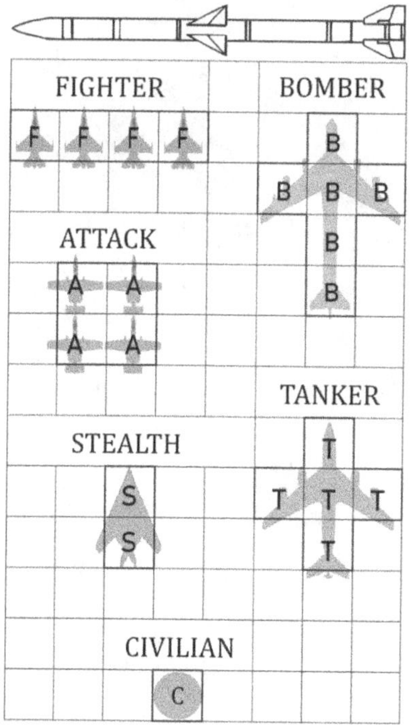

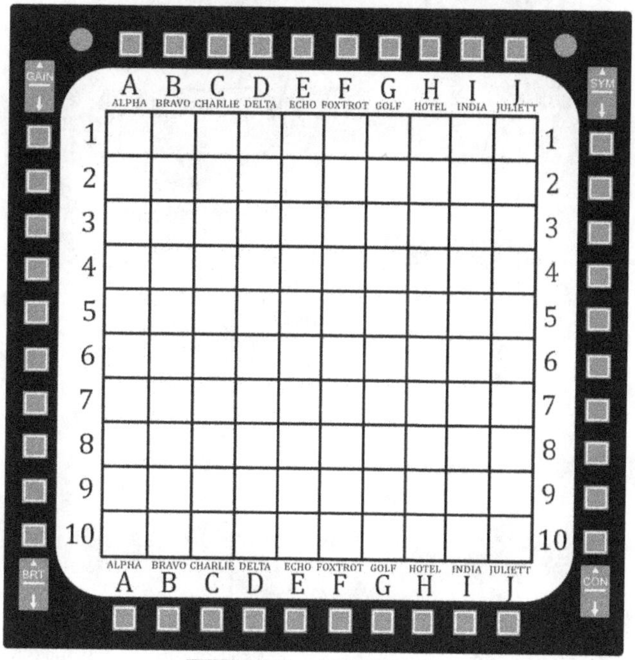

☒ HIT   ◯ MISS

Enemy Call Sign: _____

KEY

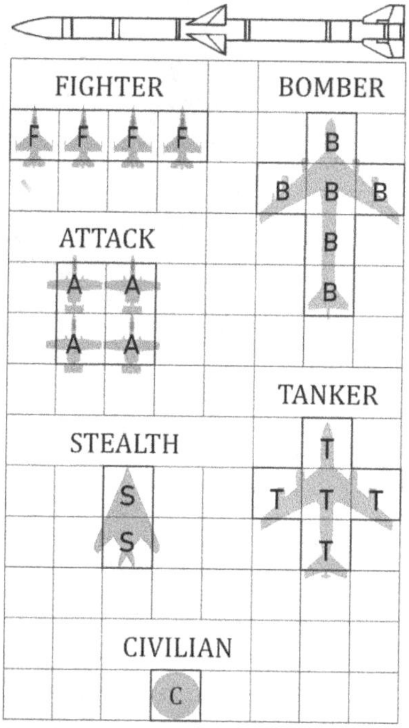

FIGHTER
F F F F

BOMBER
B
B B B
B

ATTACK
A   A
A   A

STEALTH
S
S

TANKER
T
T T T
T

CIVILIAN
C

ENEMY AIRSPACE

	A	B	C	D	E	F	G	H	I	J	
	ALPHA	BRAVO	CHARLIE	DELTA	ECHO	FOXTROT	GOLF	HOTEL	INDIA	JULIETT	
1											1
2											2
3											3
4											4
5											5
6											6
7											7
8											8
9											9
10											10
	ALPHA	BRAVO	CHARLIE	DELTA	ECHO	FOXTROT	GOLF	HOTEL	INDIA	JULIETT	
	A	B	C	D	E	F	G	H	I	J	

☒ HIT   ◯ MISS

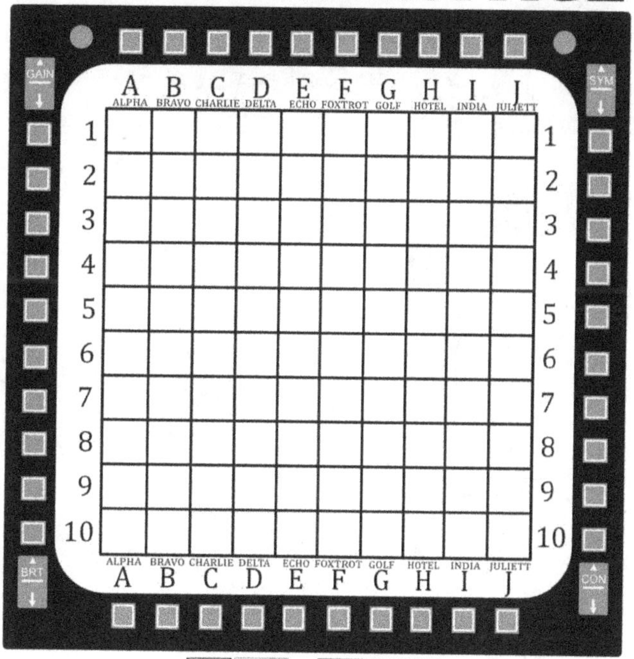

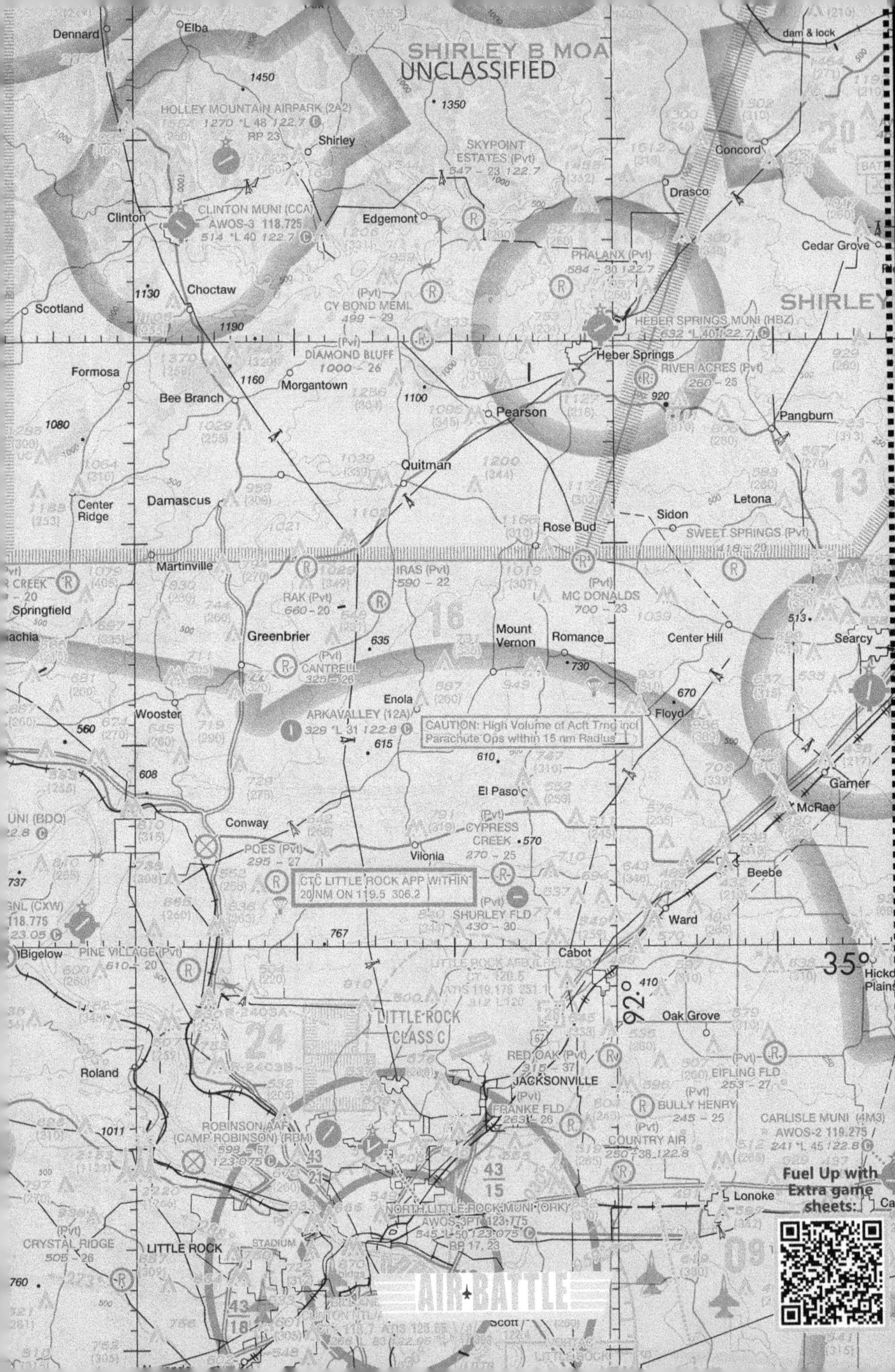

SHIRLEY B MOA
UNCLASSIFIED
Dennard
Elba
HOLLEY MOUNTAIN AIRPARK (2A2)
Shirley
SKYPOINT ESTATES (Pvt)
547 - 23 122.7
CLINTON MUNI (CCA)
AWOS-3 118.725
514 *L 40 122.7
Clinton
Edgemont
Concord
Drasco
Cedar Grove
PHALANX (Pvt)
584 - 30 122.7
Choctaw
Scotland
CY BOND MEML
499 - 29
HEBER SPRINGS MUNI (HBZ)
632 *L 40 122.7
SHIRLEY
DIAMOND BLUFF
1000 - 26
Heber Springs
RIVER ACRES (Pvt)
260 - 25
Formosa
Bee Branch
Morgantown
Pearson
Pangburn
Quitman
Damascus
Center Ridge
Letona
Sidon
Rose Bud
SWEET SPRINGS (Pvt)
Martinville
IRAS (Pvt)
590 - 22
RAK (Pvt)
660 - 20
MC DONALDS
700 - 23
Springfield
Greenbrier
Mount Vernon
Romance
Center Hill
Searcy
CANTRELL
325 - 26
Enola
ARKAVALLEY (12A)
329 *L 31 122.8
CAUTION: High Volume of Acft Trng incl Parachute Ops within 15 nm Radius
Wooster
Floyd
El Paso
Garner
McRae
Conway
POES (Pvt)
295 - 27
CYPRESS CREEK
270 - 25
Vilonia
Beebe
CTC LITTLE ROCK APP WITHIN 20 NM ON 119.5 306.2
SHURLEY FLD
430 - 30
Ward
Bigelow
PINE VILLAGE (Pvt)
610 - 20
Cabot
35°
92°
Hickory Plains
Oak Grove
LITTLE ROCK CLASS C
Roland
RED OAK (Pvt)
315 - 37
EIFLING FLD
253 - 27
JACKSONVILLE
FRANKE FLD
263 - 26
BULLY HENRY
245 - 25
ROBINSON AAF (CAMP ROBINSON) (RBM)
COUNTRY AIR
250 - 38 122.8
CARLISLE MUNI (4M3)
AWOS-2 119.275
241 *L 45 122.8
Lonoke
NORTH LITTLE ROCK MUNI (ORK)
AWOS-3PT 123.775
545 *L 50 123.075
RP 17, 23
CRYSTAL RIDGE
505 - 26
LITTLE ROCK
STADIUM
Scott
AIR BATTLE

Fuel Up with Extra game sheets:

FOLD ALONG DOTTED LINE AND TEAR

FOLD ALONG DOTTED LINE AND TEAR

Call Sign: _____

KEY

MY AIRSPACE

FIGHTER	BOMBER
F F F F	B B B / B / B

| ATTACK | |
| A A / A A | |

| STEALTH | TANKER |
| S / S | T T T / T |

| CIVILIAN | |
| C | |

MY AIRSPACE

GAIN SYM

	A	B	C	D	E	F	G	H	I	J
ALPHA	BRAVO	CHARLIE	DELTA	ECHO	FOXTROT	GOLF	HOTEL	INDIA	JULIETT

1
2
3
4
5
6
7
8
9
10

A B C D E F G H I J
ALPHA BRAVO CHARLIE DELTA ECHO FOXTROT GOLF HOTEL INDIA JULIETT

BRT CON

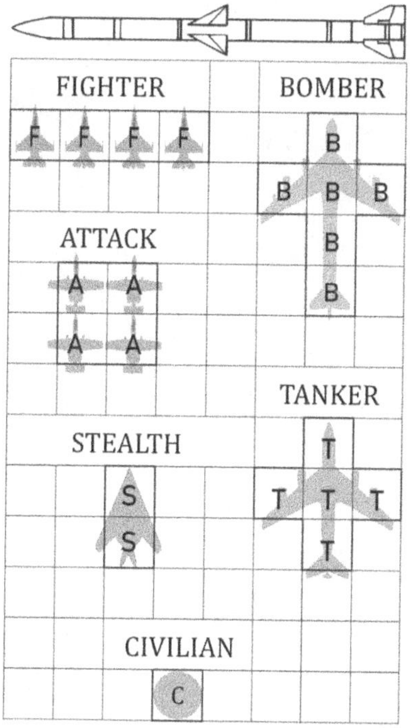

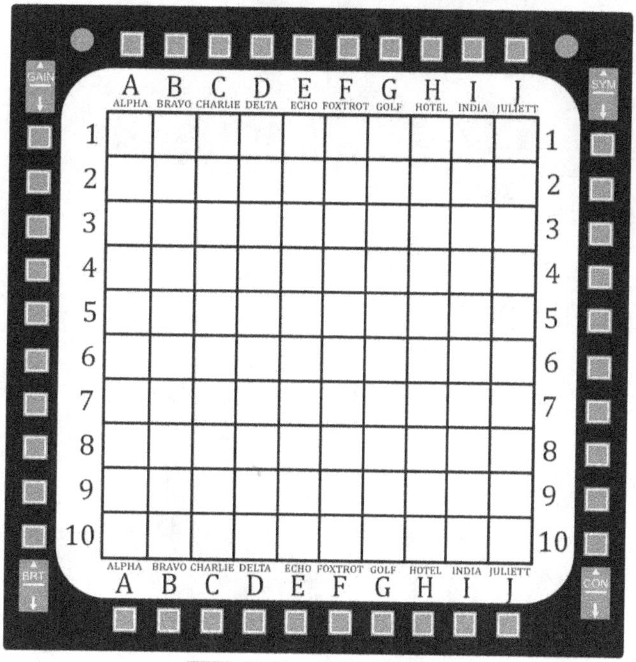

☒ HIT   ◯ MISS

Enemy Call Sign: _____

KEY

ENEMY AIRSPACE

FIGHTER	BOMBER
F F F F	B / B B B / B

| ATTACK | |
| A A / A A | |

| STEALTH | TANKER |
| S / S | T / T T T / T |

| CIVILIAN | |
| C | |

GAIN SYM

	A	B	C	D	E	F	G	H	I	J
ALPHA	BRAVO	CHARLIE	DELTA	ECHO	FOXTROT	GOLF	HOTEL	INDIA	JULIETT

1
2
3
4
5
6
7
8
9
10

A B C D E F G H I J
ALPHA BRAVO CHARLIE DELTA ECHO FOXTROT GOLF HOTEL INDIA JULIETT

BRT CON

☒ HIT   ◯ MISS

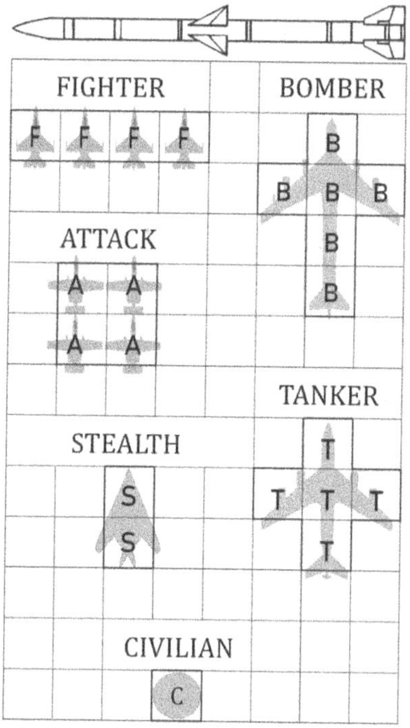

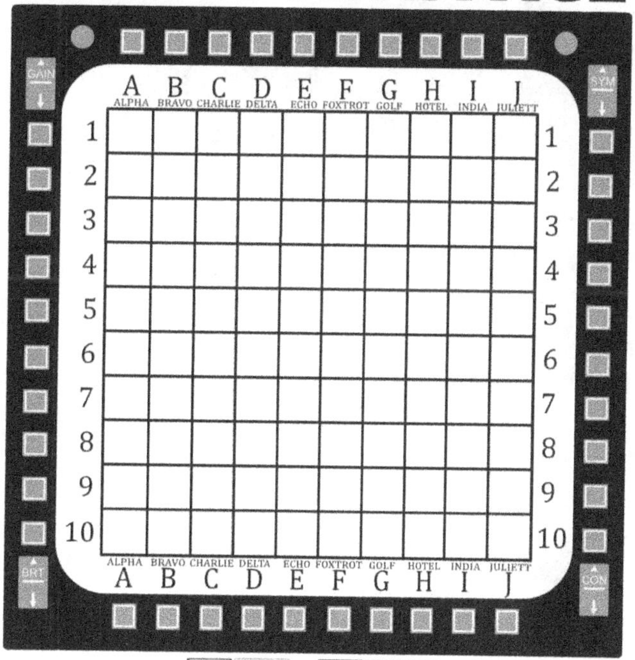

105

Onyx
Weldon

MOUNTAINS

WALKER PASS
5246

6696

4000

UNCLASSIFIED

golf course

RIDGECREST
TERA (Pvt)

R-251

a Mesa

7294

6500

6901

LA MOA

R WILDERNESS AREAS

ranches

microwave towers

INYOKERN (IYK)
2457 *L 71 122.8 ©
RP 20

bldgs

school

3483

IR425

IR200

IR211

MOA EXCLUDES AIRSPACE
1500' AGL AND BELOW

6274

KELSO VALLEY (Pvt)
4074 – 34

5997

RED ROCK CANYON
STATE PARK

5244

radomes

station

4974

6429

VR 1262

Garlock

Randsburg
substation

Johannesburg
Red Mountain
5261

GRAND MOUNTAIN RCO
RIVERSIDE

5203

IR211

IR425

ANSITING
ON 133.65

6707

6698

IR211-VR1262

IR200

2000

MOA EXCLUDES AIRSPACE
500' AGL AND BELOW

houses

CALIFORNIA
CITY MUNI (L71)
AWOS-1 120.875
2454 *L 60 122.7 ©
RP 24

3310

4584

street pattern

56

street patterns

California City

3145

MOJAVE

radomes

MOJAVE SPACE PORT
RUTAN FLD (MHV)
CT 121.6 ©
AWOS-3 132.22
260 *L 60
RP 22, 26

2500

EDWARDS AF AUX
NORTH BASE (9L2)
2299 *L 60

plant

(Pvt)
BORON AIRSTRIP
2499 – 24

Mojave

2862

ranch

EDWARDS
116.4 11 EDW

VR 1262

4190

oil

plant

MOA EXCLUDES AIRSPACE
4800' MSL AND BELOW

35°

118°

3404
bldgs

MOA EXCLUDES AIRSPACE
1500' AGL AND BELOW

ROSAMOND
SKYPARK (L00)
2415 *L 36 122.9 ©
RP

3206

EDWARDS AFB (EDW)
CT - 120
ATIS 127.425 269.9
2311 *L 150

DESERT

WILLOW
SPRINGS
(Pvt)

race track

OYOTE RANCH
2600 26

Rosamond

BUCKHORN
MOA

3424

(Pvt)
SUN HILL RA
2984

73

2572

TLE BUTTES
QUE AIRFIELD
2433 - 29

GENESA WV - FOX
AIRFIELD (WJF)
AIRFIELD 120.9

prison

LANCASTER

BUCKHORN
SOUTH

CAUTION: Unmanned Aircraft system operations
conducted in this area below 18,000 MSL. See
and avoid responsibility

3583
4120

Fuel Up with
Extra game
sheets:

3651

45

EL MIRAGE FLD
ADELANTO
2856 – 64

PALMDALE
PLANT 42
CT 120.7
ATIS 118.079
120

PALMDALE
PALMDALE
115.55 GXP 002 PMD

HANSEN (Pvt)
2885 - 59 122.8

school

AIR BATTLE

3500

5200

LAKE
PALMDALE

GRAY BUTTE FLD
3035 – 80

KREY F
3042

4850

5217

3581

PALMDALE ASOS 411 GXA

TAC INSET

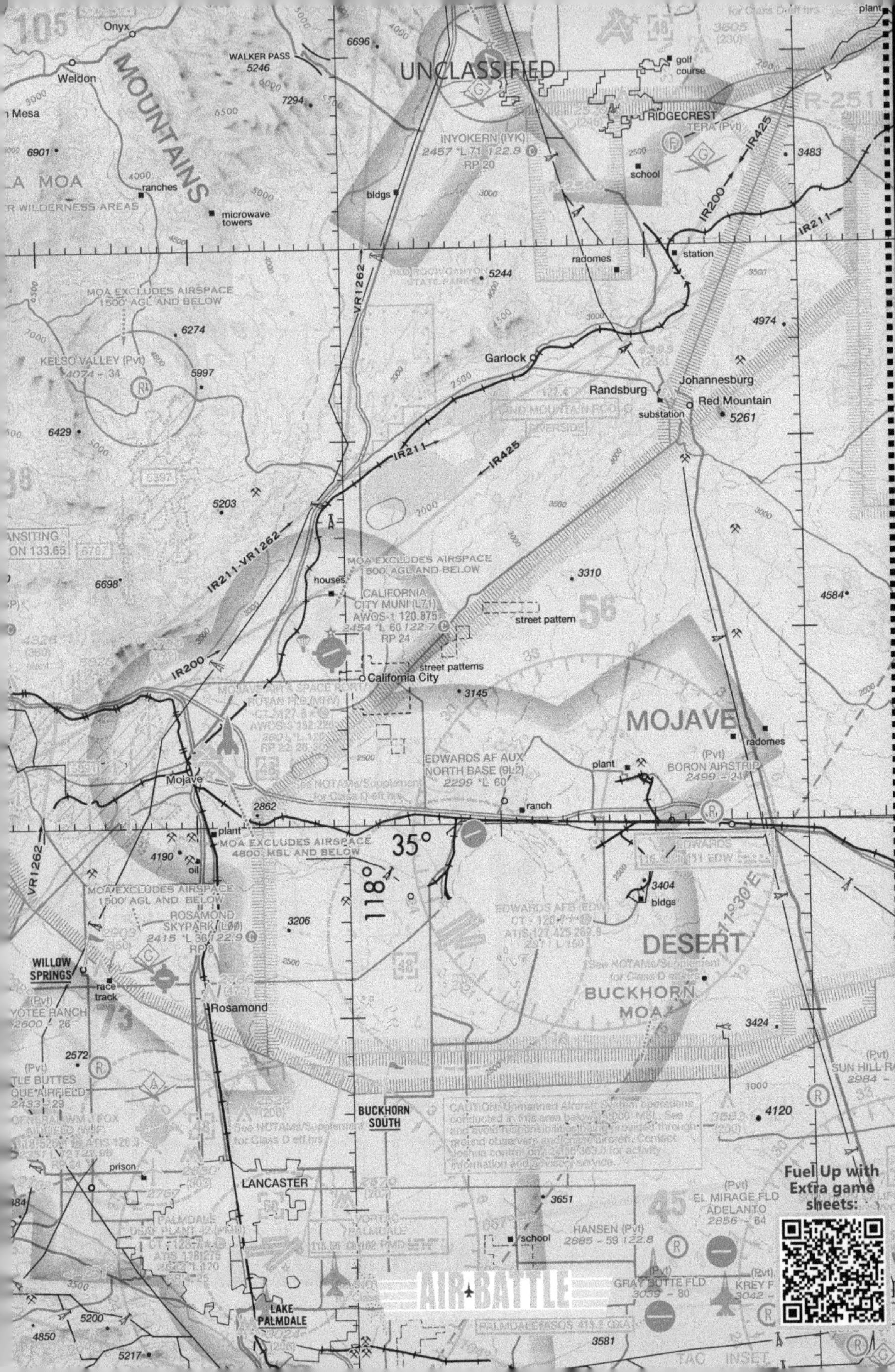

FOLD ALONG DOTTED LINE AND TEAR

Call Sign: ______________

AIR BATTLE

KEY

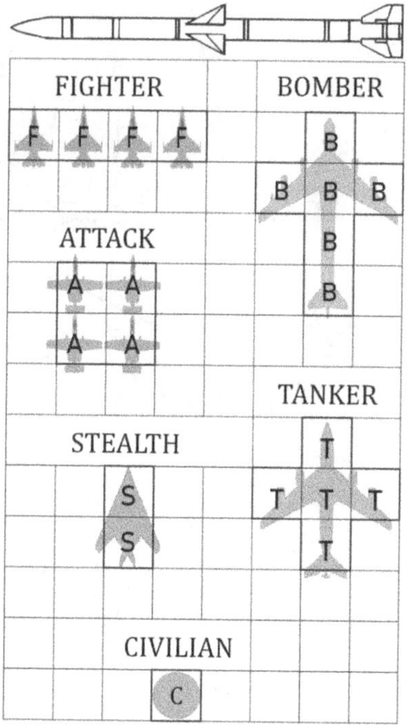

MY AIRSPACE

	A ALPHA	B BRAVO	C CHARLIE	D DELTA	E ECHO	F FOXTROT	G GOLF	H HOTEL	I INDIA	J JULIETT	
1											1
2											2
3											3
4											4
5											5
6											6
7											7
8											8
9											9
10											10
	ALPHA A	BRAVO B	CHARLIE C	DELTA D	ECHO E	FOXTROT F	GOLF G	HOTEL H	INDIA I	JULIETT J	

GAIN SYM BRT CON

HIT MISS

Enemy Call Sign: _________

KEY

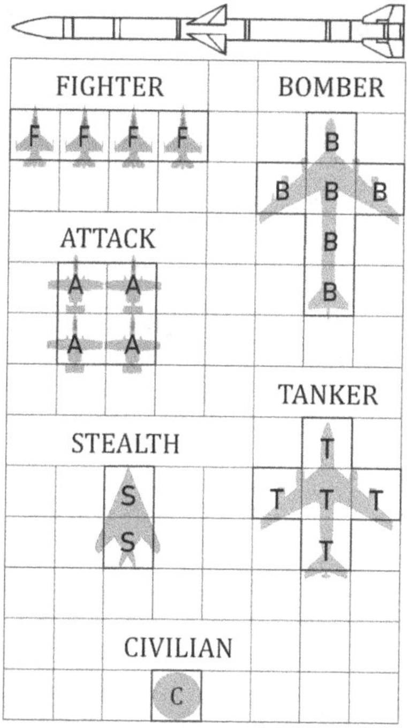

ENEMY AIRSPACE

	A ALPHA	B BRAVO	C CHARLIE	D DELTA	E ECHO	F FOXTROT	G GOLF	H HOTEL	I INDIA	J JULIETT	
1											1
2											2
3											3
4											4
5											5
6											6
7											7
8											8
9											9
10											10
	ALPHA A	BRAVO B	CHARLIE C	DELTA D	ECHO E	FOXTROT F	GOLF G	HOTEL H	INDIA I	JULIETT J	

GAIN SYM BRT CON

HIT MISS

FOLD ALONG DOTTED LINE AND TEAR

UNCLASSIFIED
(Pvt) JULIAN HINDS PUMP PLANT AIRSTRIP
CAUTION: Intensive Parachute Activity
solar farm
Avoid plant 1
towers
VR 227
IR216
IR217
VR1266
CHUCKWALLA MOUNTAINS
4504
2799
3080
ABEL NORTH MOA
RESTRICTED R-2507N
3446
2051
2580
VR1266-1267-1268
RESTRICTED R-2507E
ABEL NORTH MOA EXCLUDED WHEN R-2507 N, S & E ARE ACTIVE
2064
2700
RESTRICTED R-2507S
Niland
ABEL SOUTH MOA EXCLUDED WHEN R-2507W & R-2512 ARE ACTIVE
prison
CLIFF HATFIELD MEML (CLR)
RP 26
Calipatria
KANE EAST MOA
ABEL SOUTH MOA
Wiest
BRAWLEY MUNI (BWC)
RP 26
Westmorland
480
Glamis
Brawley
580
115°
101
R-2512
KANE SOUTH MOA
ABEL BRAVO MOA
ABEL BRAVO MOA EXCLUDED WHEN R-2512 IS ACTIVE
Imperial
HOLTVILLE (L04)
substation
AIR BATTLE

Fuel Up with Extra game sheets!

FOLD ALONG DOTTED LINE AND TEAR

FOLD ALONG DOTTED LINE AND TEAR

Call Sign: _____

KEY

MY AIRSPACE

FIGHTER

F F F F

BOMBER

B
B B B
B
B

ATTACK

A A
A A

TANKER

T
T T T
T

STEALTH

S
S

CIVILIAN

C

	A ALPHA	B BRAVO	C CHARLIE	D DELTA	E ECHO	F FOXTROT	G GOLF	H HOTEL	I INDIA	J JULIETT	
1											1
2											2
3											3
4											4
5											5
6											6
7											7
8											8
9											9
10											10

A ALPHA B BRAVO C CHARLIE D DELTA E ECHO F FOXTROT G GOLF H HOTEL I INDIA J JULIETT

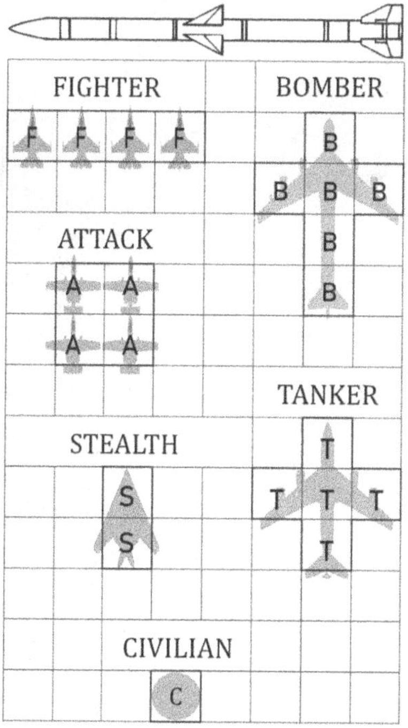

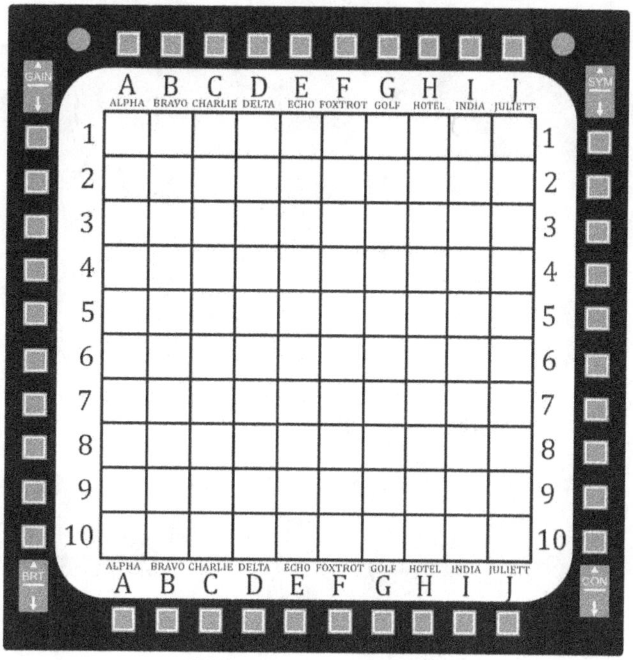

⊠ HIT   ◯ MISS

Enemy Call Sign: _____

KEY

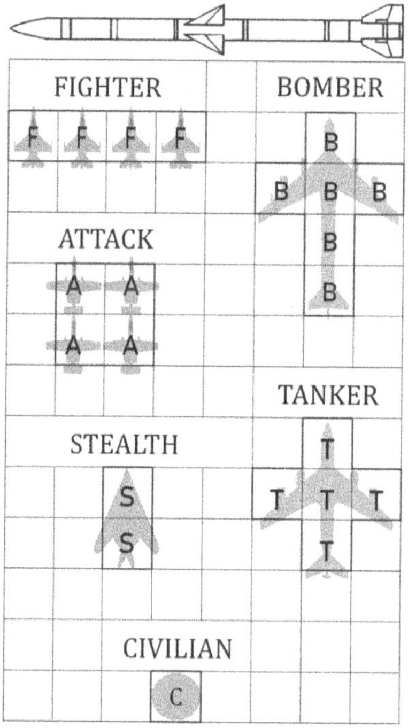

ENEMY AIRSPACE

FIGHTER

F F F F

BOMBER

B
B B B
B
B

ATTACK

A A
A A

TANKER

T
T T T
T

STEALTH

S
S

CIVILIAN

C

	A ALPHA	B BRAVO	C CHARLIE	D DELTA	E ECHO	F FOXTROT	G GOLF	H HOTEL	I INDIA	J JULIETT	
1											1
2											2
3											3
4											4
5											5
6											6
7											7
8											8
9											9
10											10

A ALPHA B BRAVO C CHARLIE D DELTA E ECHO F FOXTROT G GOLF H HOTEL I INDIA J JULIETT

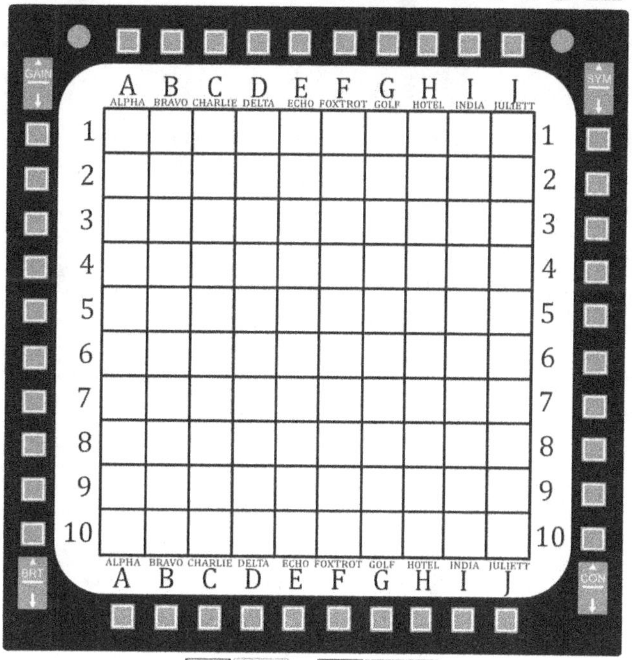

⊠ HIT   ◯ MISS

FOLD ALONG DOTTED LINE AND TEAR

UNCLASSIFIED

71

MOA EXCLUDES AIRSPACE
3000' AGL AND BELOW

MOA EXCLUDES AIRSPACE
3000' AGL AND BELOW

36°

5492

5920

5252

·-229   5384

4766

Shoshone
· 3048

SHOSHONE (L61)
1568 L 24 122.9 ©
RP 33

SUGARLOAF
PEAK
· 4820

DEATH VALLEY
NATIONAL PARK

4751

MOA EXCLUDES AIRSPACE
1500' AGL AND BELOW

2688   Tecopa

OWLSHEAD MOUNTAINS

· 4409

microwave
tower

65

SHOSHONE

57

· 4666
← VR1215   ← IR212

2592

MOA EXCLUDES AIRSPACE
3000' AGL AND BELOW

dunes

· 1460

5103

VR1215

AVAWATZ
PASS
4175

· 4879

4810   5384

· 6168

5560

RESTRICTED
R-2502N   · 5295

3313
(204)

R-2502

GOLDSTONE/GTS
3038 ~ 60   (Pvt)

· 4835   4880

3270

3231
(205)

R-2502E

BICYCLE LAKE AAF (BYS)
2350 L 96

3497

VR1214-1215

BAKE
922
12
R

· 5063

water ⌖ Fort Irwin

58

4534

MOA EXCLUDES AIRSPACE
BELOW 3000' AGL

56

3661

tower

■ towers

3456

3624

4526 ·   ← VR1218

AIR BATTLE

plant

BARSTOW
MOA

SILVER
SOUTH

rest
area

Call Sign: _____

 AIR✦BATTLE

KEY

FIGHTER
F F F F

BOMBER
B
B B B
B
B

ATTACK
A A
A A

STEALTH
S
S

TANKER
T
T T T
T

CIVILIAN
C

MY AIRSPACE

	A ALPHA	B BRAVO	C CHARLIE	D DELTA	E ECHO	F FOXTROT	G GOLF	H HOTEL	I INDIA	J JULIETT	
1											1
2											2
3											3
4											4
5											5
6											6
7											7
8											8
9											9
10											10
	A ALPHA	B BRAVO	C CHARLIE	D DELTA	E ECHO	F FOXTROT	G GOLF	H HOTEL	I INDIA	J JULIETT	

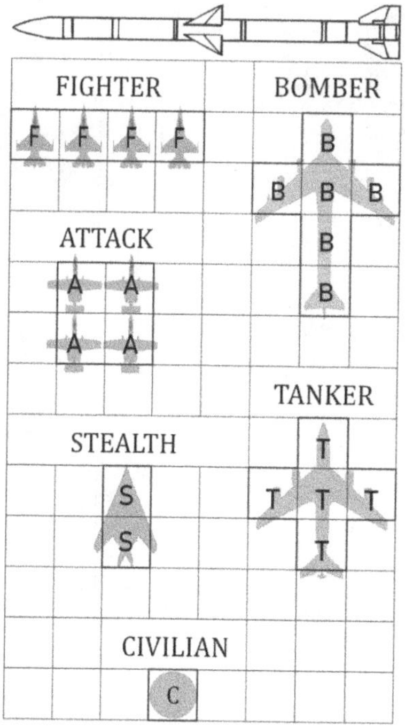

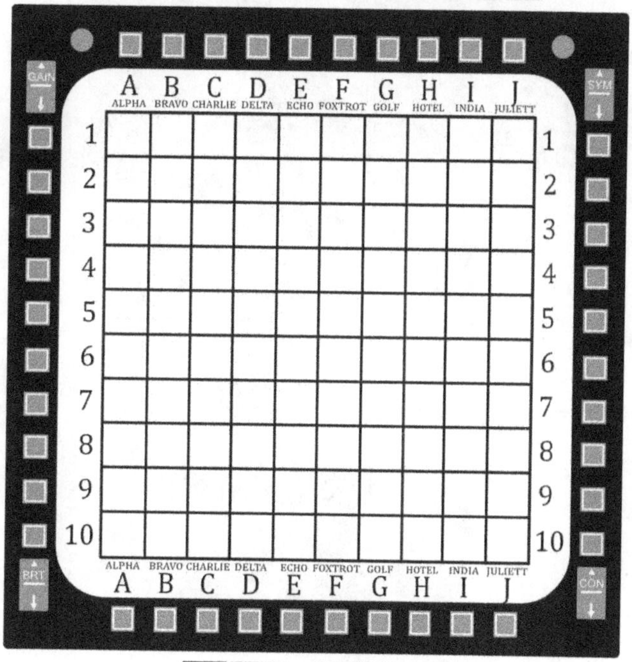

☒ HIT   ◯ MISS

Enemy Call Sign: _____

KEY

FIGHTER
F F F F

BOMBER
B
B B B
B

ATTACK
A A
A A

STEALTH
S
S

TANKER
T
T T T
T

CIVILIAN
C

ENEMY AIRSPACE

	A ALPHA	B BRAVO	C CHARLIE	D DELTA	E ECHO	F FOXTROT	G GOLF	H HOTEL	I INDIA	J JULIETT	
1											1
2											2
3											3
4											4
5											5
6											6
7											7
8											8
9											9
10											10
	A ALPHA	B BRAVO	C CHARLIE	D DELTA	E ECHO	F FOXTROT	G GOLF	H HOTEL	I INDIA	J JULIETT	

☒ HIT   ◯ MISS

FOLD ALONG DOTTED LINE AND TEAR

FOLD ALONG DOTTED LINE AND TEAR

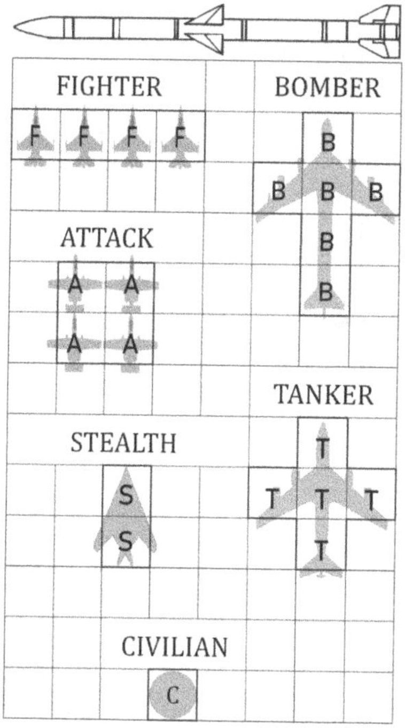

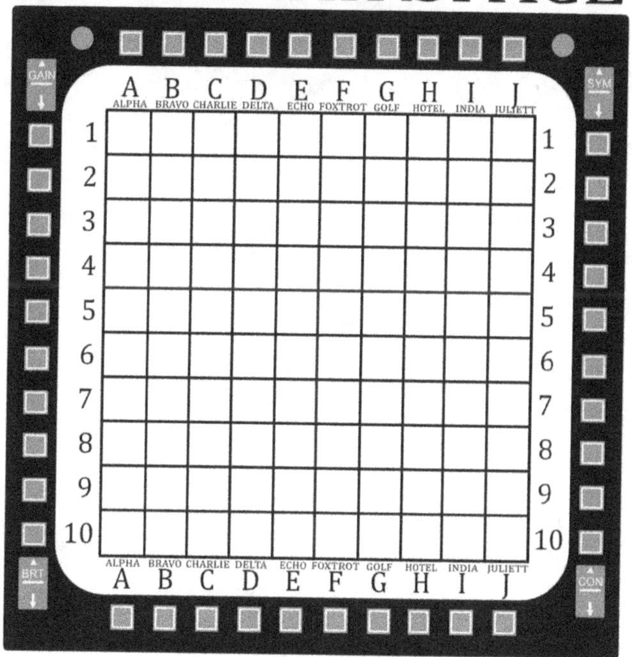

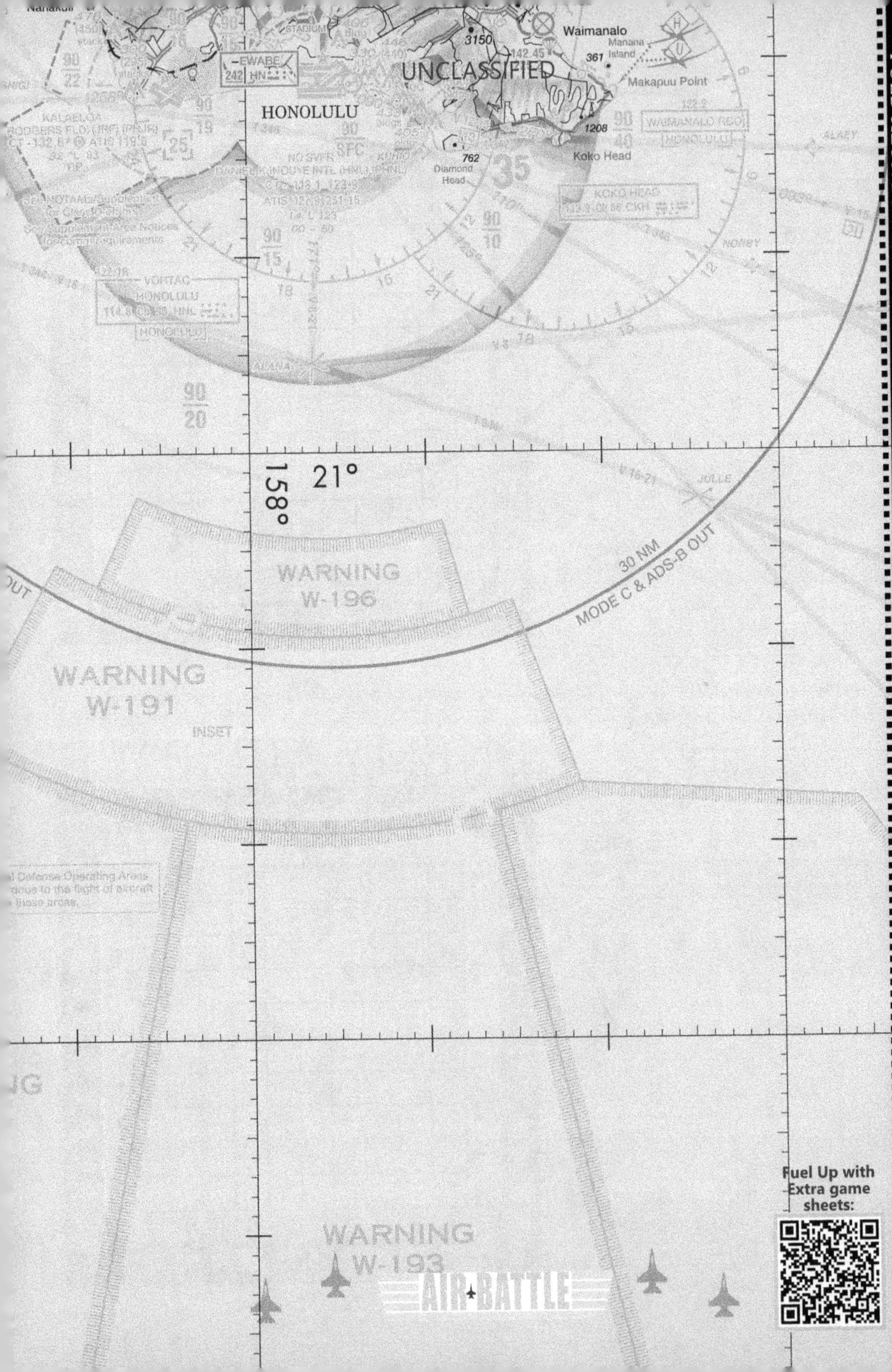

Waimanalo
3150
Manana Island
361
UNCLASSIFIED
Makapuu Point
HONOLULU
1208
Koko Head
762
Diamond Head
21°
158°
WARNING
W-196
30 NM
MODE C & ADS-B OUT
WARNING
W-191
INSET
WARNING
W-193
AIR BATTLE

Fuel Up with Extra game sheets:

FOLD ALONG DOTTED LINE AND TEAR

FOLD ALONG DOTTED LINE AND TEAR

Call Sign: _____

KEY

MY AIRSPACE

FIGHTER	BOMBER
F F F F	B B B / B / B

ATTACK

A A / A A

STEALTH

S / S

TANKER

T / T T T / T

CIVILIAN

C

MY AIRSPACE grid:

	A ALPHA	B BRAVO	C CHARLIE	D DELTA	E ECHO	F FOXTROT	G GOLF	H HOTEL	I INDIA	J JULIETT
1										
2										
3										
4										
5										
6										
7										
8										
9										
10										

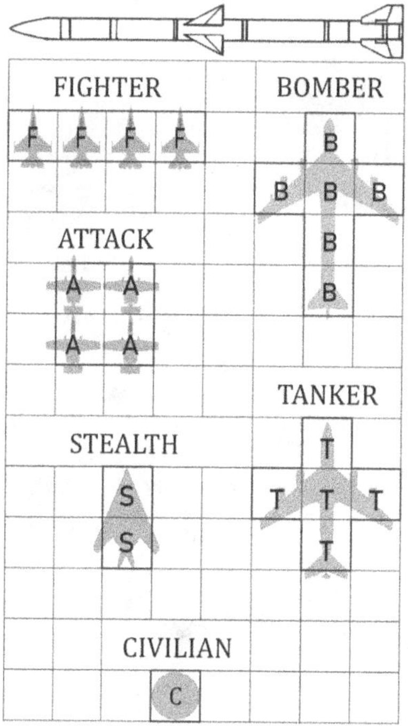

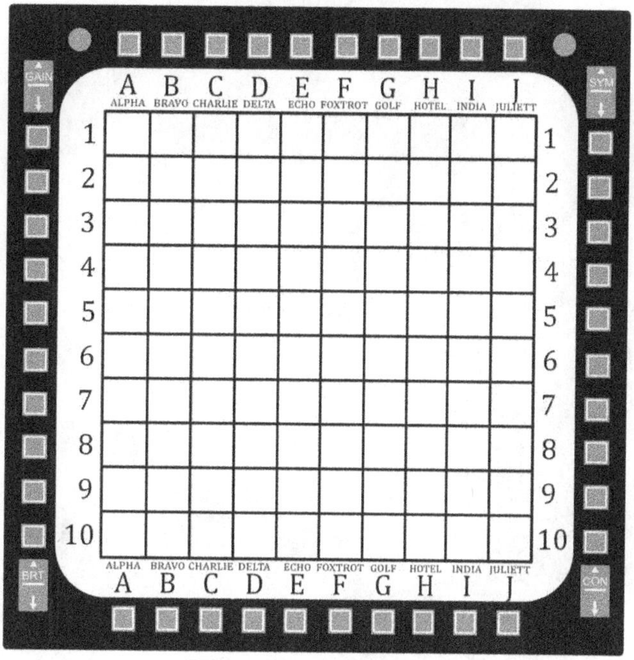

⊠ HIT   ◯ MISS

Enemy Call Sign: _____

KEY

ENEMY AIRSPACE

FIGHTER	BOMBER
F F F F	B B B / B / B

ATTACK

A A / A A

STEALTH

S / S

TANKER

T / T T T / T

CIVILIAN

C

ENEMY AIRSPACE grid:

	A ALPHA	B BRAVO	C CHARLIE	D DELTA	E ECHO	F FOXTROT	G GOLF	H HOTEL	I INDIA	J JULIETT
1										
2										
3										
4										
5										
6										
7										
8										
9										
10										

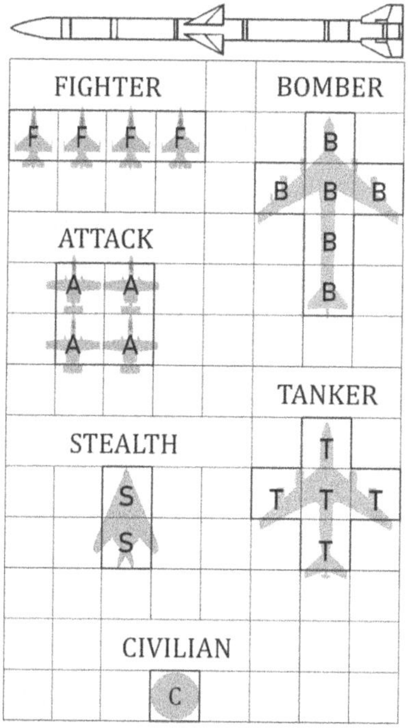

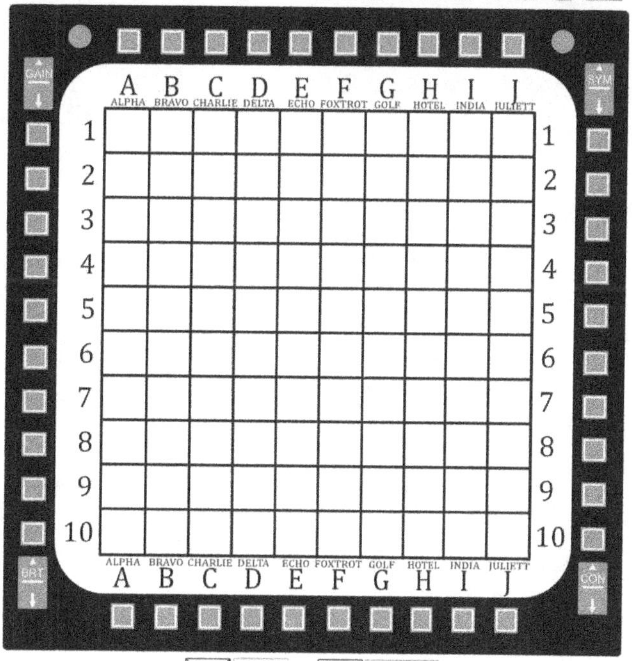

⊠ HIT   ◯ MISS

FOLD ALONG DOTTED LINE AND TEAR

70
SFC

lock and dam

Barling

Fort Chaffee

UNCLASSIFIED

R-2402C

Roseville

(Pvt)
ETNA
536 – 21

PARIS MUNI
430 'L 27
122.9

Branch   Ratcliff

Caulksville

Carbon City   Paris

ARROWHEAD ASSAULT STRIP

CHARLESTON

R-2402B

HOG A MOA
EXCLUDES R-2402B
WHEN ACTIVE

70
15

R-2402A

GREENWOOD

1033

BOONEVILLE MUNI (4M2)
468 'L 32 122.8

Magazine

VR1130

VR1113

1093   Barber

VR1102
VR1103
VR1104

BOONEVILLE

Blue Mountain

Sugar Grove

Abbott

Ione

hospital

MOA
EXCLUDES AIRSPACE
1500' AGL AND BELOW

Mansfield

Hartford

IR117

831
(268)

935
(307)

29

IR120
IR121
IR164

VR189
IR120

2439

CAUTION - RAPIDLY
RISING TERRAIN

1986

35°

microwave tower

2403

Hon

985
(256)

946

1500

Wal

Cauthron

Waldron

CREEK

Gravelly

IDLY RISING TERRAIN

CAUTION DURING PERIODS
OW CEILING AND VISIBILITY

MOA
EXCLUDES AIRSPACE
1500' AGL AND BELOW

WALDRON MUNI (M27)
205 'L 36 122.9

DUTCH

VR1103-1104

1382

1294
(305)

Parks

Boles

HOG A MOA

27

1782

Eagleton

2570

BLUE MT

2623

2285

Sims

2681

2165

CAUTION - RAPIDLY
RISING TERRAIN

HOG B MOA

Oden

Pencil Bluff
Fuel Up with
Extra game
sheets.

Rocky   Mena

Cherry Hill

Potter

Board Camp

AIR BATTLE

HOG B MOA

1890

MENA INTERMOUNTAIN MUNI (MEZ)
AWOS-3 118.025
1080 'L 55 122.8

1550

Call Sign: _____

KEY

MY AIRSPACE

FIGHTER	BOMBER
F F F F	B / B B B / B / B

ATTACK	
A A / A A	

STEALTH	TANKER
S / S	T / T T T / T

CIVILIAN	
C	

My Airspace grid, columns A–J (ALPHA BRAVO CHARLIE DELTA ECHO FOXTROT GOLF HOTEL INDIA JULIETT), rows 1–10.

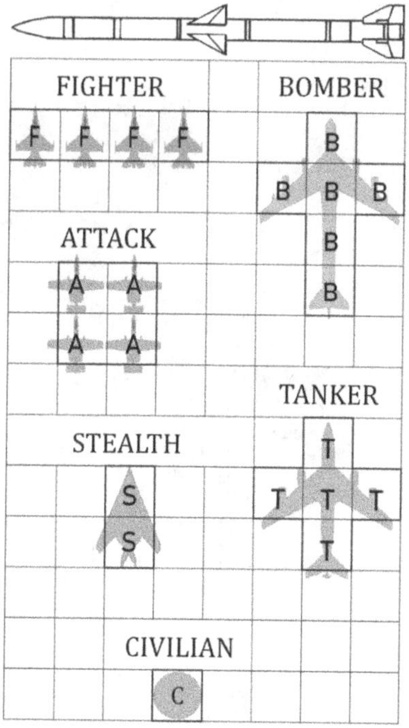

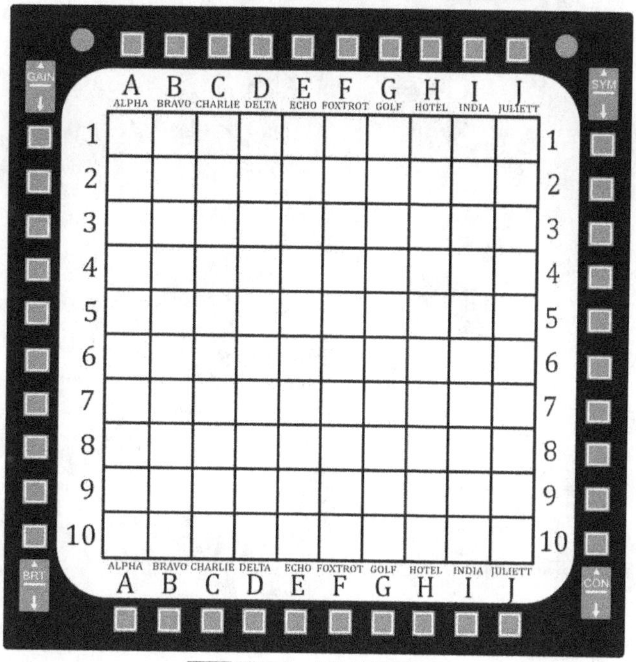

☒ HIT   ◯ MISS

Enemy Call Sign: _____

KEY

ENEMY AIRSPACE

FIGHTER	BOMBER
F F F F	B / B B B / B

ATTACK	
A A / A A	

STEALTH	TANKER
S / S	T / T T T / T

CIVILIAN	
C	

Enemy Airspace grid, columns A–J (ALPHA BRAVO CHARLIE DELTA ECHO FOXTROT GOLF HOTEL INDIA JULIETT), rows 1–10.

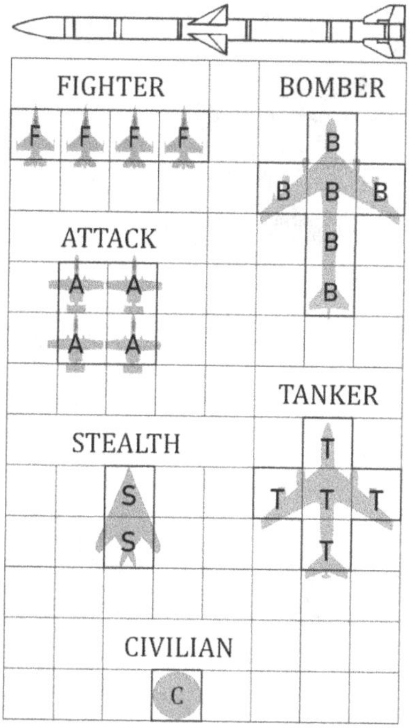

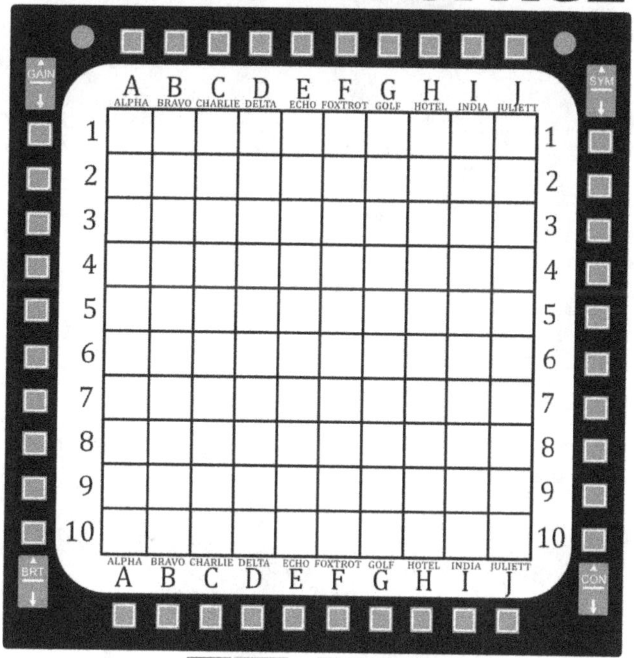

☒ HIT   ◯ MISS

FOLD ALONG DOTTED LINE AND TEAR

UNCLASSIFIED

MERIDIAN 1 WEST MOA

AIR BATTLE

Fuel Up with Extra game sheets:

MERIDIAN 2 EAST MOA

Call Sign: _____

KEY

MY AIRSPACE

FIGHTER

F F F F

BOMBER

B
B B B
B
B

ATTACK

A A
A A

STEALTH

S
S

TANKER

T
T T T
T

CIVILIAN

C

	A	B	C	D	E	F	G	H	I	J	
	ALPHA	BRAVO	CHARLIE	DELTA	ECHO	FOXTROT	GOLF	HOTEL	INDIA	JULIETT	
1											1
2											2
3											3
4											4
5											5
6											6
7											7
8											8
9											9
10											10
	ALPHA	BRAVO	CHARLIE	DELTA	ECHO	FOXTROT	GOLF	HOTEL	INDIA	JULIETT	
	A	B	C	D	E	F	G	H	I	J	

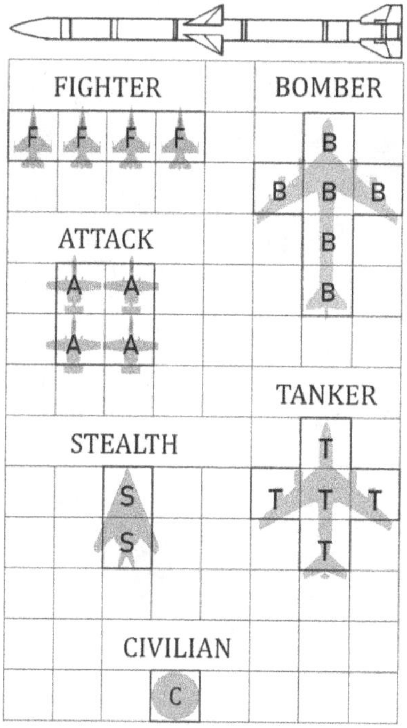

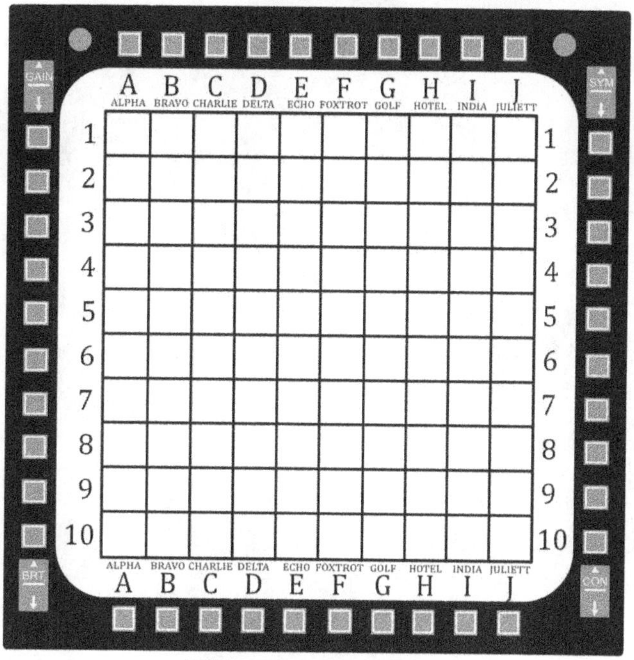

⊠ HIT   ◯ MISS

Enemy Call Sign: _____

KEY

ENEMY AIRSPACE

FIGHTER

F F F F

BOMBER

B
B B B
B
B

ATTACK

A A
A A

STEALTH

S
S

TANKER

T
T T T
T

CIVILIAN

C

	A	B	C	D	E	F	G	H	I	J	
	ALPHA	BRAVO	CHARLIE	DELTA	ECHO	FOXTROT	GOLF	HOTEL	INDIA	JULIETT	
1											1
2											2
3											3
4											4
5											5
6											6
7											7
8											8
9											9
10											10
	ALPHA	BRAVO	CHARLIE	DELTA	ECHO	FOXTROT	GOLF	HOTEL	INDIA	JULIETT	
	A	B	C	D	E	F	G	H	I	J	

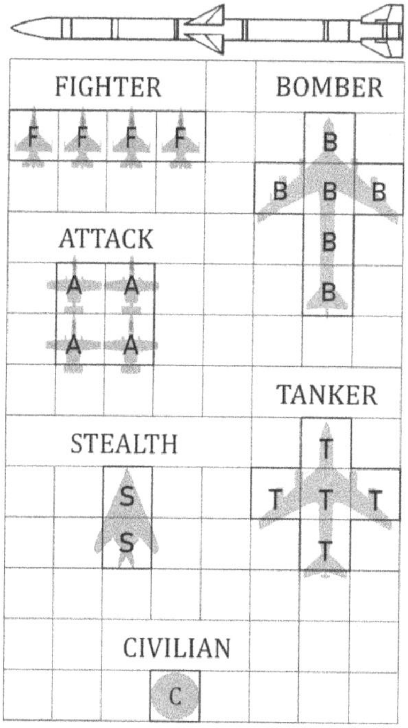

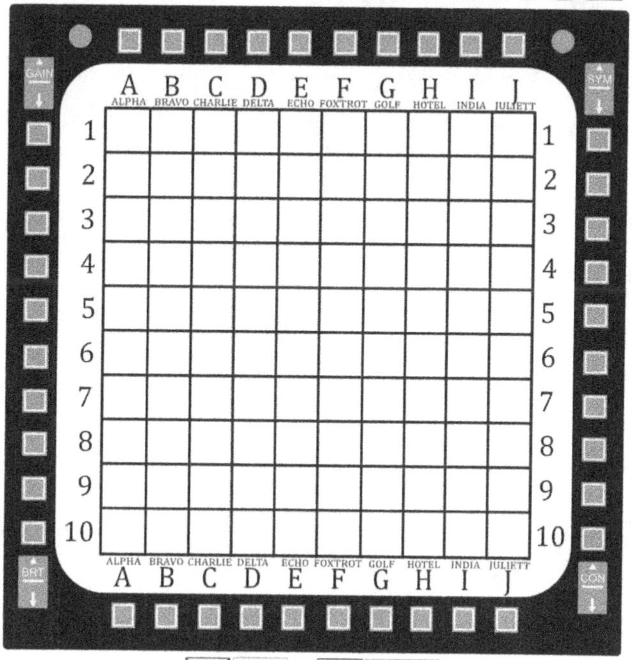

⊠ HIT   ◯ MISS

FOLD ALONG DOTTED LINE AND TEAR

UNCLASSIFIED

COLUMBUS 3 MOA

COLUMBUS 1 MOA

COLUMBUS 3 MOA

CTC COLUMBUS-ARP WITHIN
20 NM ON 135.6 323.275

AIR BATTLE

Call Sign: _____

KEY

MY AIRSPACE

FIGHTER

F F F F

BOMBER

B
B B B
B
B

ATTACK

A A
A A

TANKER

T
T T T
T

STEALTH

S
S

CIVILIAN

C

	A	B	C	D	E	F	G	H	I	J	
	ALPHA	BRAVO	CHARLIE	DELTA	ECHO	FOXTROT	GOLF	HOTEL	INDIA	JULIETT	
1											1
2											2
3											3
4											4
5											5
6											6
7											7
8											8
9											9
10											10

ALPHA BRAVO CHARLIE DELTA ECHO FOXTROT GOLF HOTEL INDIA JULIETT
A B C D E F G H I J

☒ HIT   ◯ MISS

Enemy Call Sign: _____

KEY

ENEMY AIRSPACE

FIGHTER

F F F F

BOMBER

B
B B B
B
B

ATTACK

A A
A A

TANKER

T
T T T
T

STEALTH

S
S

CIVILIAN

C

	A	B	C	D	E	F	G	H	I	J	
	ALPHA	BRAVO	CHARLIE	DELTA	ECHO	FOXTROT	GOLF	HOTEL	INDIA	JULIETT	
1											1
2											2
3											3
4											4
5											5
6											6
7											7
8											8
9											9
10											10

ALPHA BRAVO CHARLIE DELTA ECHO FOXTROT GOLF HOTEL INDIA JULIETT
A B C D E F G H I J

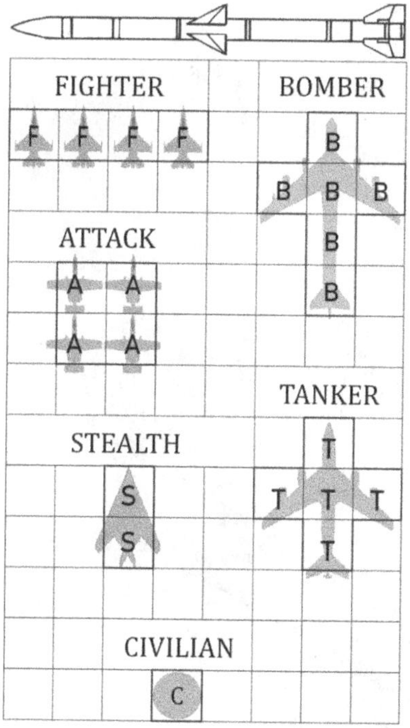

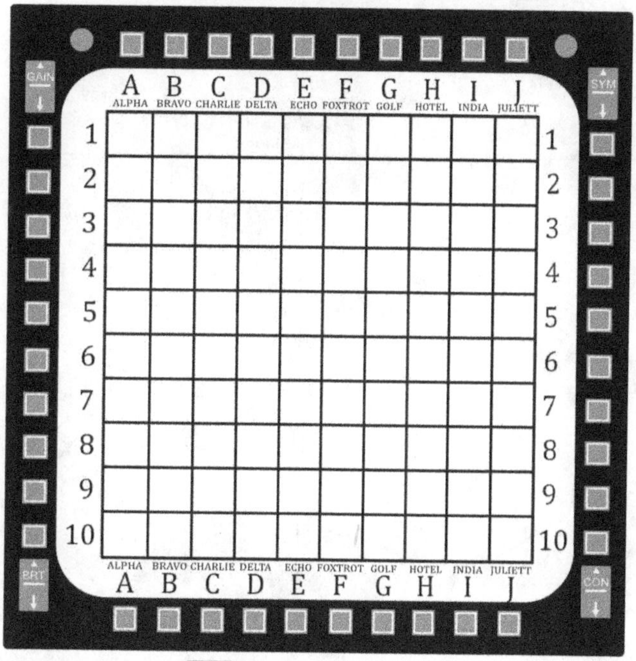

☒ HIT   ◯ MISS

FOLD ALONG DOTTED LINE AND TEAR

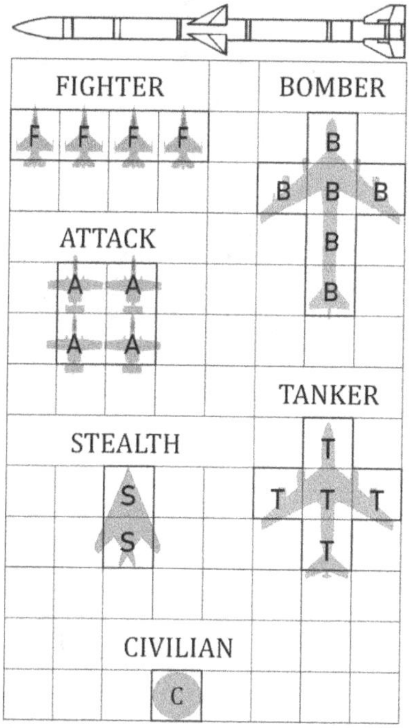

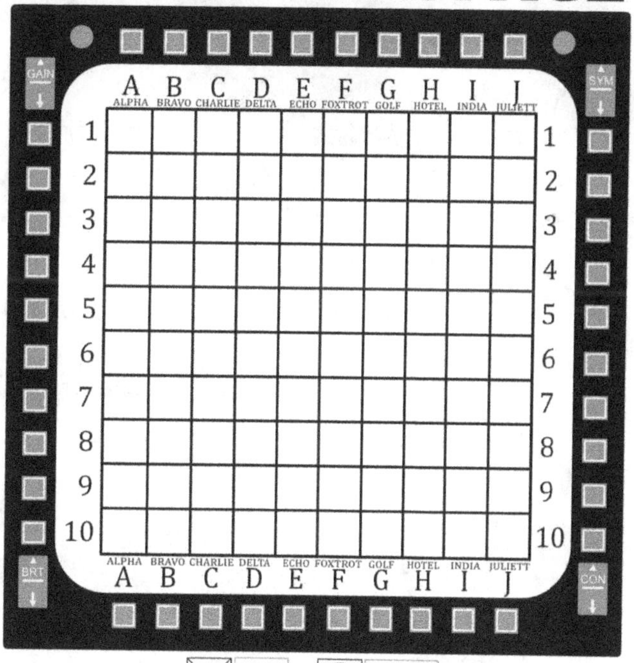

Fuel Up with
Extra game
sheets!

FOLD ALONG DOTTED LINE AND TEAR

FOLD ALONG DOTTED LINE AND TEAR

Call Sign: _____

KEY

MY AIRSPACE

FIGHTER   BOMBER

ATTACK

TANKER

STEALTH

CIVILIAN

	A	B	C	D	E	F	G	H	I	J	
	ALPHA	BRAVO	CHARLIE	DELTA	ECHO	FOXTROT	GOLF	HOTEL	INDIA	JULIETT	
1											1
2											2
3											3
4											4
5											5
6											6
7											7
8											8
9											9
10											10

ALPHA BRAVO CHARLIE DELTA ECHO FOXTROT GOLF HOTEL INDIA JULIETT
A B C D E F G H I J

☒ HIT   ◯ MISS

Enemy Call Sign: _____

KEY

ENEMY AIRSPACE

FIGHTER   BOMBER

ATTACK

TANKER

STEALTH

CIVILIAN

	A	B	C	D	E	F	G	H	I	J	
	ALPHA	BRAVO	CHARLIE	DELTA	ECHO	FOXTROT	GOLF	HOTEL	INDIA	JULIETT	
1											1
2											2
3											3
4											4
5											5
6											6
7											7
8											8
9											9
10											10

ALPHA BRAVO CHARLIE DELTA ECHO FOXTROT GOLF HOTEL INDIA JULIETT
A B C D E F G H I J

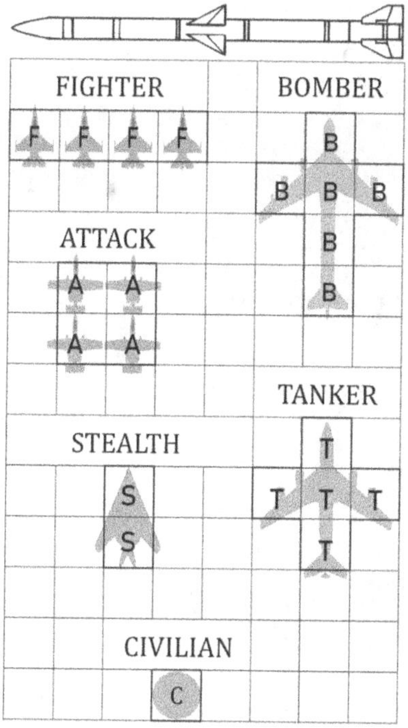

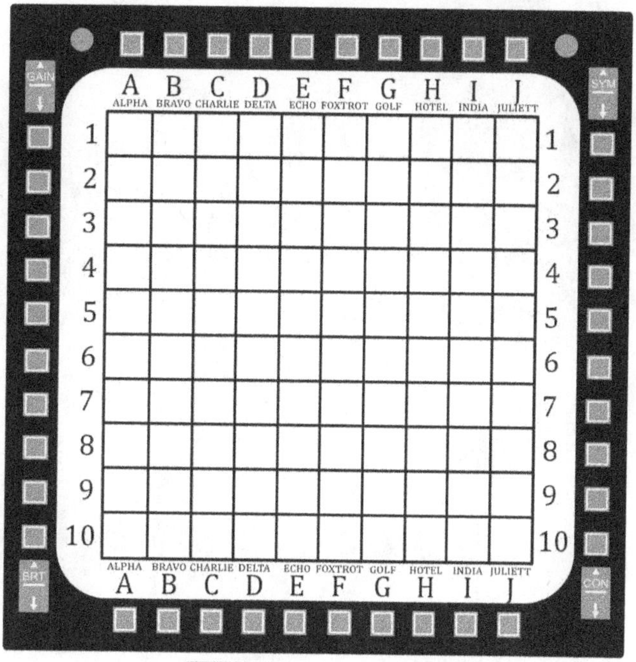

☒ HIT   ◯ MISS

FOLD ALONG DOTTED LINE AND TEAR

FOLD ALONG DOTTED LINE AND TEAR

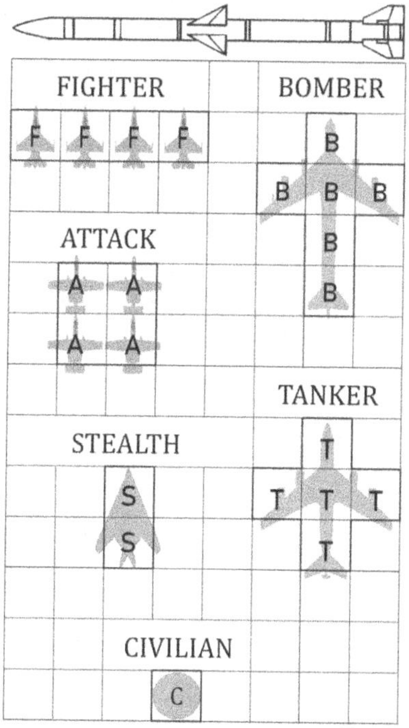

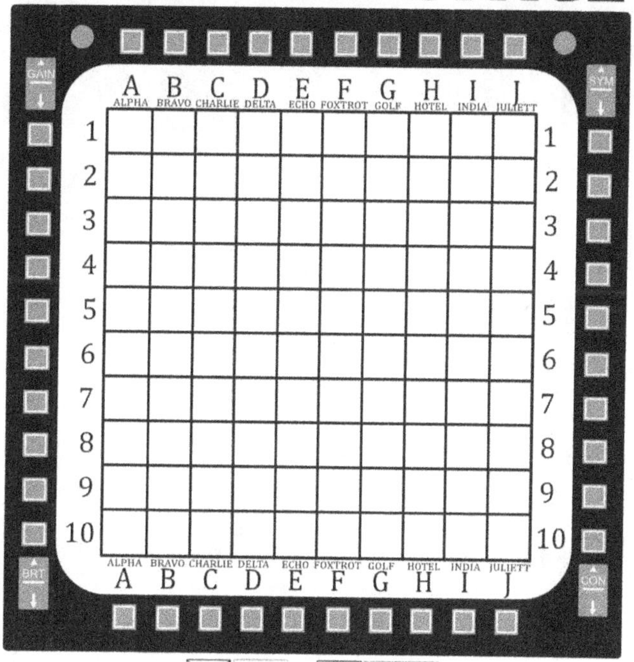

Satsuma
UNCLASSIFIED
POMONA LANDING (Pvt)
50 – 275
Welaka
R-2906
LITTLE LAKE GEORGE WILDERNESS
THUNDERBIRD AIR PARK (Pvt)
67 – 29 122.8
VR1009
JIM FINLAY FARM (Pvt)
40 – 24
MOUNT ROYAL (Pvt)
60 – 30
00 – 24
Crescent City
SKINNERS WHOLESALE NURSERY (Pvt)
20 – 34
MOA EXCLUDES
E WITHIN R-2906
WHEN ACTIVE
EAGLES NEST AERODROME (Pvt)
63 – 32
Georgetown
43 – 33
MORNINGWOOD (Pvt)
40 – 40
VR1040
VR1041
A-293
CAUTION: High volume of flight training surface to 4000' MSL
R-2907 B & C
Salt Springs
R-2907A
PALATKA 1 MOA EXCLUDES THE AIRSPACE WITHIN R-2907 A & B AND R-2910 A & D WHEN ACTIVE
LAKE DISSTON
PIERSON MUNI (2J8)
63 – 26 122.9
RP 23
JUNIPER PRAIRIE WILDERNESS
VR1039
LAFAY
R-2910 D & E
R-2910 A
Astor Park
LAKE WOODRUFF NATIONAL WILDLIFE REFUGE
ALEXANDER SPRINGS WILDERNESS
star
marina
VR1009
LAKES AIRPARK (Pvt)
100 – 25
USFS
75
(Emerg only)
DELAND MUNI-SIDNEY H TAYLOR FLD
AWOS-3 119.575
79 *L 60 123.075
BILLIES BAY WILDERNESS
DEEP WOODS RANCH (Pvt)
45 – 28
Starkes Ferry
ROCKING G RANCH (Pvt)
67 – 41
Altoona
R-2910 B
BRADSHAW (Pvt)
55 – 21
Umatilla
See NOTAMs/Supplement for Class D/E (sfc) eff hrs
AIR BATTLE
water
UMATILLA MUNI (X23)
106 *L 29 122.9
Cassia
ORLANDO CLASS B
Fuel Up with Extra game sheets:

FOLD ALONG DOTTED LINE AND TEAR

FOLD ALONG DOTTED LINE AND TEAR

FOLD ALONG DOTTED LINE AND TEAR

Call Sign: ______________

AIR BATTLE

MY AIRSPACE

KEY

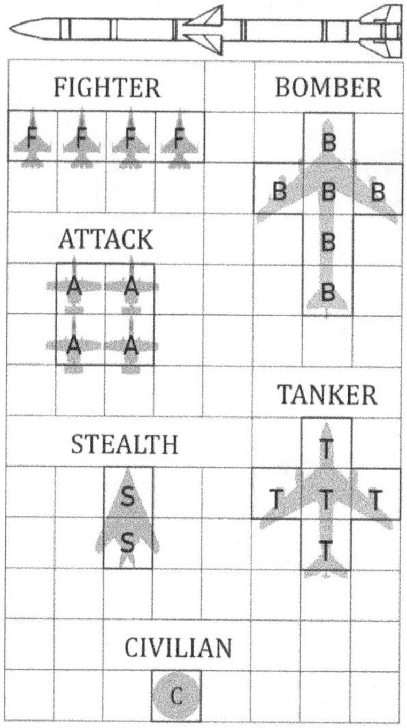

	A ALPHA	B BRAVO	C CHARLIE	D DELTA	E ECHO	F FOXTROT	G GOLF	H HOTEL	I INDIA	J JULIETT	
1											1
2											2
3											3
4											4
5											5
6											6
7											7
8											8
9											9
10											10
	ALPHA A	BRAVO B	CHARLIE C	DELTA D	ECHO E	FOXTROT F	GOLF G	HOTEL H	INDIA I	JULIETT J	

GAIN SYM BRT CON

☒ HIT ◯ MISS

FOLD ALONG DOTTED LINE AND TEAR

Enemy Call Sign: __________

ENEMY AIRSPACE

KEY

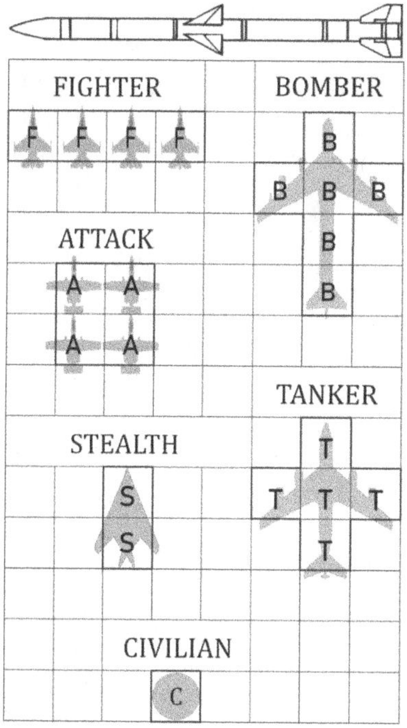

	A ALPHA	B BRAVO	C CHARLIE	D DELTA	E ECHO	F FOXTROT	G GOLF	H HOTEL	I INDIA	J JULIETT	
1											1
2											2
3											3
4											4
5											5
6											6
7											7
8											8
9											9
10											10
	ALPHA A	BRAVO B	CHARLIE C	DELTA D	ECHO E	FOXTROT F	GOLF G	HOTEL H	INDIA I	JULIETT J	

GAIN SYM BRT CON

☒ HIT ◯ MISS

Fuel Up with Extra game sheets:

FOLD ALONG DOTTED LINE AND TEAR

FOLD ALONG DOTTED LINE AND TEAR

Call Sign: _____

KEY

MY AIRSPACE

FIGHTER — F F F F

BOMBER — B / B B B / B / B

ATTACK — A A / A A

STEALTH — S / S

TANKER — T / T T T / T

CIVILIAN — C

	A ALPHA	B BRAVO	C CHARLIE	D DELTA	E ECHO	F FOXTROT	G GOLF	H HOTEL	I INDIA	J JULIETT	
1											1
2											2
3											3
4											4
5											5
6											6
7											7
8											8
9											9
10											10

ALPHA BRAVO CHARLIE DELTA ECHO FOXTROT GOLF HOTEL INDIA JULIETT
A B C D E F G H I J

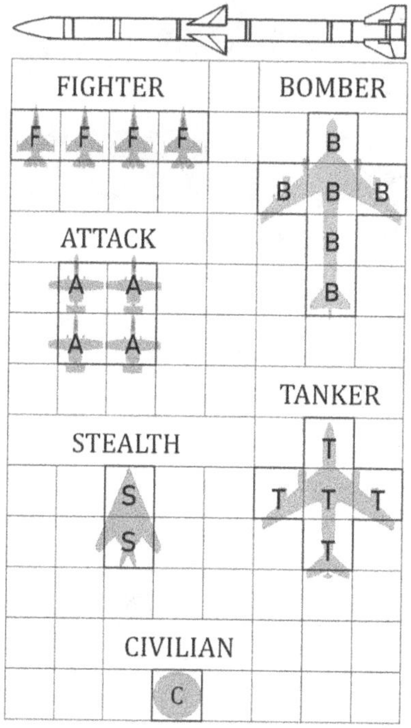

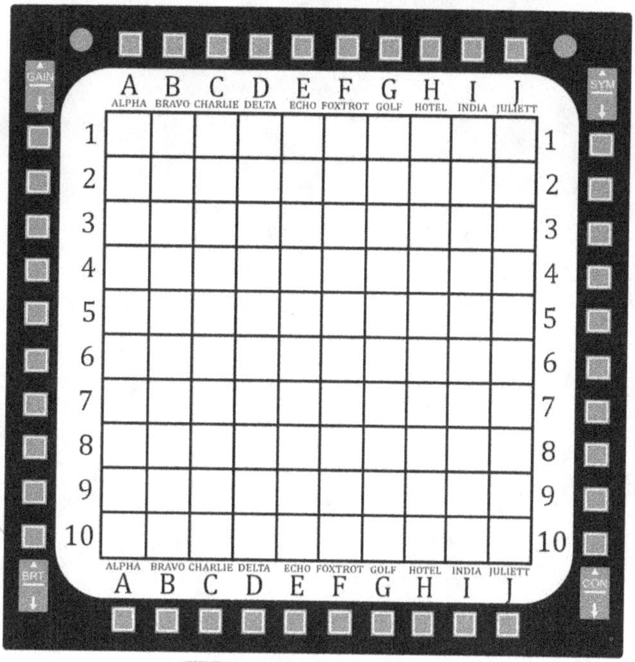

⊠ HIT   ◯ MISS

Enemy Call Sign: _____

KEY

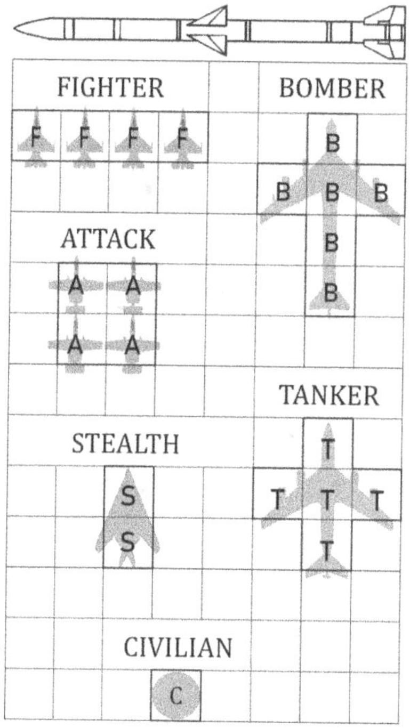

ENEMY AIRSPACE

FIGHTER — F F F F

BOMBER — B / B B B / B / B

ATTACK — A A / A A

STEALTH — S / S

TANKER — T / T T T / T

CIVILIAN — C

	A ALPHA	B BRAVO	C CHARLIE	D DELTA	E ECHO	F FOXTROT	G GOLF	H HOTEL	I INDIA	J JULIETT	
1											1
2											2
3											3
4											4
5											5
6											6
7											7
8											8
9											9
10											10

ALPHA BRAVO CHARLIE DELTA ECHO FOXTROT GOLF HOTEL INDIA JULIETT
A B C D E F G H I J

⊠ HIT   ◯ MISS

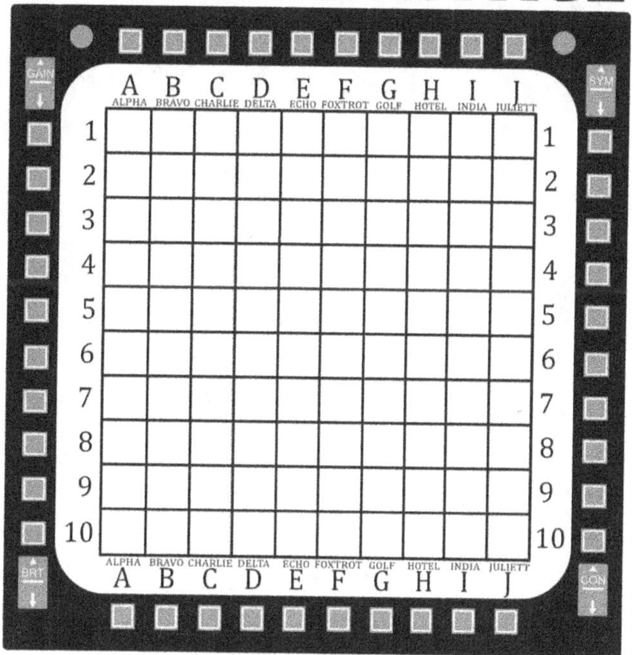

UNCLASSIFIED
BAGDAD (E51)
Bagdad
Signal
Yava
Hillside
BAGDAD 1 MOA
GLADDEN 1 MOA
BUCKSKIN MOUNTAINS
HARCUVAR MOUNTAINS
HARQUAHALA MTNS
Swansea
ranch
bldgs
towers
FLYING DARE'S RANCH
CUNNINGHAM PASS
OUTBACK RANCH AIRSTRIP
SAMPLEYS
Aguila
EAGLE ROOST AIRPARK
Gladden
Wenden
Salome
Utting
WESTERN SKY AIRPARK
INDIAN HILLS AIRPARK
settlement
Vicksburg
Hope
Brenda
WICKENBURG MUNI
AWOS-3 121.375
Congress
Piedmont
abandoned
rocky
radio facility
ALERT AREA A-231
CONCENTRATED STUDENT JET TRANSITION TRAINING
TONOPAH
Tonopah
MAULDIN AIRSTRIP
power plant
pumping station
EAGLETAIL
Wintersburg
VR245
VR242
IR254
IR250
IR214
VR1268
VR231
IR218
VR243
VR1267A
34°
113°

AIR BATTLE

Fuel Up with Extra game sheets

FOLD ALONG DOTTED LINE AND TEAR

FOLD ALONG DOTTED LINE AND TEAR

FOLD ALONG DOTTED LINE AND TEAR

Call Sign: ________________

AIR BATTLE

KEY

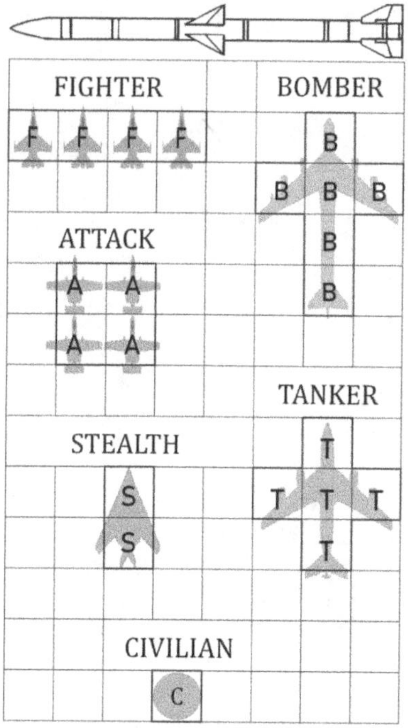

FIGHTER
F F F F
BOMBER
B
B B B
B
B
ATTACK
A A
A A
TANKER
T
T T T
T
STEALTH
S
S
CIVILIAN
C

MY AIRSPACE

	A ALPHA	B BRAVO	C CHARLIE	D DELTA	E ECHO	F FOXTROT	G GOLF	H HOTEL	I INDIA	J JULIETT	
1											1
2											2
3											3
4											4
5											5
6											6
7											7
8											8
9											9
10											10
	ALPHA A	BRAVO B	CHARLIE C	DELTA D	ECHO E	FOXTROT F	GOLF G	HOTEL H	INDIA I	JULIETT J	

GAIN SYM BRT CON

☒ HIT ◯ MISS

FOLD ALONG DOTTED LINE AND TEAR

Enemy Call Sign: __________

KEY

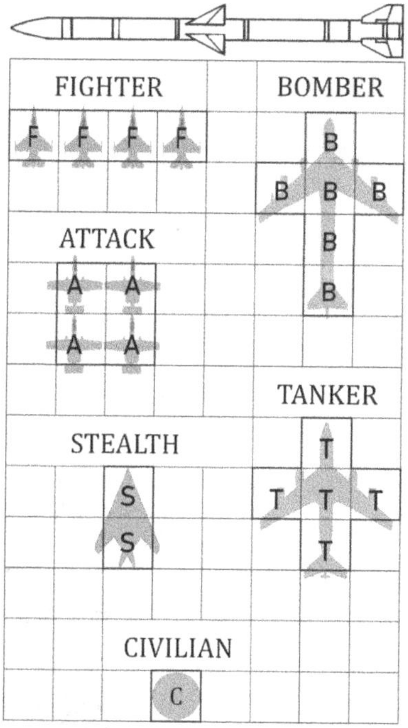

FIGHTER
F F F F
BOMBER
B
B B B
B
B
ATTACK
A A
A A
TANKER
T
T T T
T
STEALTH
S
S
CIVILIAN
C

ENEMY AIRSPACE

	A ALPHA	B BRAVO	C CHARLIE	D DELTA	E ECHO	F FOXTROT	G GOLF	H HOTEL	I INDIA	J JULIETT	
1											1
2											2
3											3
4											4
5											5
6											6
7											7
8											8
9											9
10											10
	ALPHA A	BRAVO B	CHARLIE C	DELTA D	ECHO E	FOXTROT F	GOLF G	HOTEL H	INDIA I	JULIETT J	

GAIN SYM BRT CON

☒ HIT ◯ MISS

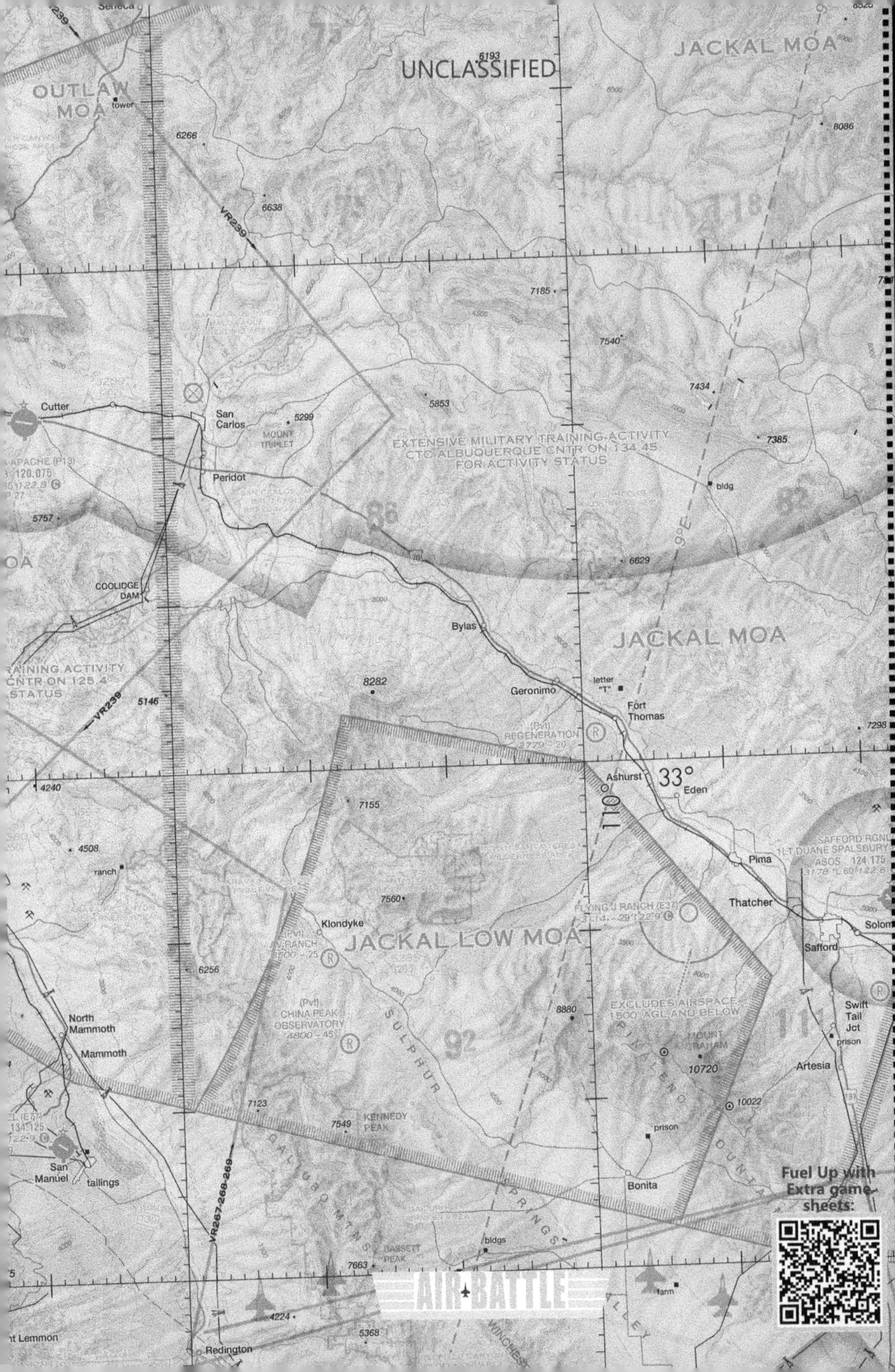
UNCLASSIFIED
JACKAL MOA
OUTLAW MOA
tower
6193
6266
6638
8086
VR239
7185
7540
7434
7385
5853
Cutter
San Carlos
MOUNT TRIPLET
5299
EXTENSIVE MILITARY TRAINING ACTIVITY
CTC ALBUQUERQUE CNTR ON 134.45
FOR ACTIVITY STATUS
Peridot
bldg
5757
6629
COOLIDGE DAM
Bylas
JACKAL MOA
RAINING ACTIVITY
CNTR ON 125.4
STATUS
8282
Geronimo
letter "T"
Fort Thomas
5146
(Pvt)
REGENERATION
2779 - 20
7298
4240
Ashurst
33°
Eden
7155
4508
ranch
Pima
SAFFORD RGNL
1LT DUANE SPALSBURY
ASOS 124.175
Thatcher
7560
FLYING J RANCH (E34)
Klondyke
JACKAL LOW MOA
Safford
Solomon
6256
8880
EXCLUDES AIRSPACE
1500 AGL AND BELOW
(Pvt)
CHINA PEAK
OBSERVATORY
4800 - 45
SULPHUR
North Mammoth
Mammoth
MOUNT GRAHAM
10720
Swift Tail Jct
prison
Artesia
7123
7549
KENNEDY PEAK
10022
prison
San Manuel
tailings
Bonita
VR267-268-269
bldgs
7663
BASSETT PEAK
farm
4224
5368
Redington
Lemmon

AIR BATTLE

Fuel Up with Extra game sheets:

FOLD ALONG DOTTED LINE AND TEAR

FOLD ALONG DOTTED LINE AND TEAR

FOLD ALONG DOTTED LINE AND TEAR

AIR BATTLE

Call Sign: ______________

KEY

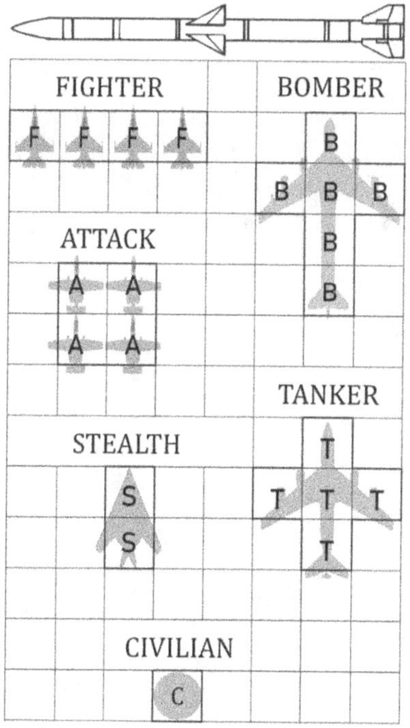
FIGHTER
F F F F
BOMBER
B
B B B
B
B
ATTACK
A A
A A
TANKER
T
T T T
T
STEALTH
S
S
CIVILIAN
C

MY AIRSPACE

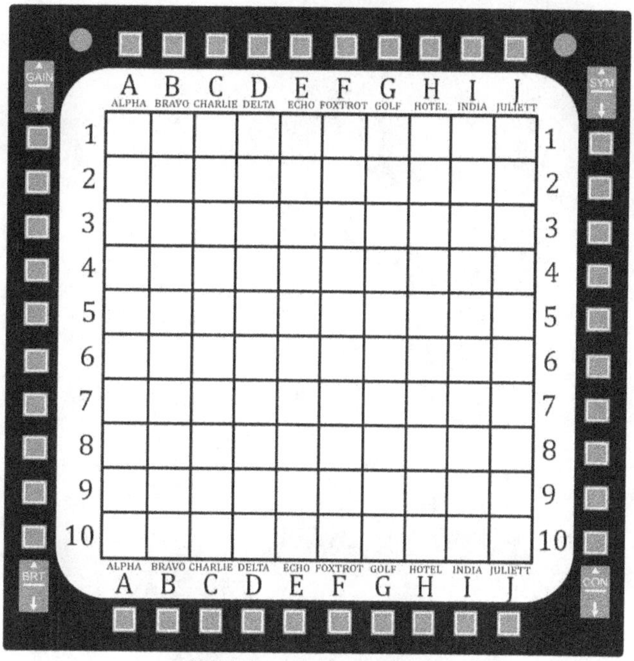
GAIN
SYM
A B C D E F G H I J
ALPHA BRAVO CHARLIE DELTA ECHO FOXTROT GOLF HOTEL INDIA JULIETT
1 2 3 4 5 6 7 8 9 10
BRT
CON

HIT MISS

Enemy Call Sign: __________

KEY

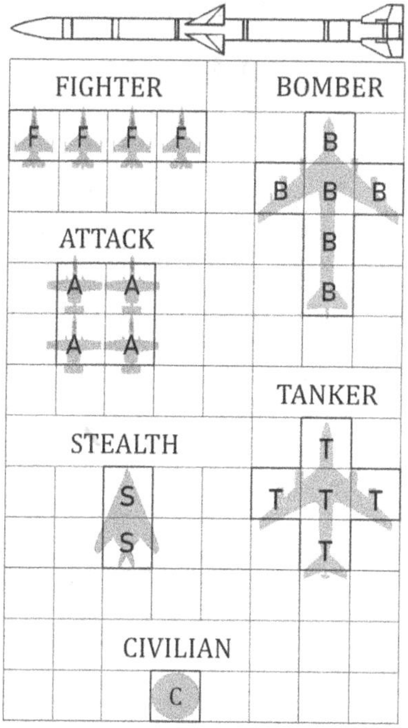
FIGHTER
F F F F
BOMBER
B
B B B
B
B
ATTACK
A A
A A
TANKER
T
T T T
T
STEALTH
S
S
CIVILIAN
C

ENEMY AIRSPACE

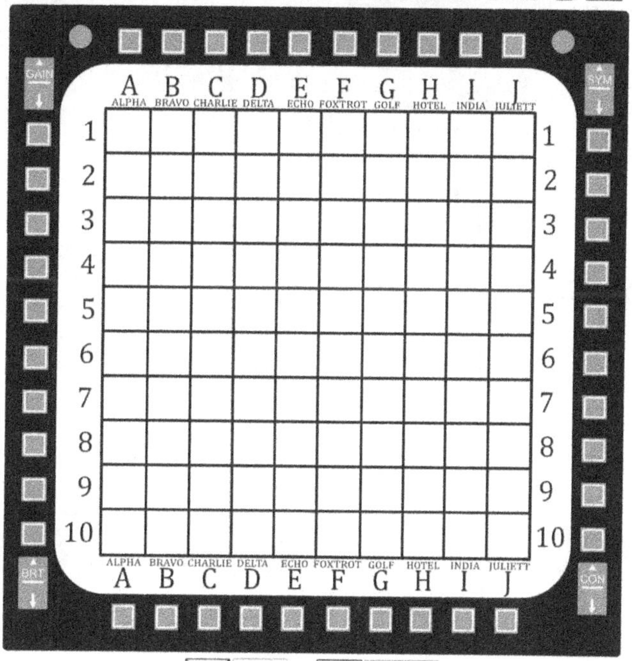
GAIN
SYM
A B C D E F G H I J
ALPHA BRAVO CHARLIE DELTA ECHO FOXTROT GOLF HOTEL INDIA JULIETT
1 2 3 4 5 6 7 8 9 10
BRT
CON

HIT MISS

FOLD ALONG DOTTED LINE AND TEAR

UNCLASSIFIED

MASSEY FARM
1632 – 13

LAKE HAVASU CITY (HII)
AWOS-3 119-025
793.1580 122-2 ®
RP 14

VR290

(Pvt)
SAGEBRUSH
TRAILS ESTATES
1964 – 40

5325

3471

5100
CROSSMAN PEAK

2926

3694

2274
street
pattern

VR256

2986

4882

2560

TURTLE MOA

CHEMEHUEVI VALLEY (II0)
634 122-2 ®

LAKE
HAVASU
CITY

1221

2700

IR252

3789

NRO
GENE WASH
RESERVOIR

IR250

3763

WHIPPLE MOUNTAINS

4130

2768

IR213-214

Milligan

4331

2695

2173

2113

3141

substation

Vidal
Jct

AVI SUQUINCA (P-20)
AWLPORT 132.75
663.1560 122-725 ®

Cienaga
Springs

1983

3330

(Pvt)
IRON MOUNTAIN
PUMPING PLANT
690 – 5 ®

IR255

Vidal

Parker

letter "P"
on hills

1665

Rice

street
pattern

IR256

IR255

2667

VR296

2254

VR1267-1268

996

2116

IR217

1797

CACTUS R

VR1267-1268

IR214

34°

4347

115°

18

QUAIL MOA

Bouse

114°

34°

IR214

3043

IR290

3852

IR218

3381

IR250

1420

2273

JALAPENO RANCH
1040 – 19

Uttin

3619

IR218

40

2822

IR250

2329

2880

solar
farm

2830

BLYTHE (BLH)
ASOS 120.175
400 1L-65 122-8 ®

2765

Quartzsite

towers

Brend

VR296

CAUTION: Intensive
Parachute Activity

128-15
power
plant

bldgs

settlement

3640

VR266

Avoid direct overflight of power plant

houses

VR1267-1268

BLYTHE (BLH)
ASOS 120.175
400 1L-65 122-8 ®

Blythe

Ehrenberg

VR1267A

prisons

3316

3640

190

Ripley

CALIFORNIA
ARIZONA

2747

2851

2653

2051

3446

3960

VR1266-1267-1268

Palo Verde

bldgs

2660

4580

1780

bldgs

3640

29

ABEL NORTH
MOA
ABEL NORTH IS EXCLUDED
WHEN R-2507 A, S & C ARE ACTIVE

2562

2768

2622

3240

2700

RESTRICTED
R-2507E

(Pvt)
WALTERS CAMP
305

AIR BATTLE

Fuel Up with
Extra game
sheets:

480

RR Siding

ABEL
EAST MOA

Glamis

3800

Call Sign: _____

KEY

MY AIRSPACE

FIGHTER
F F F F

BOMBER
B
B B B
B
B

ATTACK
A A
A A

TANKER
T
T T T
T

STEALTH
S
S

CIVILIAN
C

My Airspace grid: columns A–J (ALPHA BRAVO CHARLIE DELTA ECHO FOXTROT GOLF HOTEL INDIA JULIETT), rows 1–10

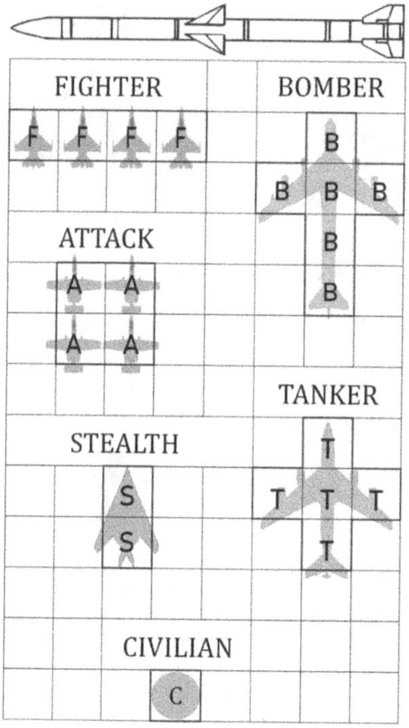

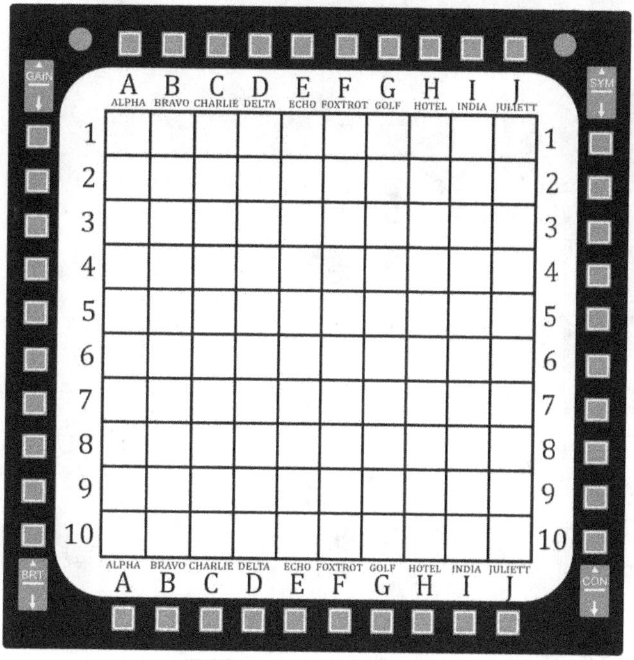

☒ HIT ◯ MISS

Enemy Call Sign: _____

KEY

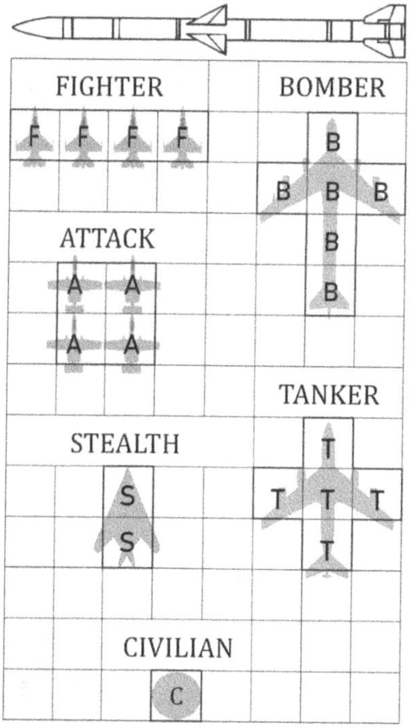

ENEMY AIRSPACE

FIGHTER
F F F F

BOMBER
B
B B B
B

ATTACK
A A
A A

TANKER
T
T T T
T

STEALTH
S
S

CIVILIAN
C

Enemy Airspace grid: columns A–J (ALPHA BRAVO CHARLIE DELTA ECHO FOXTROT GOLF HOTEL INDIA JULIETT), rows 1–10

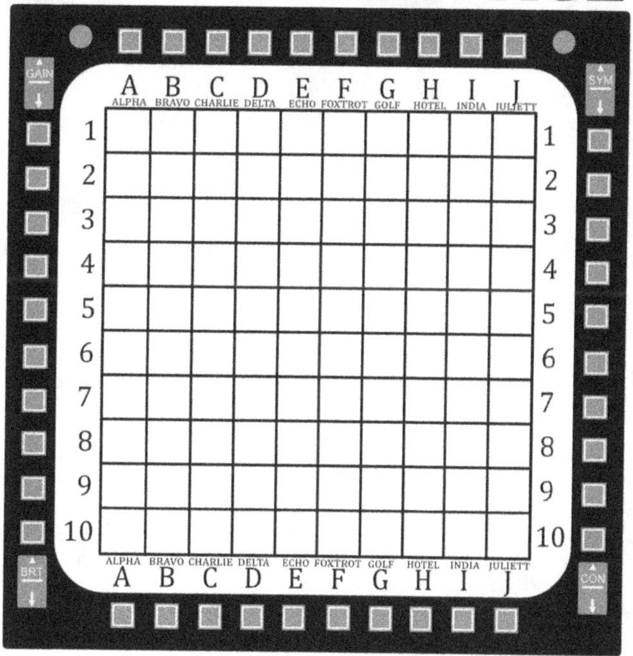

☒ HIT ◯ MISS

FOLD ALONG DOTTED LINE AND TEAR

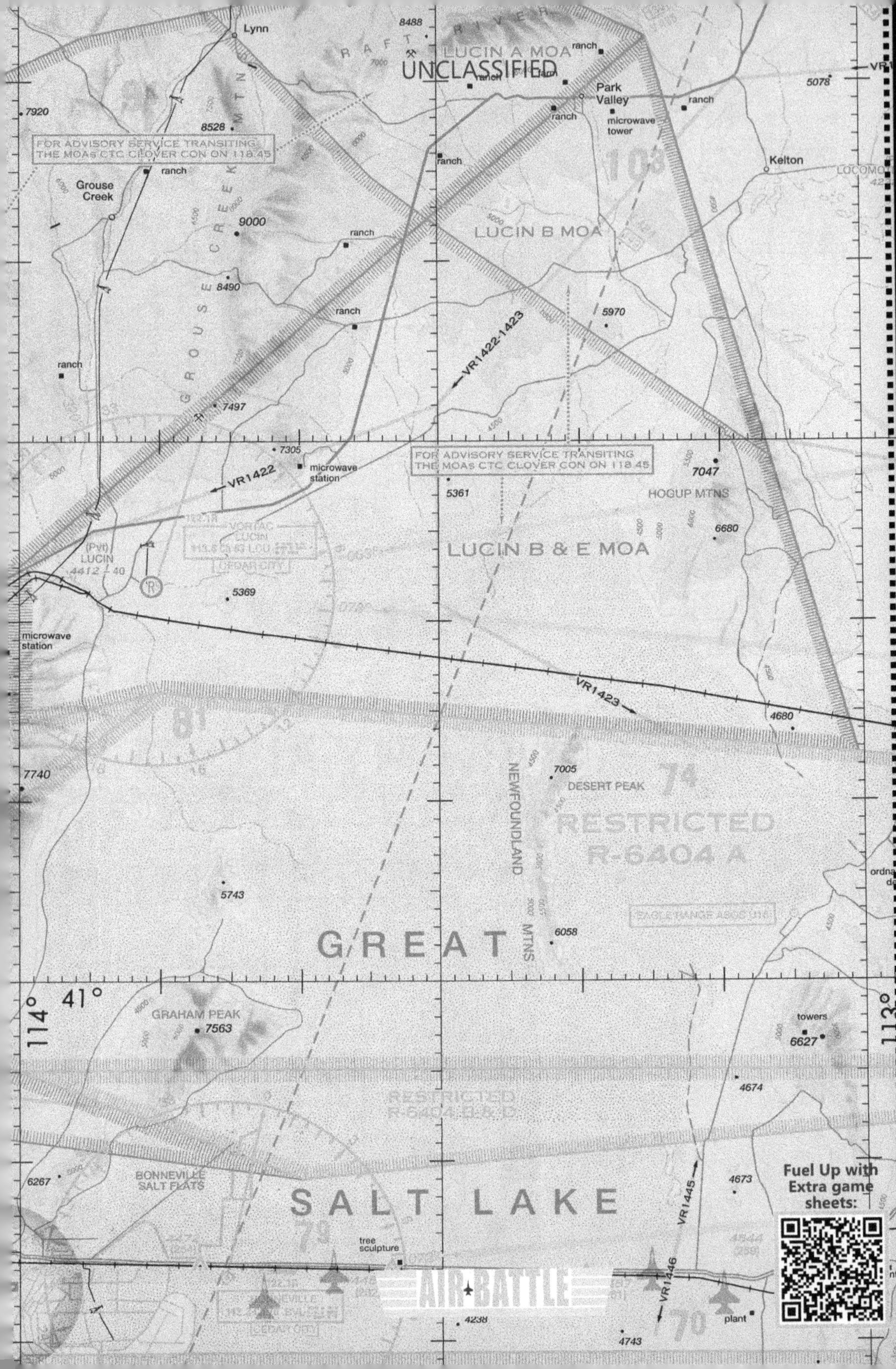
UNCLASSIFIED
LUCIN A MOA
LUCIN B MOA
LUCIN B & E MOA
FOR ADVISORY SERVICE TRANSITING THE MOAs CTC CLOVER CON ON 118.45
FOR ADVISORY SERVICE TRANSITING THE MOAs CTC CLOVER CON ON 118.45
Lynn
Park Valley
microwave tower
Kelton
Grouse Creek
GROUSE CREEK MTN
RAFT RIVER
VR1422-1423
VR1422
VR1423
VR1445
VR1446
microwave station
microwave station
(Pvt) LUCIN 4412 40
HOGUP MTNS
NEWFOUNDLAND MTNS
DESERT PEAK
RESTRICTED R-6404 A
RESTRICTED R-6404 B & D
GREAT SALT LAKE
GRAHAM PEAK
BONNEVILLE SALT FLATS
tree sculpture
towers
plant
ranch
8488
7920
8528
9000
8490
7497
7305
5361
5369
5970
7047
6680
5078
4680
7005
7740
5743
6058
7563
6627
4674
4673
6267
4238
4743
114°
41°
113°
AIR BATTLE

Fuel Up with Extra game sheets:

FOLD ALONG DOTTED LINE AND TEAR

FOLD ALONG DOTTED LINE AND TEAR

Call Sign: _____

KEY

FIGHTER	BOMBER

ATTACK	

STEALTH	TANKER

CIVILIAN

MY AIRSPACE

GAIN

SYM

```
      A   B   C   D   E   F   G   H   I   J
   ALPHA BRAVO CHARLIE DELTA ECHO FOXTROT GOLF HOTEL INDIA JULIETT
 1                                          1
 2                                          2
 3                                          3
 4                                          4
 5                                          5
 6                                          6
 7                                          7
 8                                          8
 9                                          9
10                                         10
   ALPHA BRAVO CHARLIE DELTA ECHO FOXTROT GOLF HOTEL INDIA JULIETT
      A   B   C   D   E   F   G   H   I   J
```

BRT

CON

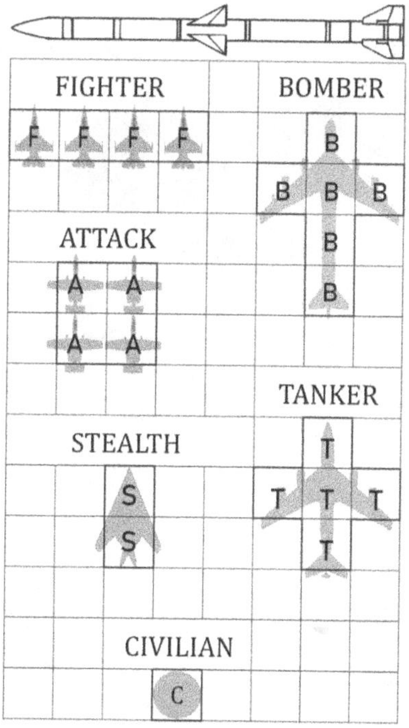

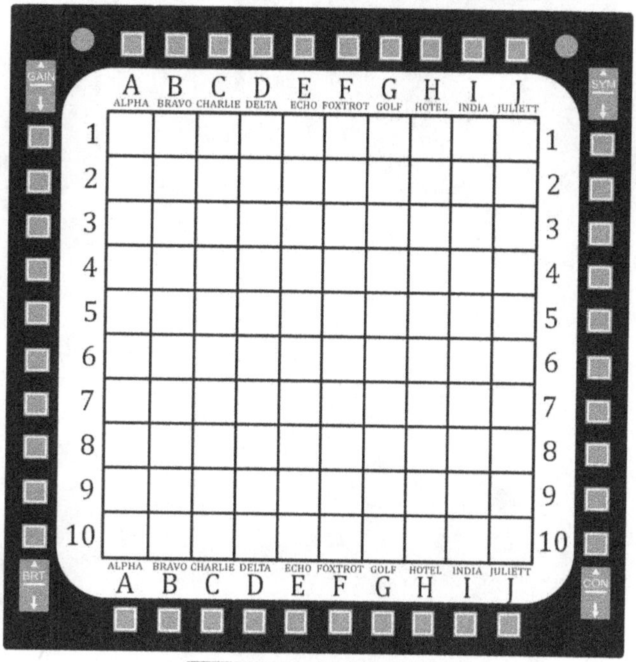

☒ HIT   ◯ MISS

Enemy Call Sign: _____

KEY

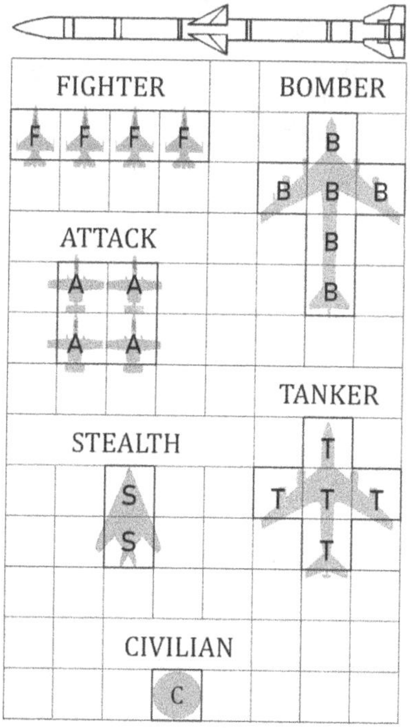

FIGHTER	BOMBER

ATTACK	

STEALTH	TANKER

CIVILIAN

ENEMY AIRSPACE

GAIN

SYM

```
      A   B   C   D   E   F   G   H   I   J
   ALPHA BRAVO CHARLIE DELTA ECHO FOXTROT GOLF HOTEL INDIA JULIETT
 1                                          1
 2                                          2
 3                                          3
 4                                          4
 5                                          5
 6                                          6
 7                                          7
 8                                          8
 9                                          9
10                                         10
   ALPHA BRAVO CHARLIE DELTA ECHO FOXTROT GOLF HOTEL INDIA JULIETT
      A   B   C   D   E   F   G   H   I   J
```

BRT

CON

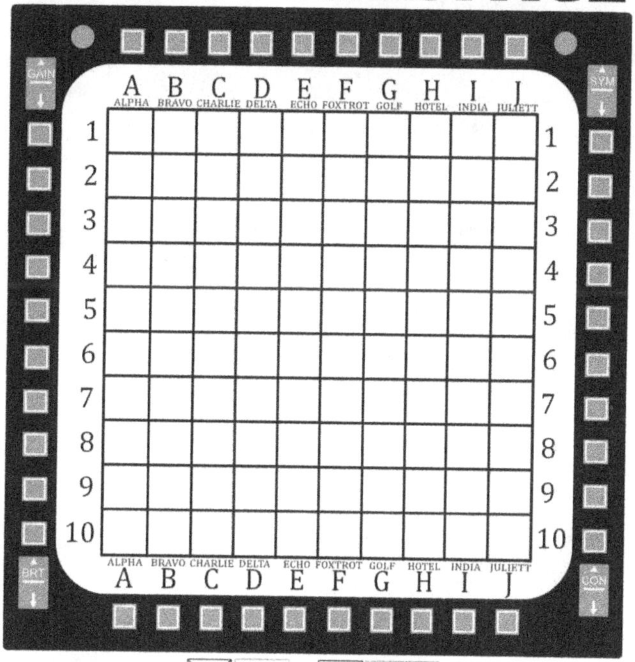

☒ HIT   ◯ MISS

FOLD ALONG DOTTED LINE AND TEAR

UNCLASSIFIED
43°
116°
42°
Grand View
Bruneau
Hammett
Glenns Ferry
King Hill
compressor station
MOA EXCLUDES AIRSPACE 500' AGL AND BELOW
RESTRICTED R-3202 LOW
WINTER CAMP BUTTE
guard station
underground pipeline
MOA REAL TIME INFORMATION CTC COWBOY 134.1 OR (208) 828-4804
JARBIDGE NORTH MOA
GRASMERE (U81)
MOA EXCLUDES AIRSPACE 1500' AGL AND BELOW
ranches
Riddle
pumping station
OWYHEE NORTH MOA
IDAHO
NEVADA
MURPHY HOT SPRINGS (U98)
settlement
Owyhee
HAT PEAK
Mountain City
Jarbidge
MATTERHORN
OWYHEE SOUTH MOA
JARBIDGE SOUTH MOA
HAYSTACK MOUNTAIN
VR1300-1304
IR302
IR303
VR391
VR389
VR1303-1305
IR303
STEVENS-CROSBY (08U)
Tuscarora
AIR BATTLE

Fuel Up with Extra game sheets:

FOLD ALONG DOTTED LINE AND TEAR

FOLD ALONG DOTTED LINE AND TEAR

Call Sign: _____

KEY

MY AIRSPACE

FIGHTER
F F F F

BOMBER
B
B B B
B
B

ATTACK
A A
A A

TANKER
T
T T T
T

STEALTH
S
S

CIVILIAN
C

MY AIRSPACE grid:

	A	B	C	D	E	F	G	H	I	J
	ALPHA	BRAVO	CHARLIE	DELTA	ECHO	FOXTROT	GOLF	HOTEL	INDIA	JULIETT
1										
2										
3										
4										
5										
6										
7										
8										
9										
10										

A B C D E F G H I J

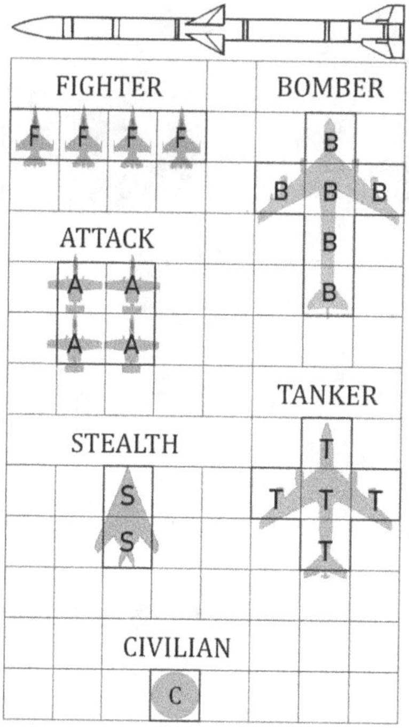

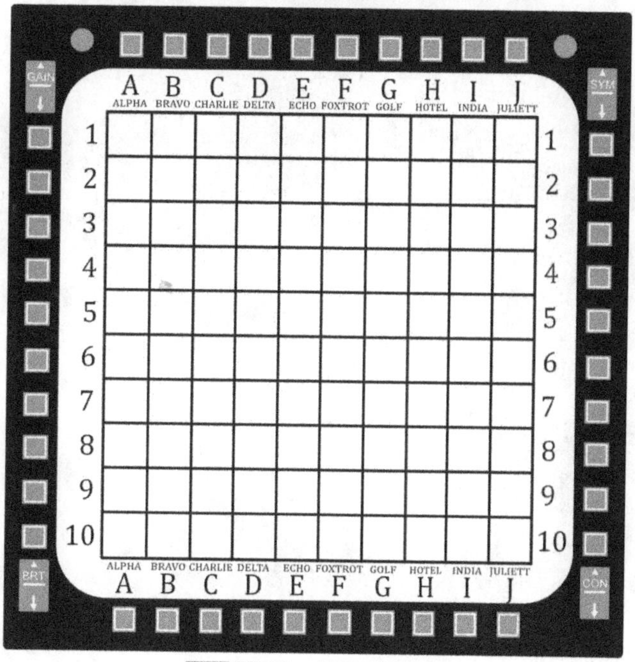

☒ HIT   ◯ MISS

Enemy Call Sign: _____

KEY

ENEMY AIRSPACE

FIGHTER
F F F F

BOMBER
B
B B B
B

ATTACK
A A
A A

TANKER
T
T T T
T

STEALTH
S
S

CIVILIAN
C

ENEMY AIRSPACE grid:

	A	B	C	D	E	F	G	H	I	J
	ALPHA	BRAVO	CHARLIE	DELTA	ECHO	FOXTROT	GOLF	HOTEL	INDIA	JULIETT
1										
2										
3										
4										
5										
6										
7										
8										
9										
10										

A B C D E F G H I J

☒ HIT   ◯ MISS

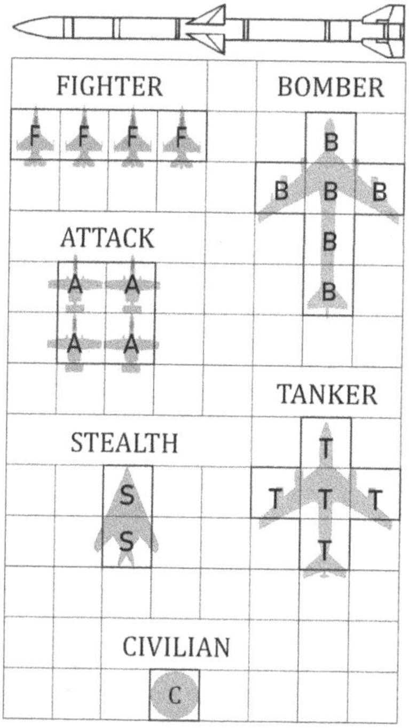

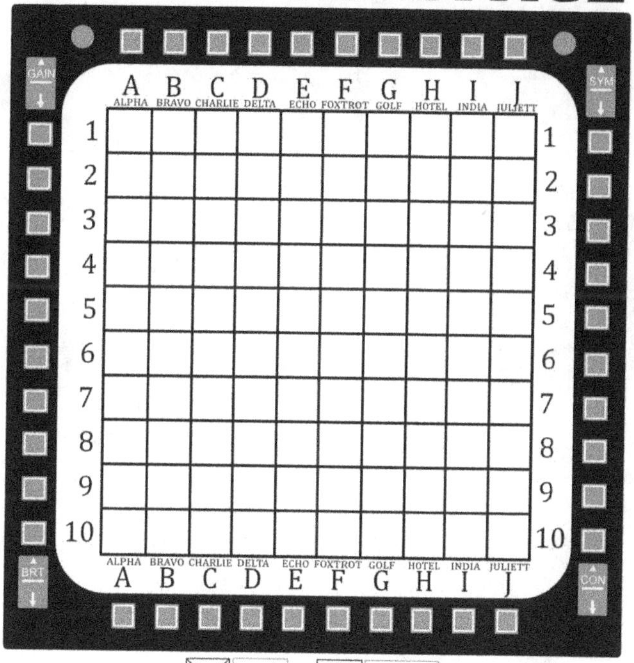

UNCLASSIFIED
CTC NELLIS APP ON 126.65 OR FLIGHT SERVICE PRIOR TO ENTERING MOA
MILITARY ACTIVITY
CTC JOSHUA CON
OR ACTIVITY STATUS
VR209-1259
IR425
IR200
IR286
VR1253
VR209
TEMPIUTE MTN
MOUNT IRISH
microwave tower
ranch
houses
farms
corral
Caliente
Etna
Elgin
Carp
Ash Springs
MOA EXCLUDES AIRSPACE 1500 AGL & BELOW
Alamo
letter "P"
EMIGRANT VALLEY
TIKABOO VALLEY
PAHRANAGAT RANGE
DELAMAR MOUNTAINS
DRY LAKE
R-4806 N
R-4806W
R-4806 E
DESERT MOA
CTC NELLIS APP ON 126.65 OR FLIGHT SERVICE PRIOR TO ENTERING MOA
37°
115°
ranch
target
targets
AYSEES PEAK
SPOTTED RANGE
INDIAN SPRINGS VALLEY
PINTWATER RANGE
SHEEP RANGE
bombing and gunnery range
bldgs
Indian Springs
MODE C & ADS-B OUT 30 NM
EXAMPLES OF CLASS B ALTITUDES
Moapa
substation
Glendale
Logandale
Overton
PERKINS FLD
solar farms
solar farm
truck stop
tower
A-481
HIGH PERFORMANCE CLIMBS & DESCENTS BY NELLIS AFB TRAINING MISSIONS
SPRING MTNS
Cold Creek
camps
radome
Mt Charleston
racetrack
plant & strip mine
MUDDY MOUNTAINS
NEVADA
ARIZONA
SEE LAS VEGAS TERMINAL AREA CHART FOR CORTEZ, ROCKS & GYPSUM VFR TRANSITION ROUTES
AIR BATTLE
LAS VEGAS
Fuel Up with Extra game sheets:

FOLD ALONG DOTTED LINE AND TEAR

FOLD ALONG DOTTED LINE AND TEAR

Call Sign: _____

KEY

MY AIRSPACE

FIGHTER

BOMBER

| F | F | F | F |

B
B B B
B
B

ATTACK

| A | | A | |
| A | | A | |

TANKER

STEALTH

| S | |
| S | |

T
T T T
T

CIVILIAN

C

MY AIRSPACE grid

	A	B	C	D	E	F	G	H	I	J	
	ALPHA	BRAVO	CHARLIE	DELTA	ECHO	FOXTROT	GOLF	HOTEL	INDIA	JULIETT	
1											1
2											2
3											3
4											4
5											5
6											6
7											7
8											8
9											9
10											10

ALPHA BRAVO CHARLIE DELTA ECHO FOXTROT GOLF HOTEL INDIA JULIETT
A B C D E F G H I J

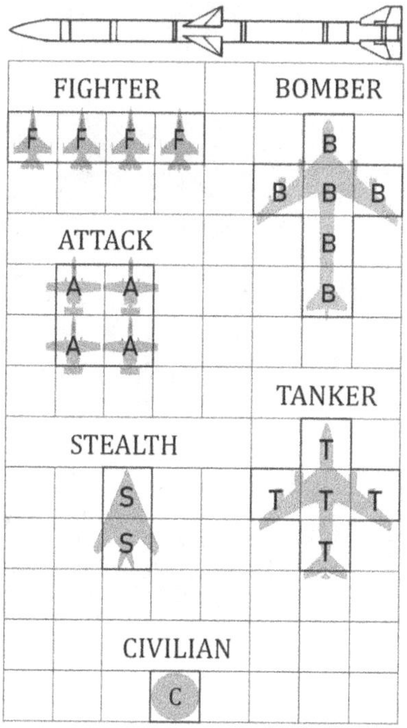

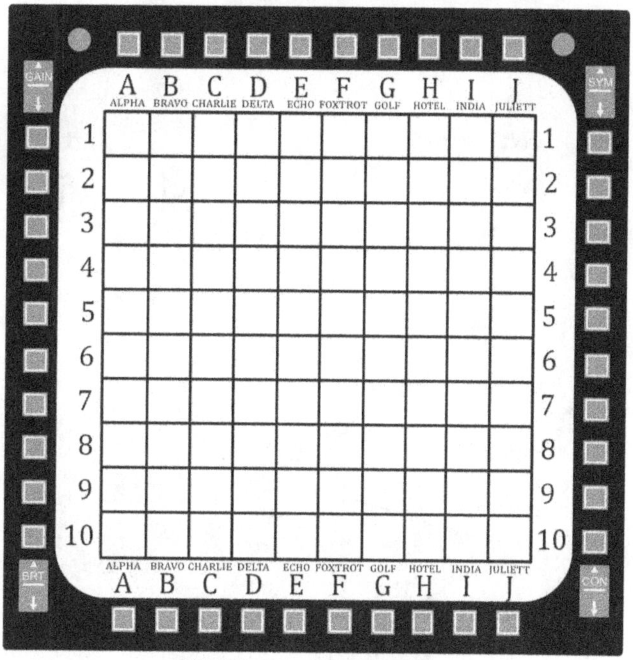

⊠ HIT   ◯ MISS

Enemy Call Sign: _____

KEY

ENEMY AIRSPACE

FIGHTER

BOMBER

| F | F | F | F |

B
B B B
B
B

ATTACK

| A | | A | |
| A | | A | |

TANKER

STEALTH

| S | |
| S | |

T
T T T
T

CIVILIAN

C

ENEMY AIRSPACE grid

	A	B	C	D	E	F	G	H	I	J	
	ALPHA	BRAVO	CHARLIE	DELTA	ECHO	FOXTROT	GOLF	HOTEL	INDIA	JULIETT	
1											1
2											2
3											3
4											4
5											5
6											6
7											7
8											8
9											9
10											10

ALPHA BRAVO CHARLIE DELTA ECHO FOXTROT GOLF HOTEL INDIA JULIETT
A B C D E F G H I J

⊠ HIT   ◯ MISS

FOLD ALONG DOTTED LINE AND TEAR

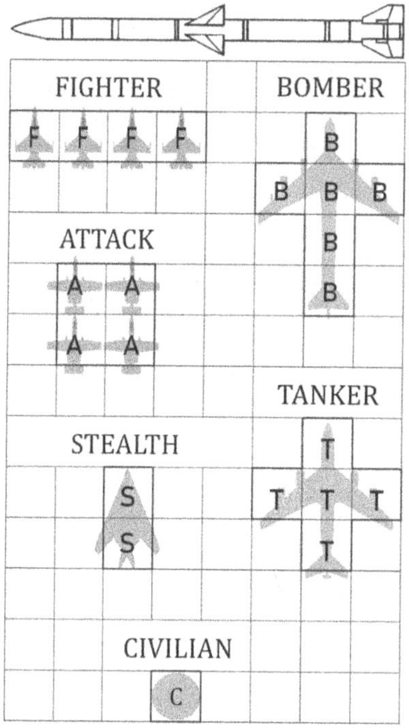

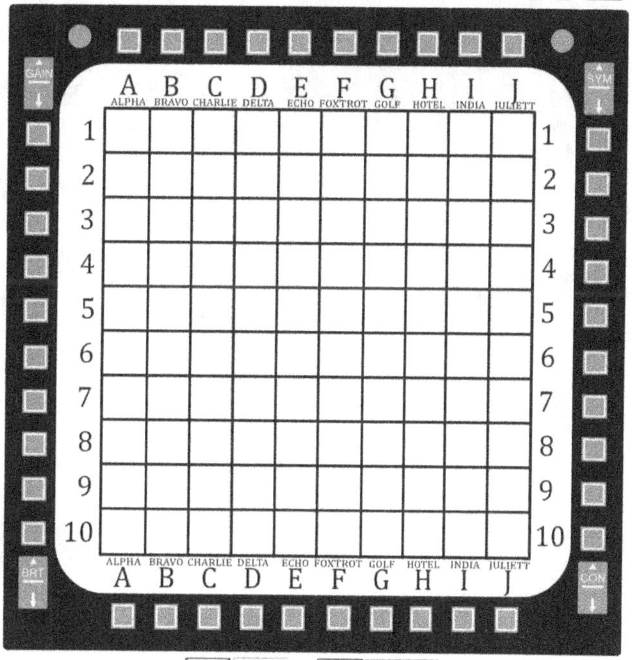

VOLK WEST MOA EXCLUDED
WHEN R-6904 A & B ARE ACTIVE
UNCLASSIFIED
firing range
R-6904A
30′
Warrens
Mather
Sprage
VOLK MOA EXCLUDES
AIRSPACE 1500' AGL
AND BELOW
NECEDAH
NATIONAL
WILDLIFE
REFUGE
NECEDAH (DAF)
919 *L 27 122.7
Wyeville
Necedah
Tomah
BLOYER FLD (Y72)
966 *L 39
122.9
VOLK
SOUTH
MOA
VOLK FLD (VOK)
CT - 127.5
ATIS 134.35 257.85
912 *L 90
(Pvt)
ACCURATE
890 - 26
Camp Douglas
See NOTAMs/Supplement
for Class D eff hrs
New
Lisbon
MOA E
1500
Hustler
MAUSTON/
NEW LISBON UNION (82C)
AWOS-3 123.925
908 *L 37 122.9
Kendall
Mauston
(Pvt)
PISHA FARM
1411 - 15
(Pvt)
MILE BLUFF
MEDICAL CENTER
ELROY (60C)
944 - 31 122.9
RP 24
Elroy
1330
Mount
Tabor
Union
Fuel Up with
Extra game
sheets:
AIR BATTLE

FOLD ALONG DOTTED LINE AND TEAR

FOLD ALONG DOTTED LINE AND TEAR

Call Sign: _____

KEY

 AIR BATTLE

MY AIRSPACE

FIGHTER	BOMBER
F F F F	B / B B B / B / B

ATTACK	
A A / A A	

STEALTH	TANKER
S / S	T T T / T

CIVILIAN
C

MY AIRSPACE

```
     A  B  C  D  E  F  G  H  I  J
   ALPHA BRAVO CHARLIE DELTA ECHO FOXTROT GOLF HOTEL INDIA JULIETT
 1                                        1
 2                                        2
 3                                        3
 4                                        4
 5                                        5
 6                                        6
 7                                        7
 8                                        8
 9                                        9
10                                       10
   ALPHA BRAVO CHARLIE DELTA ECHO FOXTROT GOLF HOTEL INDIA JULIETT
     A  B  C  D  E  F  G  H  I  J
```

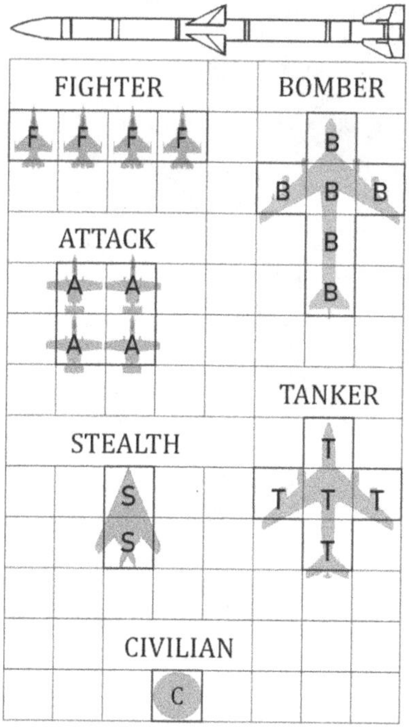

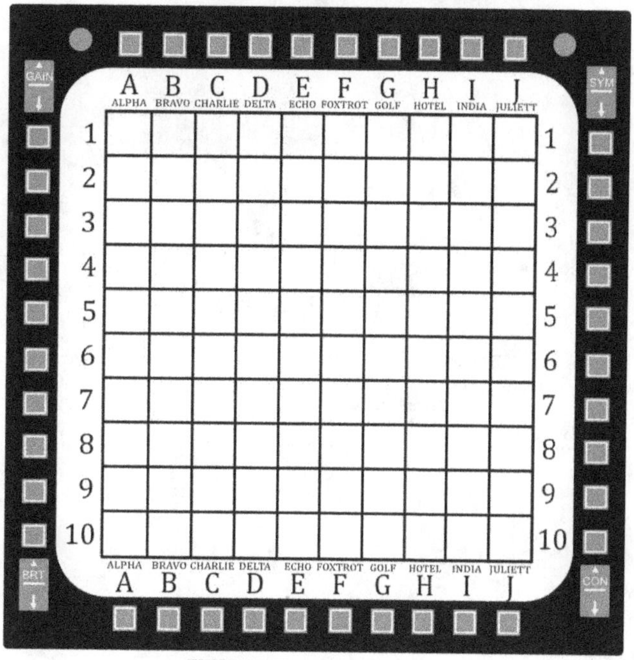

☒ HIT   ◯ MISS

Enemy Call Sign: _____

KEY

ENEMY AIRSPACE

FIGHTER	BOMBER
F F F F	B / B B B / B / B

ATTACK	
A A / A A	

STEALTH	TANKER
S / S	T / T T T / T

CIVILIAN
C

```
     A  B  C  D  E  F  G  H  I  J
   ALPHA BRAVO CHARLIE DELTA ECHO FOXTROT GOLF HOTEL INDIA JULIETT
 1                                        1
 2                                        2
 3                                        3
 4                                        4
 5                                        5
 6                                        6
 7                                        7
 8                                        8
 9                                        9
10                                       10
   ALPHA BRAVO CHARLIE DELTA ECHO FOXTROT GOLF HOTEL INDIA JULIETT
     A  B  C  D  E  F  G  H  I  J
```

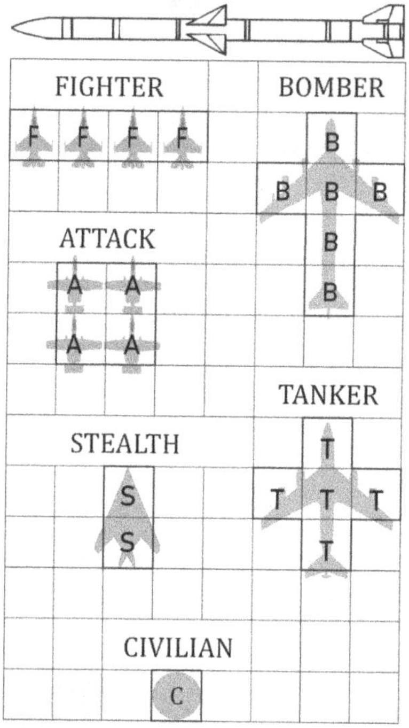

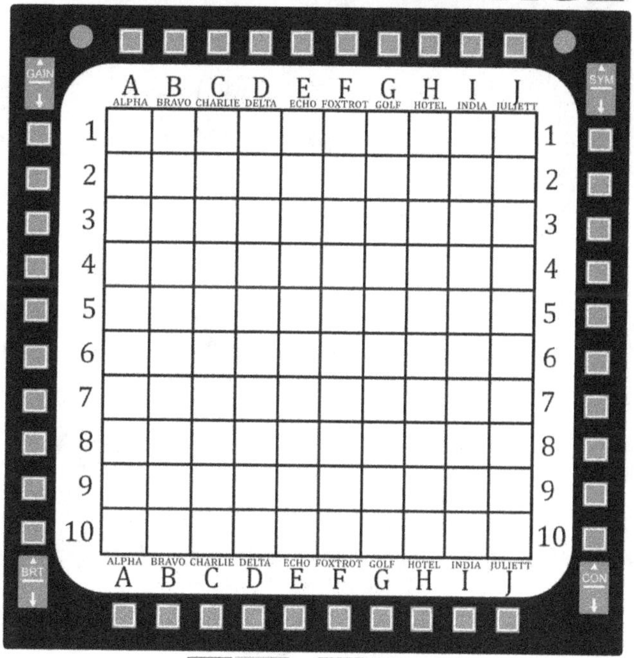

☒ HIT   ◯ MISS

FOLD ALONG DOTTED LINE AND TEAR

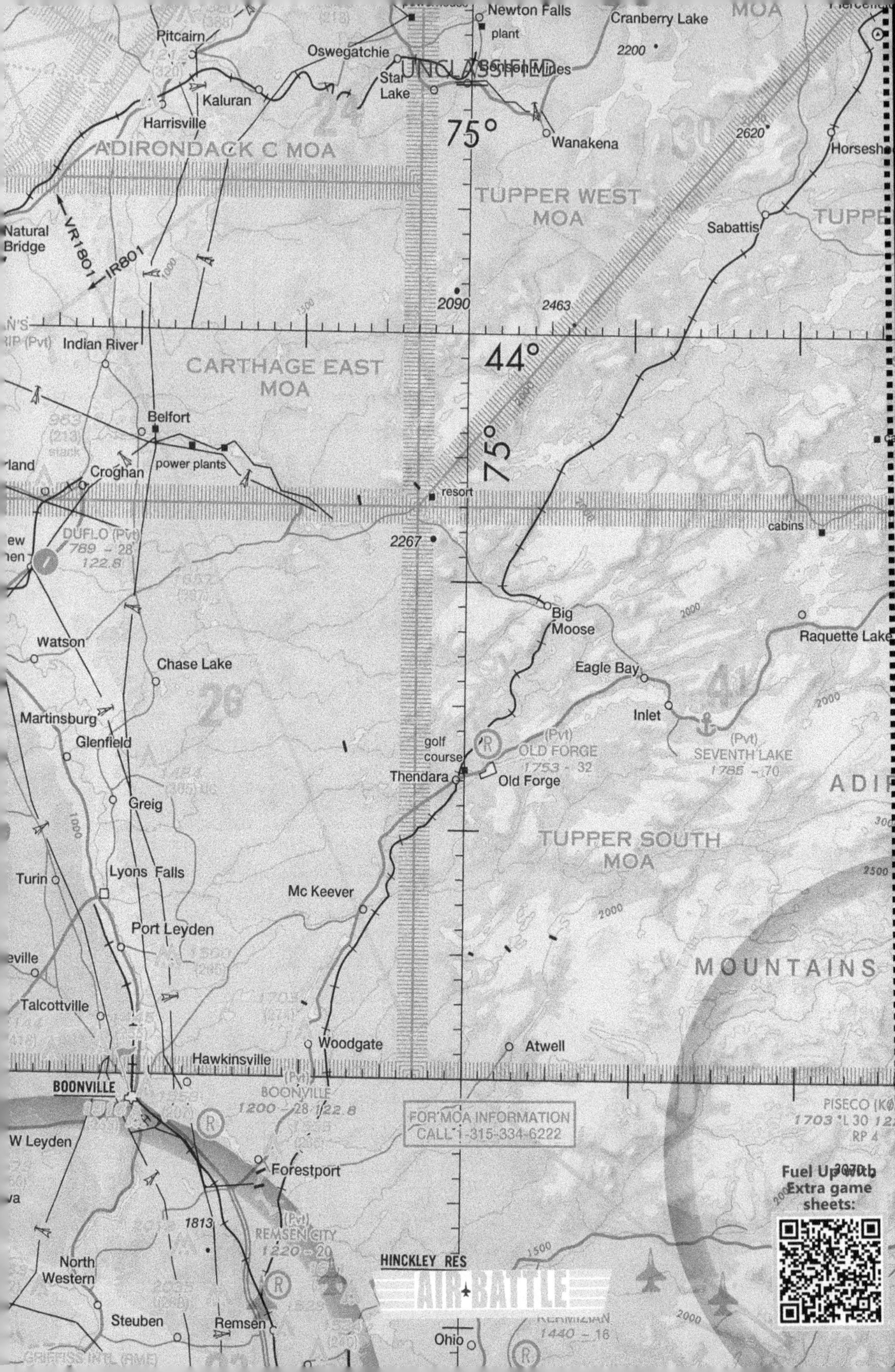

Newton Falls
plant
Cranberry Lake
MOA
Pitcairn
Oswegatchie
UNCLASSIFIED
Benson Mines
Star Lake
Kaluran
Harrisville
2200
75°
Wanakena
2620
Horseshoe
ADIRONDACK C MOA
TUPPER WEST MOA
Sabattis
Natural Bridge
VR1801
IR801
2090
2463
Indian River
CARTHAGE EAST MOA
44°
Belfort
75°
power plants
Croghan
resort
DUFLO (Pvt)
789 - 28
122.8
2267
cabins
Big Moose
Raquette Lake
Watson
Chase Lake
Eagle Bay
Inlet
Martinsburg
Glenfield
golf course
(Pvt)
OLD FORGE
1753 - 32
(Pvt)
SEVENTH LAKE
1785 - 70
Thendara
Old Forge
Greig
TUPPER SOUTH MOA
Turin
Lyons Falls
Mc Keever
Port Leyden
MOUNTAINS
Talcottville
Woodgate
Atwell
Hawkinsville
BOONVILLE
(Pvt)
BOONVILLE
1200 - 28 122.8
PISECO
1703 L 30
FOR MOA INFORMATION
CALL 1-315-334-6222
W Leyden
Forestport
Fuel Up with
Extra game
sheets:
1813
(Pvt)
REMSEN CITY
1220 - 20
North Western
HINCKLEY RES
AIR BATTLE
Steuben
Remsen
1440 - 16
Ohio

FOLD ALONG DOTTED LINE AND TEAR

FOLD ALONG DOTTED LINE AND TEAR

FOLD ALONG DOTTED LINE AND TEAR

Call Sign: ____________

AIR BATTLE

MY AIRSPACE

KEY

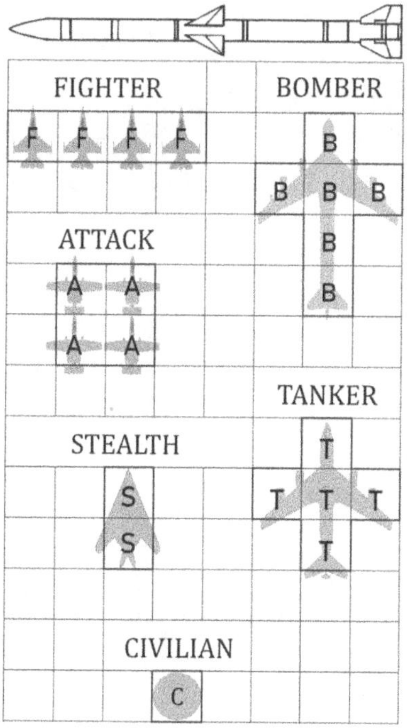

	A ALPHA	B BRAVO	C CHARLIE	D DELTA	E ECHO	F FOXTROT	G GOLF	H HOTEL	I INDIA	J JULIETT	
1											1
2											2
3											3
4											4
5											5
6											6
7											7
8											8
9											9
10											10
	ALPHA A	BRAVO B	CHARLIE C	DELTA D	ECHO E	FOXTROT F	GOLF G	HOTEL H	INDIA I	JULIETT J	

GAIN SYM BRT CON

☒ HIT ◯ MISS

FOLD ALONG DOTTED LINE AND TEAR

Enemy Call Sign: ________

ENEMY AIRSPACE

KEY

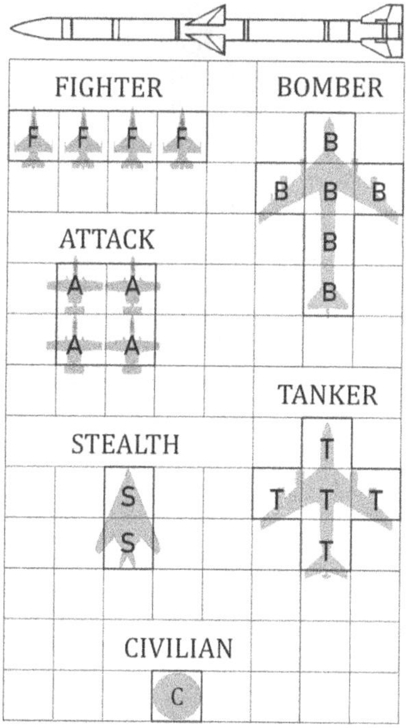

	A ALPHA	B BRAVO	C CHARLIE	D DELTA	E ECHO	F FOXTROT	G GOLF	H HOTEL	I INDIA	J JULIETT	
1											1
2											2
3											3
4											4
5											5
6											6
7											7
8											8
9											9
10											10
	ALPHA A	BRAVO B	CHARLIE C	DELTA D	ECHO E	FOXTROT F	GOLF G	HOTEL H	INDIA I	JULIETT J	

GAIN SYM BRT CON

☒ HIT ◯ MISS

sawmill
UNCLASSIFIED
Herndon
Pinedale
STADIUM
FRESNO CHANDLER
EXEC (FCH)
AWOS-3 135.225
280 L 36 123.0
RP 12
school
FRESNO
WILLIAM ROBERT
JOHNSTON MUNI (M90)
162 - 35 122.9
RP 33
Kerman
Tranquillity
A MOA
elevator
San
Joaquin
Raisin City
drag
strip
Easton
SELMA (0Q4)
305 L 22
122.8
Caruthers
Conejo
plant
Helm
230
Cantua Creek
LEMOORE C MOA
grain elevator
Burtel
Five
Points
Lanare
Riverdale
Hub
Hardwick
Westside
240
See NOTAMs/Supplement
for Class D eff hrs
AGRO-WEST (Pvt)
335 - 30
LEMOORE NAS (REEVES FLD) (NLC)
CT - 128.3 ATIS 121.575 327.15
228 L 135
STONE (Pvt)
220 - 25
Grangeville
Armona
Lemoore
HARRIS (308)
470 L 28 122.9
RP 14
Westhaven
JONES FARMS (Pvt)
199 - 19
Huron
Stratford
oil wells
NEWTON FLD (Pvt)
194 - 28
MACHADO DUSTERS (Pvt)
192 - 26
LEMOORE B MOA
elevator
substation
prison
NEW COALINGA MUNI (C80)
AWOS-3 119.275
625 L 50 122.7
RP 19, 30
STONE LAND COMPANY (Pvt)
ESTLAKE FARMS (Pvt)
192 - 36
oil
AIR BATTLE

Fuel Up with Extra game sheets:

FOLD ALONG DOTTED LINE AND TEAR

FOLD ALONG DOTTED LINE AND TEAR

Call Sign: _____

KEY

MY AIRSPACE

FIGHTER | BOMBER

F F F F | B / B B B / B / B

ATTACK | A A / A A

STEALTH | S / S

TANKER | T / T T T / T

CIVILIAN | C

	A	B	C	D	E	F	G	H	I	J	
	ALPHA	BRAVO	CHARLIE	DELTA	ECHO	FOXTROT	GOLF	HOTEL	INDIA	JULIETT	
1											1
2											2
3											3
4											4
5											5
6											6
7											7
8											8
9											9
10											10
	ALPHA	BRAVO	CHARLIE	DELTA	ECHO	FOXTROT	GOLF	HOTEL	INDIA	JULIETT	
	A	B	C	D	E	F	G	H	I	J	

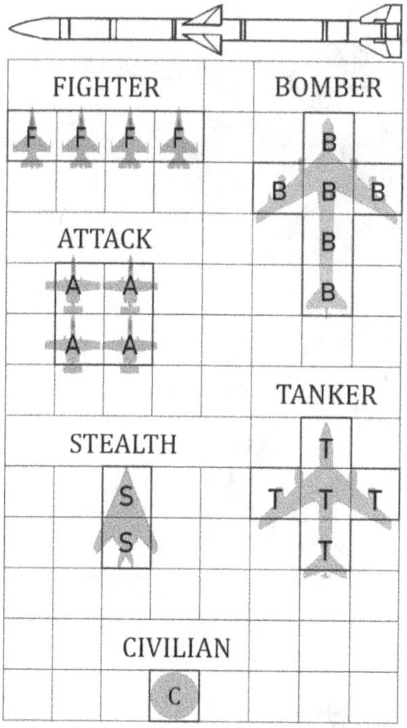

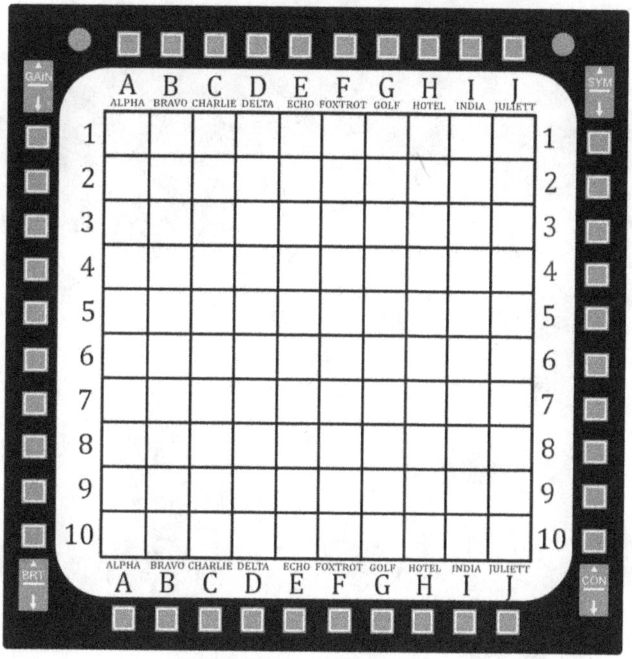

☒ HIT   ◯ MISS

Enemy Call Sign: _____

KEY

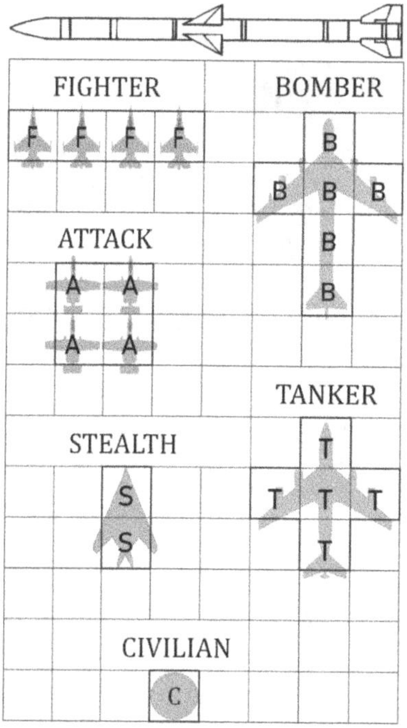

ENEMY AIRSPACE

FIGHTER | BOMBER

F F F F | B / B B B / B / B

ATTACK | A A / A A

STEALTH | S / S

TANKER | T / T T T / T

CIVILIAN | C

	A	B	C	D	E	F	G	H	I	J	
	ALPHA	BRAVO	CHARLIE	DELTA	ECHO	FOXTROT	GOLF	HOTEL	INDIA	JULIETT	
1											1
2											2
3											3
4											4
5											5
6											6
7											7
8											8
9											9
10											10
	ALPHA	BRAVO	CHARLIE	DELTA	ECHO	FOXTROT	GOLF	HOTEL	INDIA	JULIETT	
	A	B	C	D	E	F	G	H	I	J	

☒ HIT   ◯ MISS

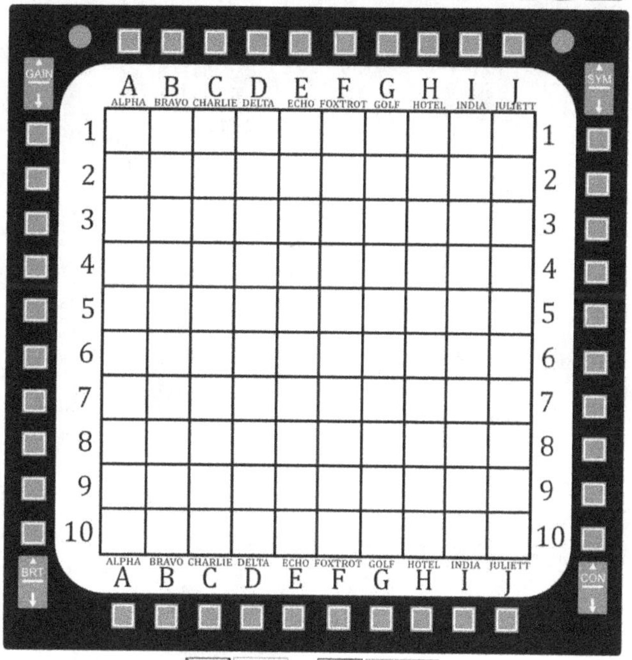

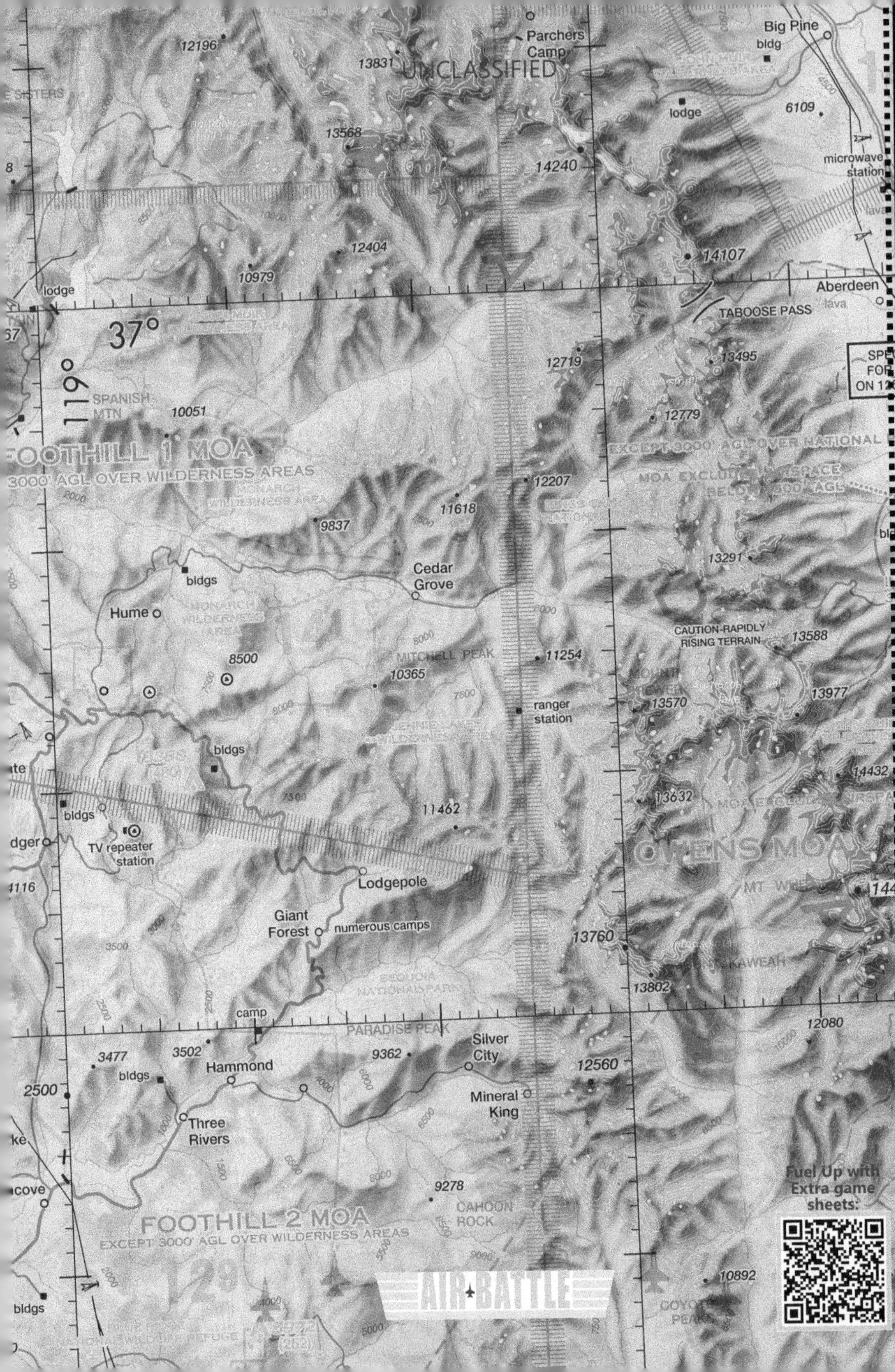

Big Pine
bldg
Parchers Camp
12196
13831
UNCLASSIFIED
lodge
6109
13568
14240
microwave station
lava
12404
10979
14107
lodge
Aberdeen
lava
TABOOSE PASS
37°
119°
12719
13495
SPANISH MTN
10051
12779
FOOTHILL 1 MOA
3000' AGL OVER WILDERNESS AREAS
EXCEPT 3000' AGL OVER NATIONAL
MOA EXCLUDES AIRSPACE BELOW 3000' AGL
12207
11618
9837
13291
bldgs
Cedar Grove
Hume
CAUTION-RAPIDLY RISING TERRAIN
13588
8500
MITCHELL PEAK
11254
10365
13977
ranger station
13570
bldgs
14432
13632
bldgs
11462
TV repeater station
OWENS MOA
Lodgepole
Giant Forest
numerous camps
13760
13802
camp
PARADISE PEAK
12080
3477
3502
9362
Silver City
Hammond
12560
bldgs
2500
Mineral King
Three Rivers
9278
CAHOON ROCK
FOOTHILL 2 MOA
EXCEPT 3000' AGL OVER WILDERNESS AREAS
10892
bldgs
AIR BATTLE
Fuel Up with Extra game sheets:

FOLD ALONG DOTTED LINE AND TEAR

FOLD ALONG DOTTED LINE AND TEAR

Call Sign: _____

KEY

MY AIRSPACE

FIGHTER	BOMBER
F F F F	B B B B B B

ATTACK	
A A A A	

STEALTH	TANKER
S S	T T T T T

CIVILIAN	
C	

MY AIRSPACE grid

A ALPHA B BRAVO C CHARLIE D DELTA E ECHO F FOXTROT G GOLF H HOTEL I INDIA J JULIETT
Rows 1-10

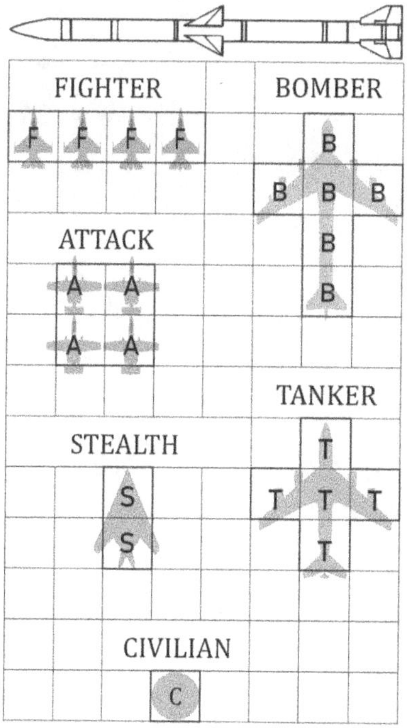

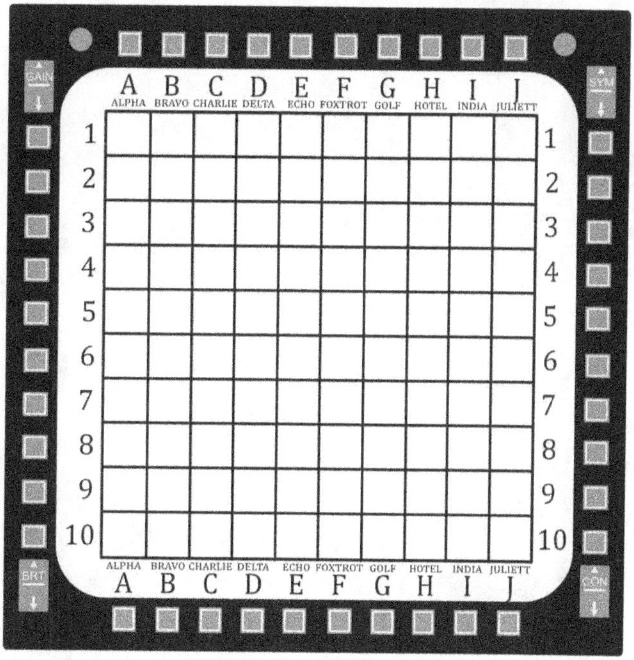

☒ HIT   ○ MISS

Enemy Call Sign: _____

KEY

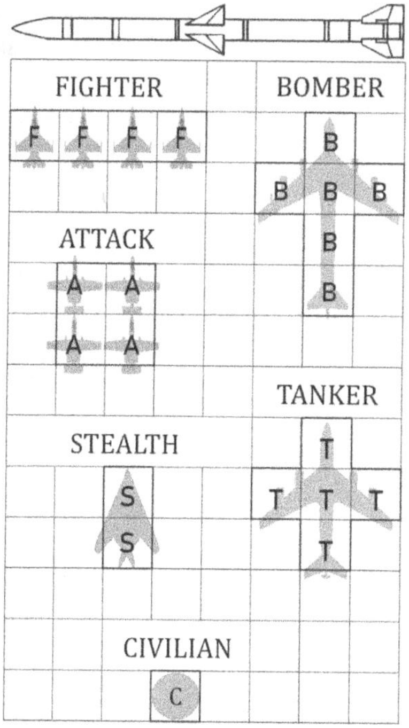

ENEMY AIRSPACE

FIGHTER	BOMBER
F F F F	B B B B B B

ATTACK	
A A A A	

STEALTH	TANKER
S S	T T T T T

CIVILIAN	
C	

ENEMY AIRSPACE grid

A ALPHA B BRAVO C CHARLIE D DELTA E ECHO F FOXTROT G GOLF H HOTEL I INDIA J JULIETT
Rows 1-10

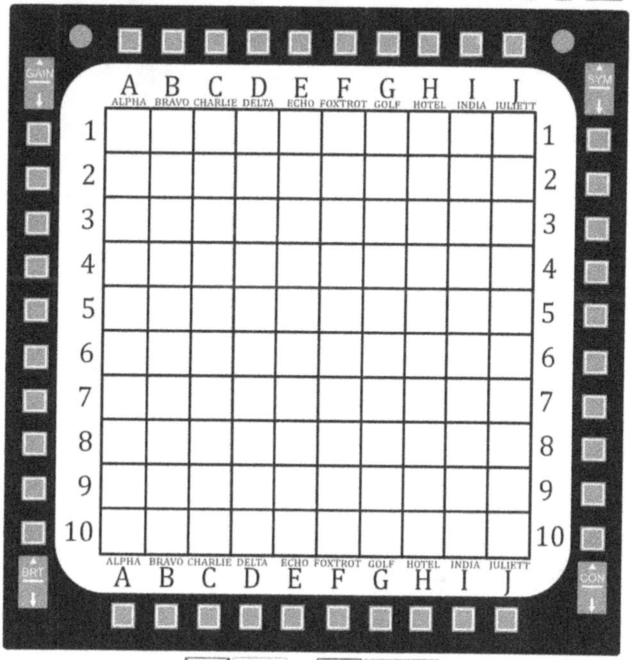

☒ HIT   ○ MISS

FOLD ALONG DOTTED LINE AND TEAR

UNCLASSIFIED
RESTRICTED
VR201
VR1250
VR1255
4664
telephone relay station
67
91
3898
7340
FALLON NATIONAL WILDLIFE REFUGE
4158
3902
FALLON NORTH 1 MOA
EXCEPT BELOW 3000' AGL OVER FALLON AND STILLWATER NWR
8785
8569
8312
FALLON MUNI (FLX)
AWOS-AV 118.25
3966 L 57 122.8
Stillwater
STILLWATER NATIONAL WILDLIFE REFUGE
Fallon
5487
6217
FALLON SOUTHWEST AIRPARK
3950 - 26
FALLON NAS
(VAN VOORHIS FLD) (NFL)
See NOTAMs/Supplement for Class D eff hrs
Salt Wells
FALLON
MOA EXCLUDED WHEN R-4
4892
68
ruins
bldgs
87
8303
MOA EXCLUDES AIRSPACE BETWEEN 2000' AGL & 8500' MSL
camp
6104
6404
MOUNTAINS
R-4810
R-4812
R-4804 A
IR206
6243
6042
SPECIAL MILITARY ACTIVITY FOR IR206 CTC OAKLAND CNTR ON 125.75 FOR ACTIVITY STATUS
7467
6084
RANCH LOW MOA EXCLUDED WHEN R-4810 IS ACTIVE
Rawhide
camp
5195
6908
plant
6597
FOR ADVISORY SERVICE TRANSITING THE MOAS CTC DESERT CON ON 126.2
FALLON SOUTH
Schurz
8102
VR1255
tower
GABBS
AIR BATTLE

Fuel Up with Extra game sheets:

FOLD ALONG DOTTED LINE AND TEAR

FOLD ALONG DOTTED LINE AND TEAR

Call Sign: _____

KEY

MY AIRSPACE

FIGHTER

BOMBER

ATTACK

STEALTH

TANKER

CIVILIAN

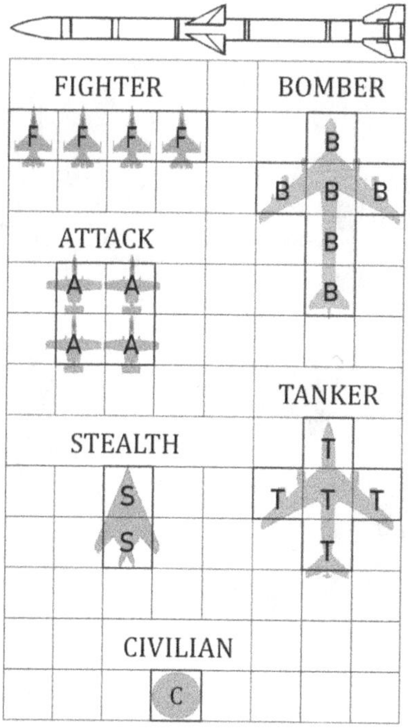

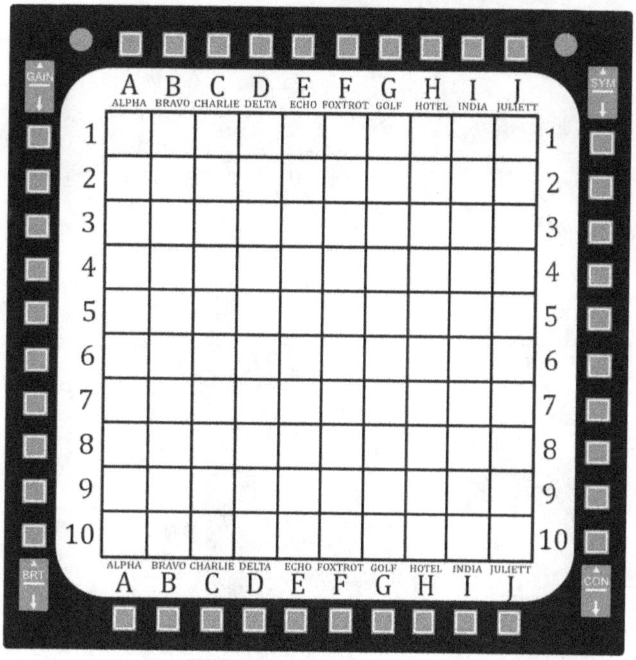

☒ HIT   ◯ MISS

Enemy Call Sign: _____

KEY

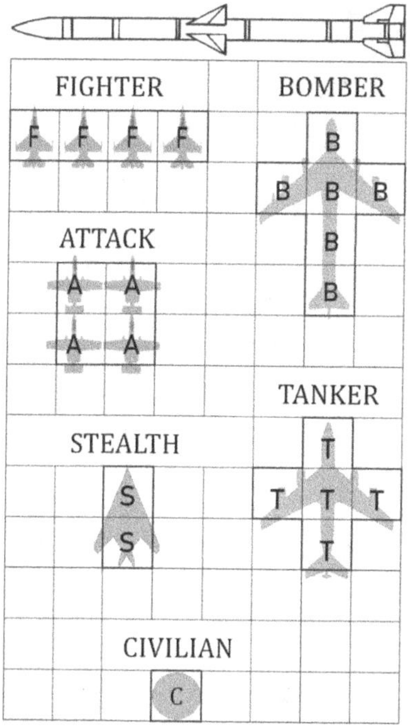

ENEMY AIRSPACE

FIGHTER

BOMBER

ATTACK

STEALTH

TANKER

CIVILIAN

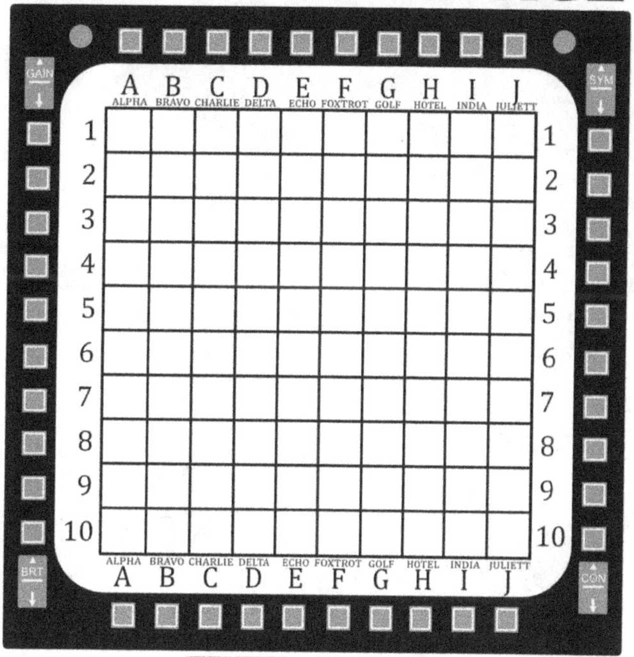

☒ HIT   ◯ MISS

FOLD ALONG DOTTED LINE AND TEAR

UNCLASSIFIED
LAUGHLIN 1 MOA
CANYON RANCH
2306 - 82
gas plant
ranch
2276
2572 (280)
2577 (326) UC
2129
FOUR SQUARE
2250 - 41
ROCKSPRINGS
SAN ANGELO
radome
Rocksprings
2397
30°
2151
BAR C RANCH
1856 - 30
underground pipeline
2410
FREEMAN RANCH
2380 - 30
2406
RNK RANCH
1945 - 44
LOMA ALTA
houses
IR170
2365
KUBIK RANCH
1955 - 23
RIO VISTA RANCH
1774 - 48
MAFRIGE RANCH INC
1847 - 42
MORNING STAR RANCH
1500 - 42 122.7
AGUA NADA RANCH
2053 - 22
101°
Carta Valley
DEVIL'S RIVER RANCH
1680 - 38
MARTIN RANCH
1724 - 27
2210
2250
INDIANHEAD RANCH
1545 - 30
ranches
CTC DEL RIO APP WITHIN 20 NM ON 119.6 259.1
PINON RANCH (Pvt)
1644 - 45
IR149 - 170
ALERT AREA A-633 A CONCENTRATED STUDENT JET TRAINING
settlement
OBJECTIONABLE
SPRING RANCH
1440 - 43
LAUGHLIN AFB
CLASS C
See NOTAMs/Supplement for Class C eff hrs
LEWIS PRIVATE
DAVIS RANCH
1390 - 31
BERTANI RANCH
1110 - 33
1369
LEONA RANCH
1720 - 42
1943
1695
TULAROSA
1397 - 38
1805
DEL RIO
51 25
51 SFC
See NOTAMs/Supplement for Class E (sfc) eff hrs
BRACKETTVILLE
solar farm
RIO PINTO RANCH
Colonia Calles
CLARK SPRINGS
ANACACHO RANCH
1043
VFR Use Only
LA FONDA
AIR BATTLE

Fuel Up with Extra game sheets:

FOLD ALONG DOTTED LINE AND TEAR

FOLD ALONG DOTTED LINE AND TEAR

FOLD ALONG DOTTED LINE AND TEAR

Call Sign: ______________

AIR BATTLE

KEY

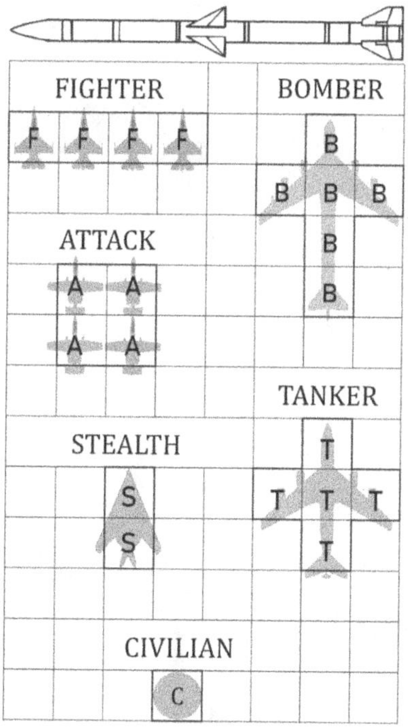

MY AIRSPACE

	A ALPHA	B BRAVO	C CHARLIE	D DELTA	E ECHO	F FOXTROT	G GOLF	H HOTEL	I INDIA	J JULIETT	
1											1
2											2
3											3
4											4
5											5
6											6
7											7
8											8
9											9
10											10
	ALPHA A	BRAVO B	CHARLIE C	DELTA D	ECHO E	FOXTROT F	GOLF G	HOTEL H	INDIA I	JULIETT J	

GAIN SYM BRT CON

☒ HIT ◯ MISS

FOLD ALONG DOTTED LINE AND TEAR

Enemy Call Sign: __________

KEY

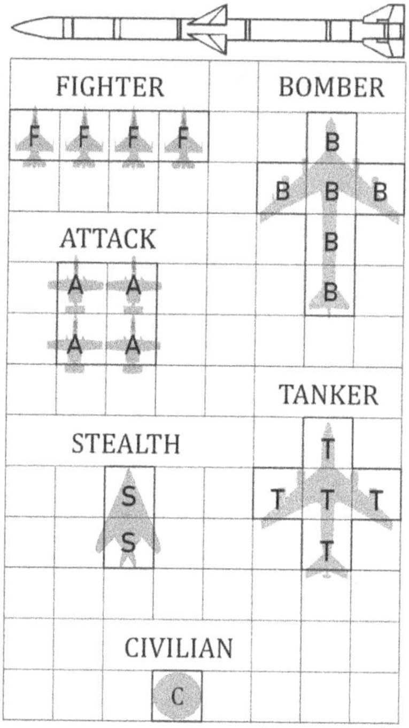

ENEMY AIRSPACE

	A ALPHA	B BRAVO	C CHARLIE	D DELTA	E ECHO	F FOXTROT	G GOLF	H HOTEL	I INDIA	J JULIETT	
1											1
2											2
3											3
4											4
5											5
6											6
7											7
8											8
9											9
10											10
	ALPHA A	BRAVO B	CHARLIE C	DELTA D	ECHO E	FOXTROT F	GOLF G	HOTEL H	INDIA I	JULIETT J	

GAIN SYM BRT CON

☒ HIT ◯ MISS

UNCLASSIFIED
OBJECTIONABLE
ZUEHL (Pvt)
592 - 29
LACKORN (Pvt)
420 - 30
Belmont
ELM CREEK
RANDOLPH AFB (RND)
New Berlin
HERITAGE AIRFIELD
(Pvt)
555 - 31
A-635
MARTINDALE AHP (MDA)
CIBOLO SEA-WILLO
517 - 25
CONCENTRATED STUDENT JET TRAINING
CTC SAN ANTONIO APP WITHIN 20 NM ON 128.05 318.1
IR148
Bebe
Cost
Leesville
Wrightsboro
oil
TALL TOWERS
RANDO
Sutherland Springs
585
Pandora
Nixon
Smiley
MIDLAKE (Pvt)
535 - 26
(Pvt)
PEELER AIRPARK
540 - 38
Stockdale
BAILEY (Pvt)
452 - 42
Westhoff
JOHN B CONNALLY RANCH
530 - 40
FLORESVILLE
Nopal
Gillett
Kosciusko
CIRCLE P RANCH (Pvt)
500 - 26
525
Poth
Pawelekville
RANDOLPH 1B MOA
VR1121
Cestohowa
Dewees
BOENING BROTHERS
(Pvt)
407 - 34
29°
VR1120
485
Yorktown
Falls City
Hobson
Panna Maria
Helena
455
98°
IR148
(Pvt)
BURRIS RANCH
448 - 33
Karnes City
Nordheim
Runge
McCoy
525
refinery
Coy City
KENEDY RGNL (2R9)
AWOS-3PT 118.45
289 L 32 123.0
RP 16
(Pvt)
CARD AIRFIELD
320 - 31
pumping station
KINGSV
Lenz
Kenedy
Fashing
prison
Choate
565
Campbellton
SAN CHRISTOVAL RANCH (Pvt)
378 - 39
Charco
414
oil field
stockyard
Burnell
refinery
(Pvt)
LANTANA RIDGE
250 - 33
Pawnee
441
Whitsett
Pettus
GOLIAD NOLF (NGT)
ASOS 353.675
322 L 80 132.875
THREE RIVERS
530
Tuleta
Mineral
plant
Normanna
325
Three Rivers
oil
refinery
Oakville
285
Beeville
183
LIVE OAK COUNTY (8T6)

Fuel Up with Extra game sheets:

FOLD ALONG DOTTED LINE AND TEAR

FOLD ALONG DOTTED LINE AND TEAR

Call Sign: _____

KEY

AIR★BATTLE

MY AIRSPACE

FIGHTER
F F F F

BOMBER
B
B B B
B
B

ATTACK
A A
A A

STEALTH
S
S

TANKER
T
T T T
T

CIVILIAN
C

MY AIRSPACE

	A	B	C	D	E	F	G	H	I	J
	ALPHA	BRAVO	CHARLIE	DELTA	ECHO	FOXTROT	GOLF	HOTEL	INDIA	JULIETT
1										
2										
3										
4										
5										
6										
7										
8										
9										
10										

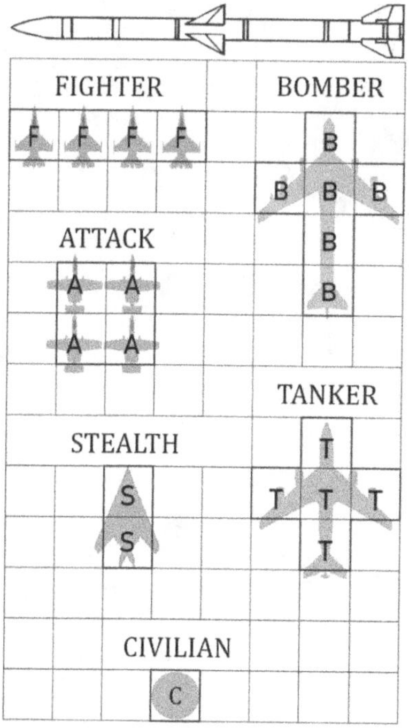

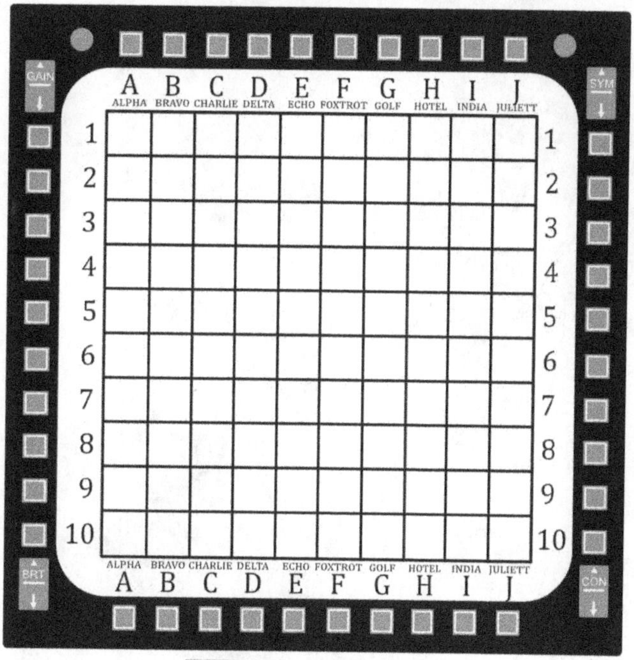

☒ HIT   ◯ MISS

Enemy Call Sign: _____

KEY

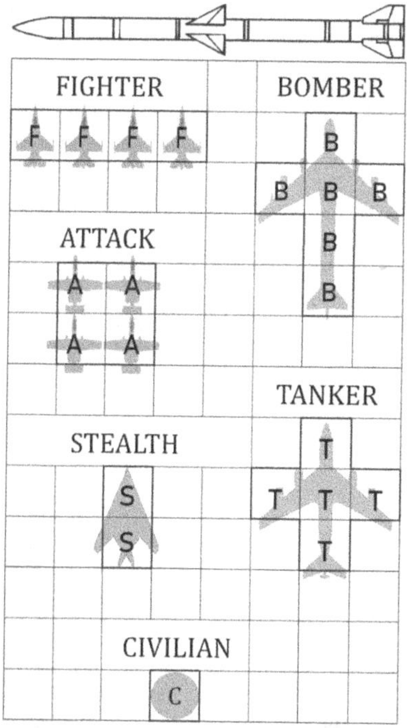

ENEMY AIRSPACE

FIGHTER
F F F F

BOMBER
B
B B B
B

ATTACK
A A
A A

STEALTH
S
S

TANKER
T
T T T
T

CIVILIAN
C

ENEMY AIRSPACE

	A	B	C	D	E	F	G	H	I	J
	ALPHA	BRAVO	CHARLIE	DELTA	ECHO	FOXTROT	GOLF	HOTEL	INDIA	JULIETT
1										
2										
3										
4										
5										
6										
7										
8										
9										
10										

☒ HIT   ◯ MISS

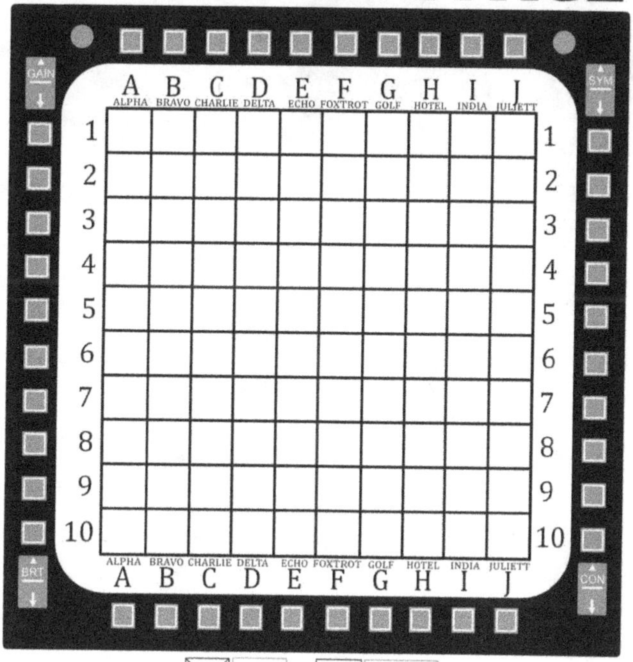

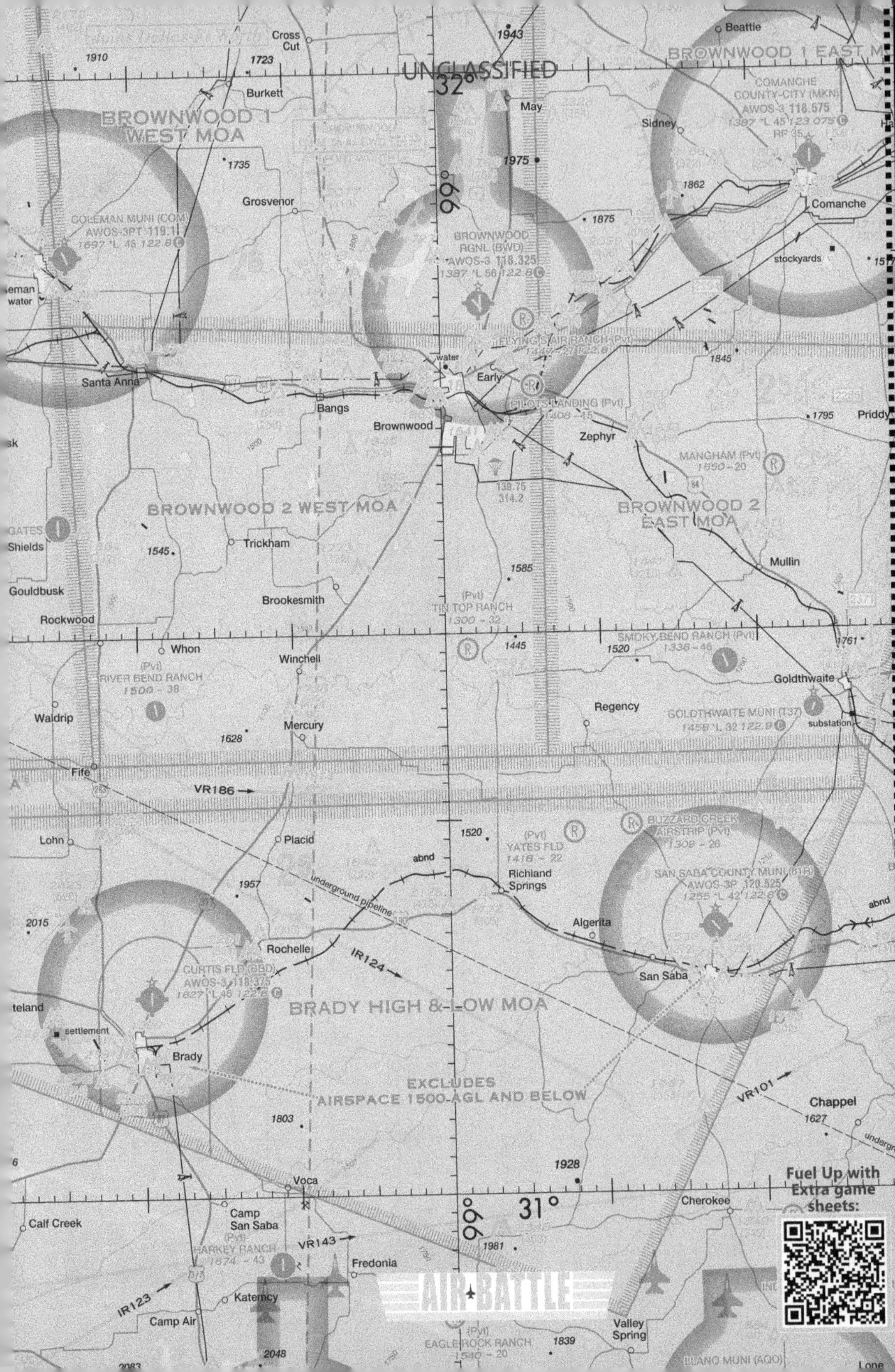
UNCLASSIFIED
32°
BROWNWOOD 1 WEST MOA
BROWNWOOD 1 EAST M
COLEMAN MUNI (COM)
AWOS-3PT 119.1
1697 L 45 122.8
BROWNWOOD RGNL (BWD)
AWOS-3 118.325
1387 L 56 122.8
COMANCHE COUNTY-CITY (MKN)
AWOS-3 118.575
1387 L 45 123.075
Cross Cut
Burkett
May
Beattie
Sidney
Grosvenor
Comanche
stockyards
Santa Anna
Bangs
Brownwood
Early
water
FLYING S AIR RANCH (Pvt)
PILOTS LANDING (Pvt)
Zephyr
Priddy
MANGHAM (Pvt)
BROWNWOOD 2 WEST MOA
BROWNWOOD 2 EAST MOA
Trickham
Shields
Gouldbusk
Brookesmith
Rockwood
TIN TOP RANCH
Mullin
Whon
Winchell
SMOKY BEND RANCH (Pvt)
RIVER BEND RANCH
Waldrip
Mercury
Regency
Goldthwaite
GOLDTHWAITE MUNI (T37)
substation
Fife
VR186
Lohn
Placid
YATES FLD
BUZZARD CREEK AIRSTRIP (Pvt)
SAN SABA COUNTY MUNI (81R)
AWOS-3P 120.525
1255 L 42 122.8
abnd
Richland Springs
underground pipeline
Algerita
Rochelle
IR124
San Saba
CURTIS FLD (BBD)
AWOS-3 118.375
1827 L 46 122.8
BRADY HIGH & LOW MOA
settlement
Brady
EXCLUDES AIRSPACE 1500 AGL AND BELOW
VR101
Chappel
Voca
31°
Cherokee
Calf Creek
Camp San Saba
HARKEY RANCH
VR143
Fredonia
IR123
Katemcy
Camp Air
AIR BATTLE
Valley Spring
EAGLE ROCK RANCH
LLANO MUNI (AQO)
Fuel Up with Extra game sheets:

FOLD ALONG DOTTED LINE AND TEAR

FOLD ALONG DOTTED LINE AND TEAR

Call Sign: _____

KEY

FIGHTER	BOMBER
F F F F	B B B B B

ATTACK

A A
A A

TANKER

STEALTH

S
S

T
T T T
T

CIVILIAN

C

MY AIRSPACE

	A	B	C	D	E	F	G	H	I	J	
	ALPHA	BRAVO	CHARLIE	DELTA	ECHO	FOXTROT	GOLF	HOTEL	INDIA	JULIETT	
1											1
2											2
3											3
4											4
5											5
6											6
7											7
8											8
9											9
10											10
	ALPHA	BRAVO	CHARLIE	DELTA	ECHO	FOXTROT	GOLF	HOTEL	INDIA	JULIETT	
	A	B	C	D	E	F	G	H	I	J	

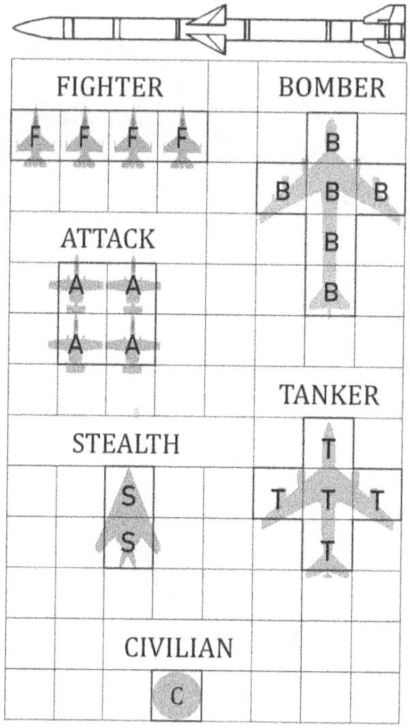

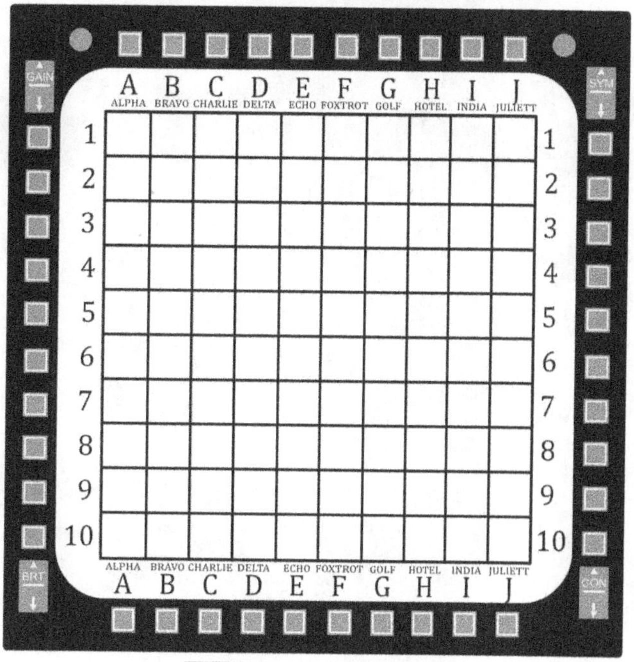

☒ HIT   ◯ MISS

Enemy Call Sign: _____

KEY

FIGHTER	BOMBER
F F F F	B B B B B

ATTACK

A A
A A

TANKER

STEALTH

S
S

T
T T T
T

CIVILIAN

C

ENEMY AIRSPACE

	A	B	C	D	E	F	G	H	I	J	
	ALPHA	BRAVO	CHARLIE	DELTA	ECHO	FOXTROT	GOLF	HOTEL	INDIA	JULIETT	
1											1
2											2
3											3
4											4
5											5
6											6
7											7
8											8
9											9
10											10
	ALPHA	BRAVO	CHARLIE	DELTA	ECHO	FOXTROT	GOLF	HOTEL	INDIA	JULIETT	
	A	B	C	D	E	F	G	H	I	J	

☒ HIT   ◯ MISS

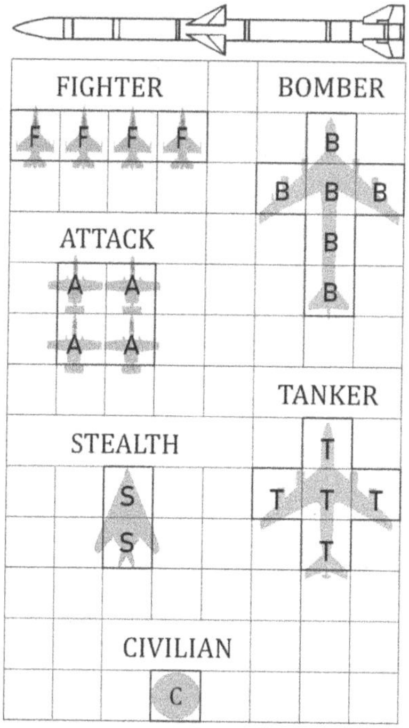

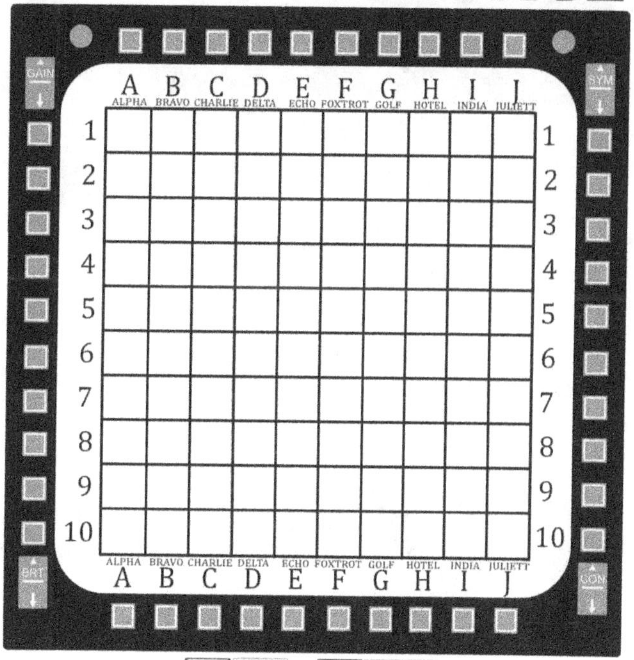

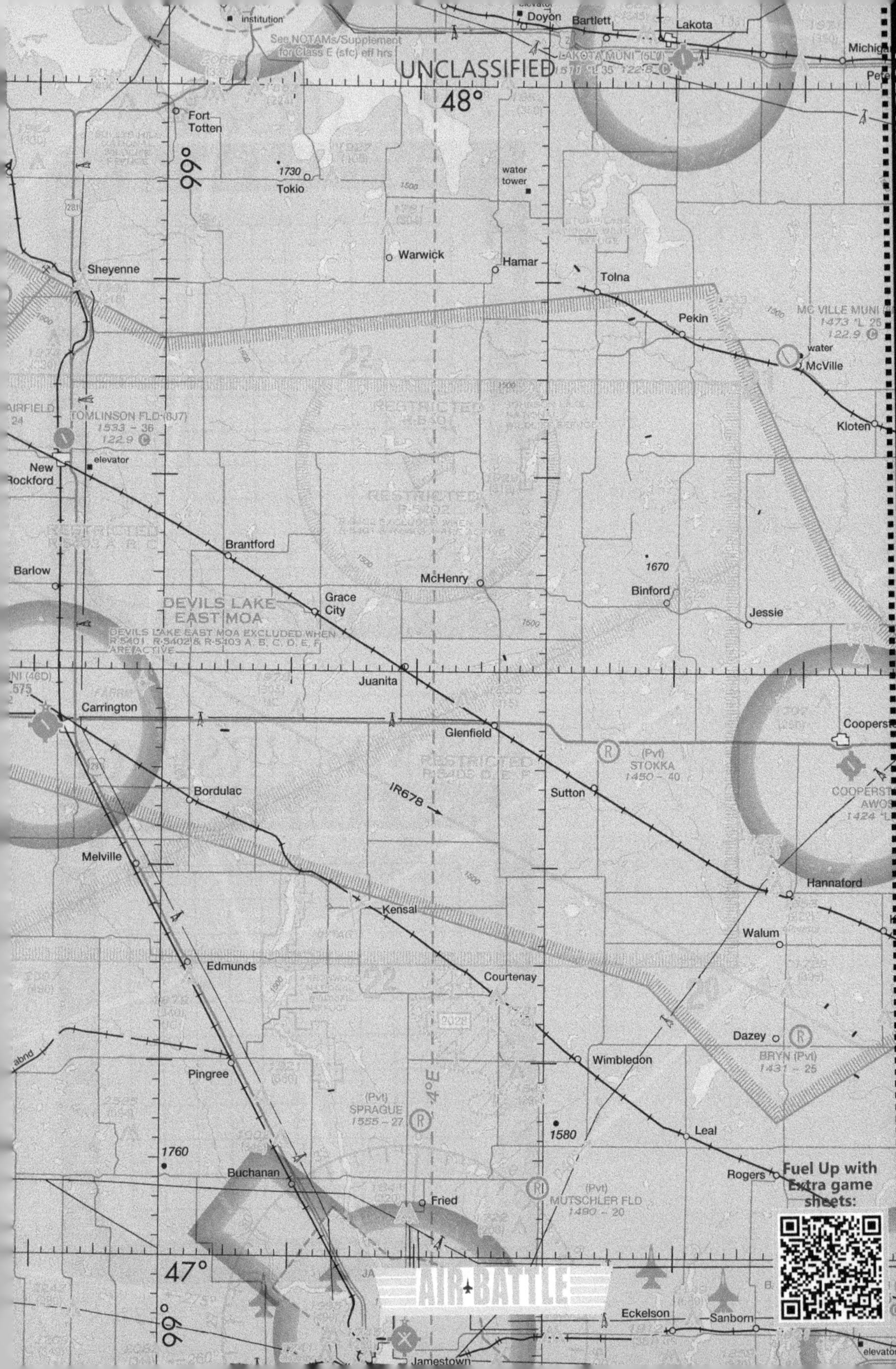

UNCLASSIFIED
48°
99°
47°
Fort Totten
Tokio
1730
water tower
Warwick
Hamar
Tolna
Pekin
McVille
MC VILLE MUNI
1473 *L 25
122.9
Kloten
Doyon
Bartlett
Lakota
LAKOTA MUNI (5L0)
Sheyenne
TOMLINSON FLD (8J7)
1533 – 36
122.9
New Rockford
elevator
Brantford
Barlow
DEVILS LAKE EAST MOA
DEVILS LAKE EAST MOA EXCLUDED WHEN R-5401, R-5402 & R-5403 A, B, C, D, E, F ARE ACTIVE
Grace City
McHenry
Binford
1670
Jessie
Juanita
Carrington
Glenfield
Cooperstown
(Pvt) STOKKA
1450 – 40
Sutton
Bordulac
IR678
Melville
Hannaford
Kensal
Walum
Edmunds
Courtenay
Dazey
BRYN (Pvt)
1431 – 25
Wimbledon
Pingree
(Pvt) SPRAGUE
1555 – 27
1580
Leal
1760
Buchanan
Rogers
Fried
(Pvt) MUTSCHLER FLD
1490 – 20
AIR BATTLE
Eckelson
Sanborn
Jamestown
elevator

Fuel Up with Extra game sheets:

FOLD ALONG DOTTED LINE AND TEAR

FOLD ALONG DOTTED LINE AND TEAR

Call Sign: _____

KEY

MY AIRSPACE

FIGHTER
F F F F

BOMBER
B
B B B
B
B

ATTACK
A A
A A

TANKER
T
T T T
T

STEALTH
S
S

CIVILIAN
C

My Airspace grid:

	A	B	C	D	E	F	G	H	I	J
	ALPHA	BRAVO	CHARLIE	DELTA	ECHO	FOXTROT	GOLF	HOTEL	INDIA	JULIETT
1										
2										
3										
4										
5										
6										
7										
8										
9										
10										

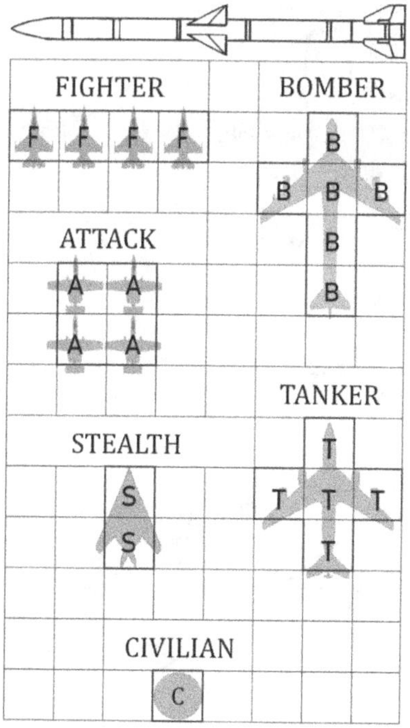

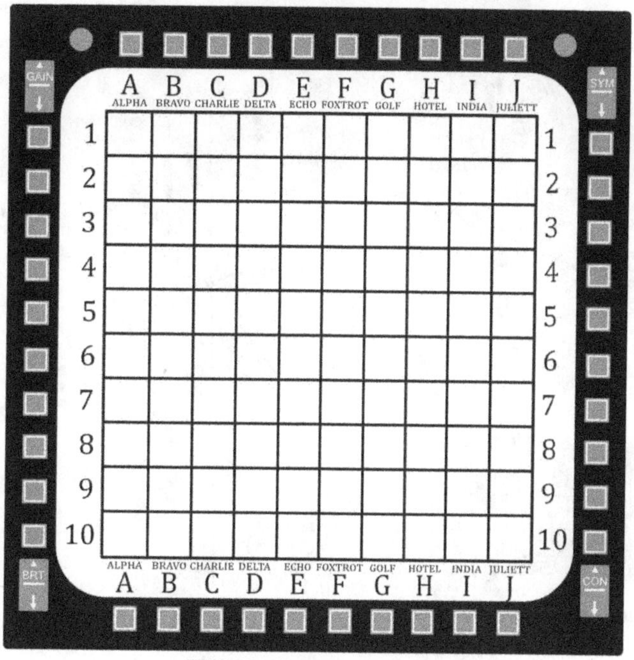

☒ HIT   ◯ MISS

Enemy Call Sign: _____

KEY

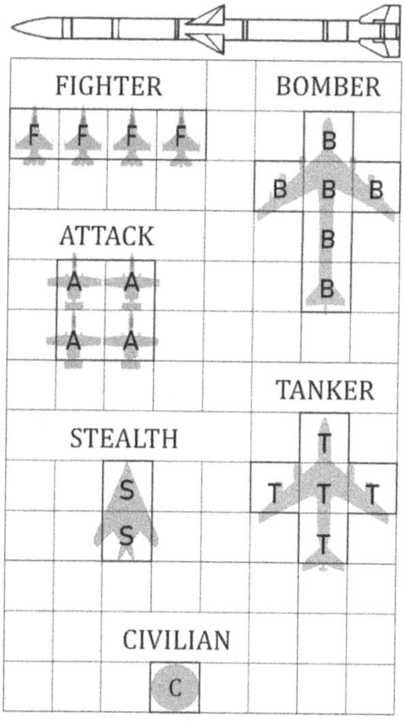

ENEMY AIRSPACE

FIGHTER
F F F F

BOMBER
B
B B B
B
B

ATTACK
A A
A A

TANKER
T
T T T
T

STEALTH
S
S

CIVILIAN
C

Enemy Airspace grid:

	A	B	C	D	E	F	G	H	I	J
	ALPHA	BRAVO	CHARLIE	DELTA	ECHO	FOXTROT	GOLF	HOTEL	INDIA	JULIETT
1										
2										
3										
4										
5										
6										
7										
8										
9										
10										

☒ HIT   ◯ MISS

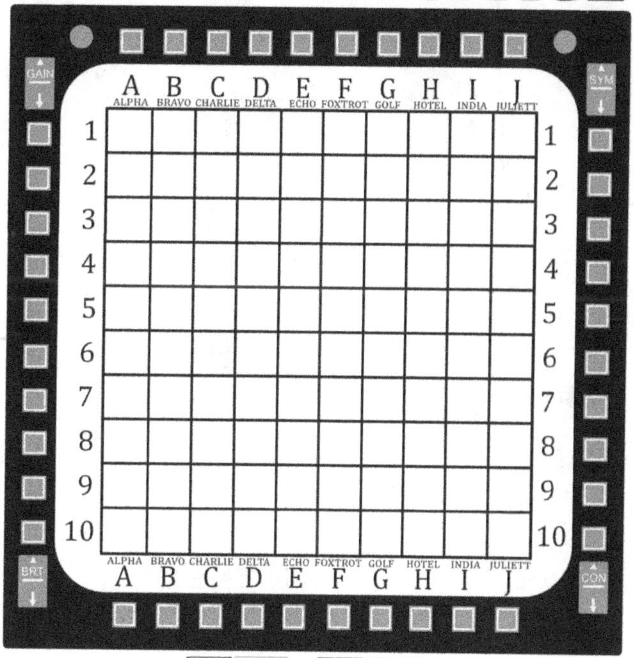

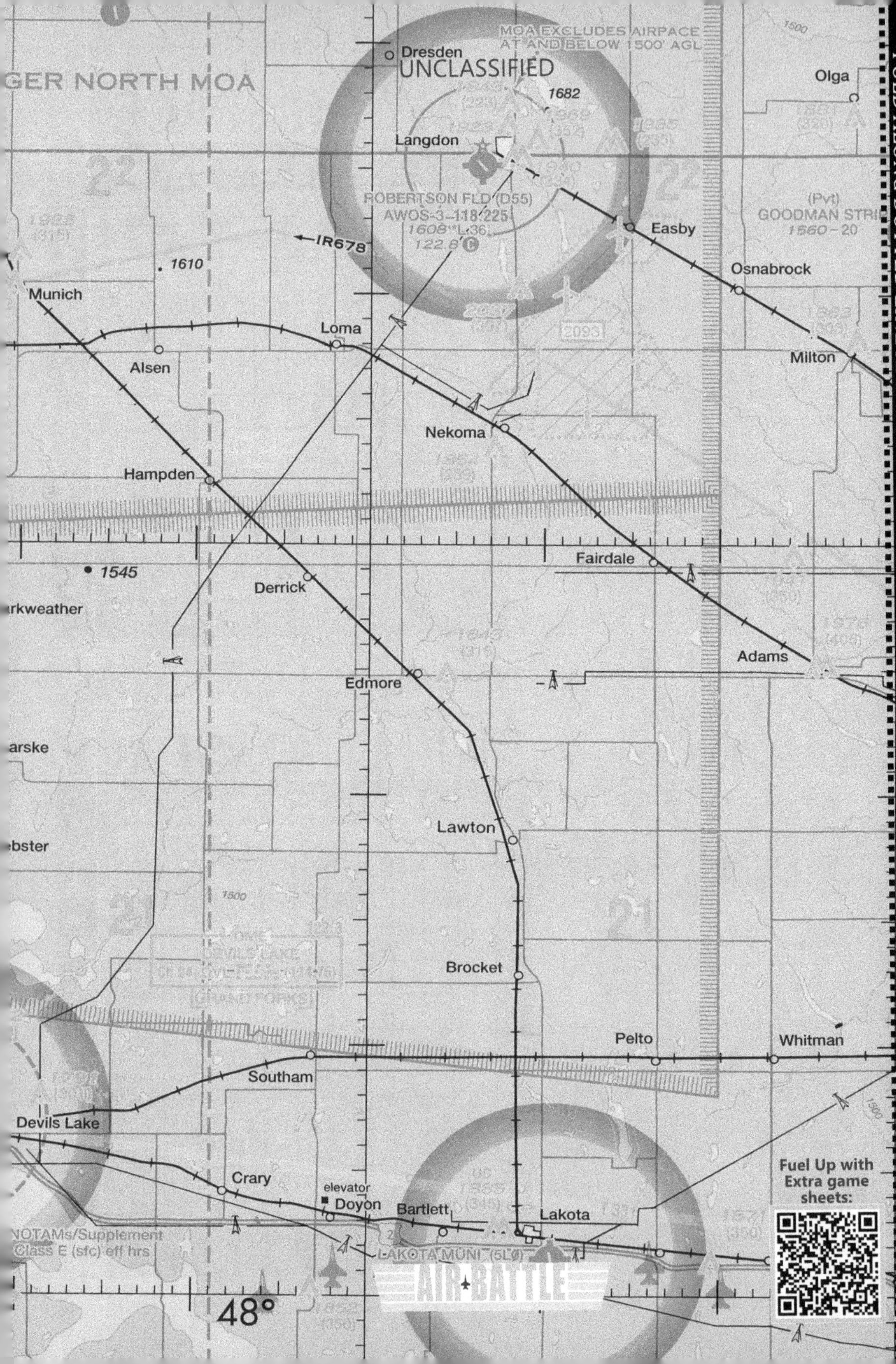

GER NORTH MOA
MOA EXCLUDES AIRPACE AT AND BELOW 1500' AGL
Dresden
UNCLASSIFIED
1682
Olga
Langdon
ROBERTSON FLD (D55)
AWOS-3 118.225
1608 L 36
122.8
IR678
(Pvt)
GOODMAN STRIP
1560 – 20
Easby
Osnabrock
1610
Munich
Loma
Alsen
Milton
2093
Nekoma
Hampden
1545
Fairdale
Derrick
rkweather
Adams
Edmore
arske
Lawton
ebster
Brocket
Pelto
Whitman
Southam
Devils Lake
Crary
elevator
Doyon
Bartlett
Lakota
NOTAMs/Supplement
Class E (sfc) eff hrs
LAKOTA MUNI (5L0)
AIR BATTLE
48°

Fuel Up with Extra game sheets:

FOLD ALONG DOTTED LINE AND TEAR

FOLD ALONG DOTTED LINE AND TEAR

Call Sign: _____

KEY

FIGHTER

F F F F

BOMBER

B
B B B
B
B

ATTACK

A A
A A

STEALTH

S
S

TANKER

T
T T T
T

CIVILIAN

C

MY AIRSPACE

	A	B	C	D	E	F	G	H	I	J	
	ALPHA	BRAVO	CHARLIE	DELTA	ECHO	FOXTROT	GOLF	HOTEL	INDIA	JULIETT	
1											1
2											2
3											3
4											4
5											5
6											6
7											7
8											8
9											9
10											10
	ALPHA	BRAVO	CHARLIE	DELTA	ECHO	FOXTROT	GOLF	HOTEL	INDIA	JULIETT	
	A	B	C	D	E	F	G	H	I	J	

☒ HIT   ◯ MISS

Enemy Call Sign: _____

KEY

FIGHTER

F F F F

BOMBER

B
B B B
B

ATTACK

A A
A A

STEALTH

S
S

TANKER

T
T T T
T

CIVILIAN

C

ENEMY AIRSPACE

	A	B	C	D	E	F	G	H	I	J	
	ALPHA	BRAVO	CHARLIE	DELTA	ECHO	FOXTROT	GOLF	HOTEL	INDIA	JULIETT	
1											1
2											2
3											3
4											4
5											5
6											6
7											7
8											8
9											9
10											10
	ALPHA	BRAVO	CHARLIE	DELTA	ECHO	FOXTROT	GOLF	HOTEL	INDIA	JULIETT	
	A	B	C	D	E	F	G	H	I	J	

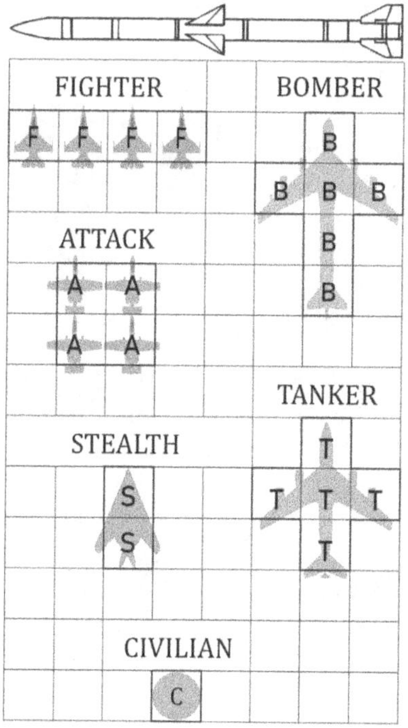

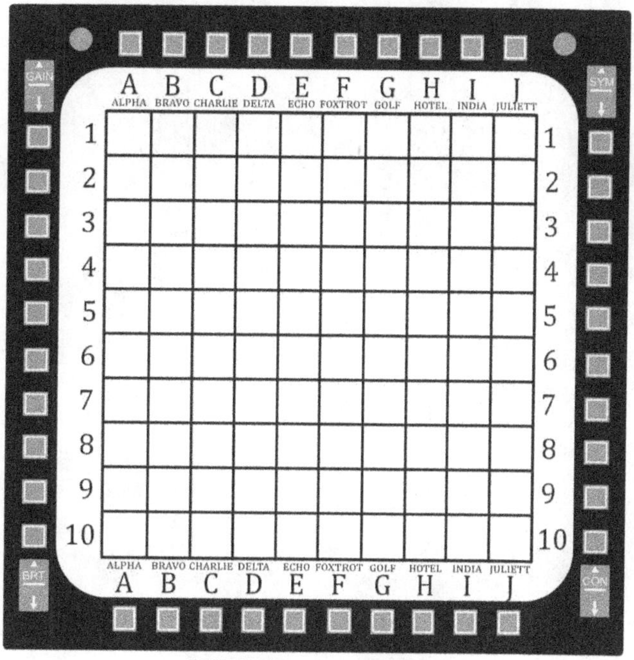

☒ HIT   ◯ MISS

FOLD ALONG DOTTED LINE AND TEAR

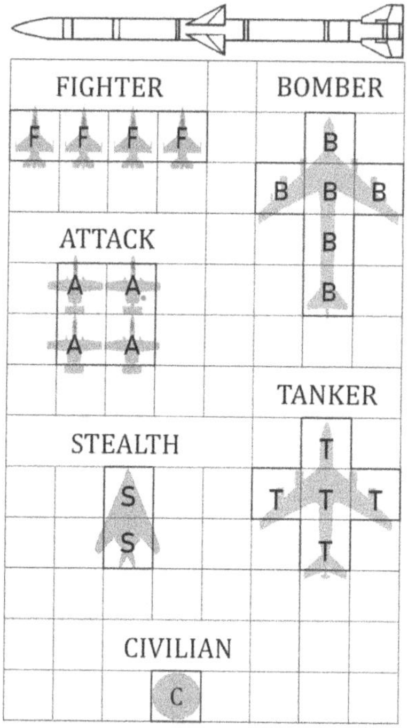

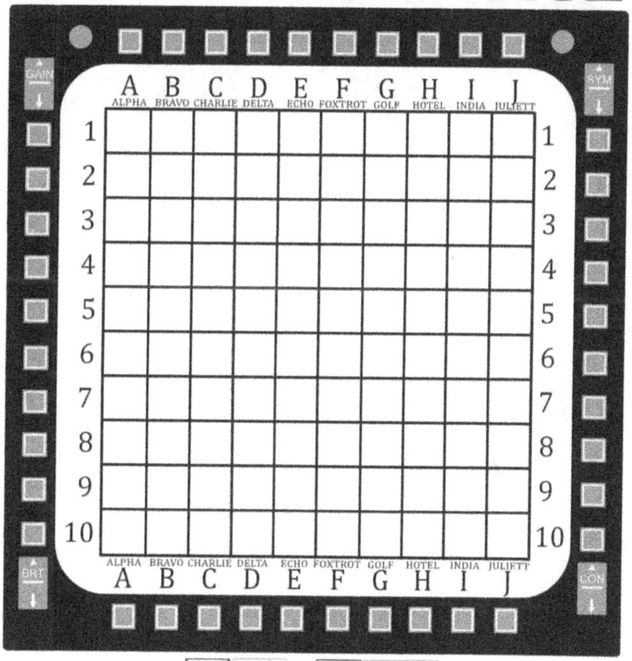

UNCLASSIFIED
Big Fork
Loman
LITTLEFORK MUNI/
HANOVER (13Y)
1145 – 30 122.9
Littlefork
MOA EXCLUDES AIRSPACE
BELOW 1500' AGL
Big Falls
BIG FALLS MUNI (7Y9)
1233 – 25 122.9
Waskish
WASKISH MUNI (VWU)
AWOS-3PT 124.175
1185 – 30
122.9
BEAVER MOA
1261
Margie
MOA EXCLUDES AIRSPACE
BELOW 1500' AGL
Shotley
1325
48°
94°
Gemmell
Kelliher
Mizpah
NORTHOME MUNI (43Y)
1430 L 32 122.9
Shooks
Northome
Effie
BIGFORK
345 FOZ
BIGFORK MUNI
1516
MOA EXCLUDES AIRSPACE
BELOW 1500' AGL
Bergville
Funkley
Wirt
Bigfork
Blackduck
Alvwood
IR606
IR605
Bass Lake
Hines
(Pvt)
LITTLE SAND
1930 – 32
Fuel Up with
Extra game
sheets:
BOWSTRING (9Y)
1372 – 25 122.9
Inger
(Pvt)
CUTFOOT SIOUX
AIR BATTLE

FOLD ALONG DOTTED LINE AND TEAR

FOLD ALONG DOTTED LINE AND TEAR

Call Sign: _____

KEY

MY AIRSPACE

FIGHTER	BOMBER
F F F F	B / B B B / B / B

| ATTACK | |
| A A / A A | TANKER |

| STEALTH | T / T T T / T |

| | CIVILIAN |
| | C |

MY AIRSPACE

	A	B	C	D	E	F	G	H	I	J	
	ALPHA	BRAVO	CHARLIE	DELTA	ECHO	FOXTROT	GOLF	HOTEL	INDIA	JULIETT	
1											1
2											2
3											3
4											4
5											5
6											6
7											7
8											8
9											9
10											10
	A	B	C	D	E	F	G	H	I	J	
	ALPHA	BRAVO	CHARLIE	DELTA	ECHO	FOXTROT	GOLF	HOTEL	INDIA	JULIETT	

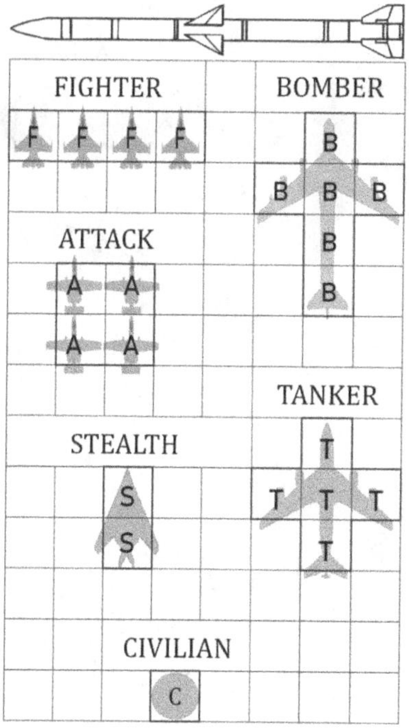

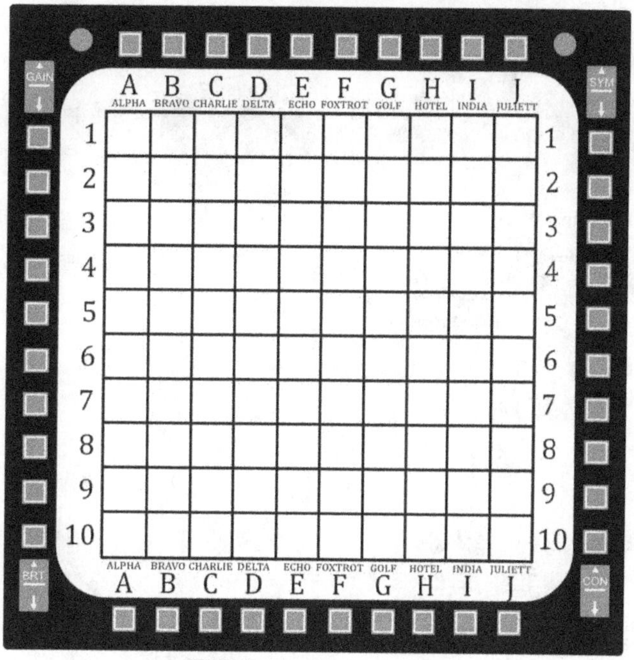

☒ HIT   ◯ MISS

Enemy Call Sign: _____

KEY

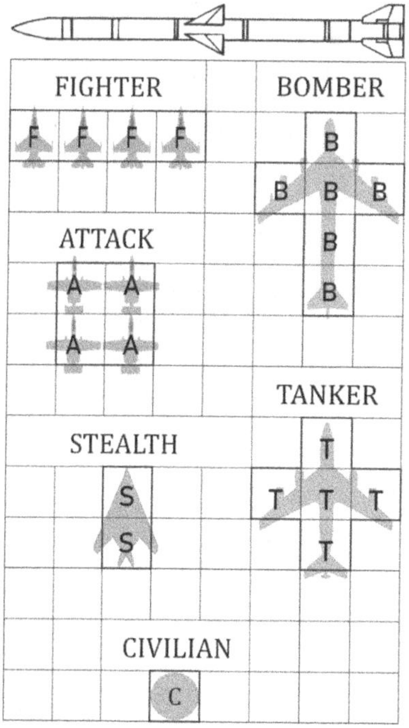

ENEMY AIRSPACE

FIGHTER	BOMBER
F F F F	B / B B B / B / B

| ATTACK | |
| A A / A A | TANKER |

| STEALTH | T / T T T / T |

| | CIVILIAN |
| | C |

ENEMY AIRSPACE

	A	B	C	D	E	F	G	H	I	J	
	ALPHA	BRAVO	CHARLIE	DELTA	ECHO	FOXTROT	GOLF	HOTEL	INDIA	JULIETT	
1											1
2											2
3											3
4											4
5											5
6											6
7											7
8											8
9											9
10											10
	A	B	C	D	E	F	G	H	I	J	
	ALPHA	BRAVO	CHARLIE	DELTA	ECHO	FOXTROT	GOLF	HOTEL	INDIA	JULIETT	

☒ HIT   ◯ MISS

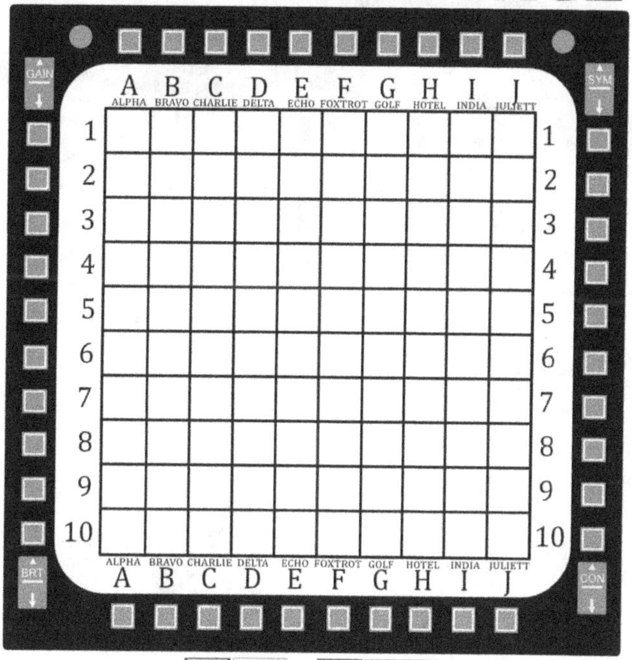

UNCLASSIFIED
Westfall
Glendale
(Pvt)
BURGERS VALLEY
1325 – 24
SALINA
Brookville
1750
ELLSWORTH MUNI (9K7)
AWOS-3PT 119.675
1633 L 45 122.7
Ellsworth
Kanopolis
Carneiro
water
VR152
VR533
VR119
VR531
VR532
warehouses
Falun
IR505
VR544
VR531
SMOKY HIGH MOA
VR552
IR513
IR526
TWISTER MOA
Lindsborg
Lorraine
VR531-532
VR138
VR534
VR535
VR536
Langley
Marquette
abnd
SMOKY MOA
VR138
VR119
Crawford
Frederick
Geneseo
FOR MOA ACTIVITY ADVISORY
MONITOR 123.25
IR526
elevator
MCPHERSON (MPR)
AWOS-3P 119.025
1498 L 55 122.8
RP 18, 26
elevator
abnd
Mitchell
Little River
Windom
refinery
Conway
Lyons
oil
VR152
VR536
refinery
oil
LYONS-RICE COUNTY MUNI (LYO)
AWOS-3P 119.925
1692 L 44 122.8
RP 17
Saxman
Groveland
Elyria
MAXWELL AVIATION (8KS)
1677 – 25 122.9
Alden
Sterling
VR119
Inman
(Pvt)
WILLYS LAKE
1631 – 19
Nickerson
Buhler
Fuel Up with
Extra game
sheets:
AIR BATTLE
HUTCHINSON
Burrton

FOLD ALONG DOTTED LINE AND TEAR

FOLD ALONG DOTTED LINE AND TEAR

Call Sign: _____

KEY

FIGHTER

BOMBER

ATTACK

STEALTH

TANKER

CIVILIAN

MY AIRSPACE

	A	B	C	D	E	F	G	H	I	J	
	ALPHA	BRAVO	CHARLIE	DELTA	ECHO	FOXTROT	GOLF	HOTEL	INDIA	JULIETT	
1											1
2											2
3											3
4											4
5											5
6											6
7											7
8											8
9											9
10											10

ALPHA BRAVO CHARLIE DELTA ECHO FOXTROT GOLF HOTEL INDIA JULIETT
A B C D E F G H I J

☒ HIT   ◯ MISS

Enemy Call Sign: _____

KEY

FIGHTER

BOMBER

ATTACK

STEALTH

TANKER

CIVILIAN

ENEMY AIRSPACE

	A	B	C	D	E	F	G	H	I	J	
	ALPHA	BRAVO	CHARLIE	DELTA	ECHO	FOXTROT	GOLF	HOTEL	INDIA	JULIETT	
1											1
2											2
3											3
4											4
5											5
6											6
7											7
8											8
9											9
10											10

ALPHA BRAVO CHARLIE DELTA ECHO FOXTROT GOLF HOTEL INDIA JULIETT
A B C D E F G H I J

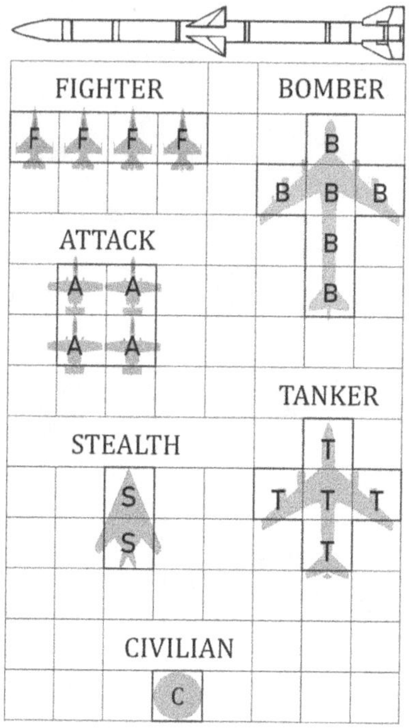

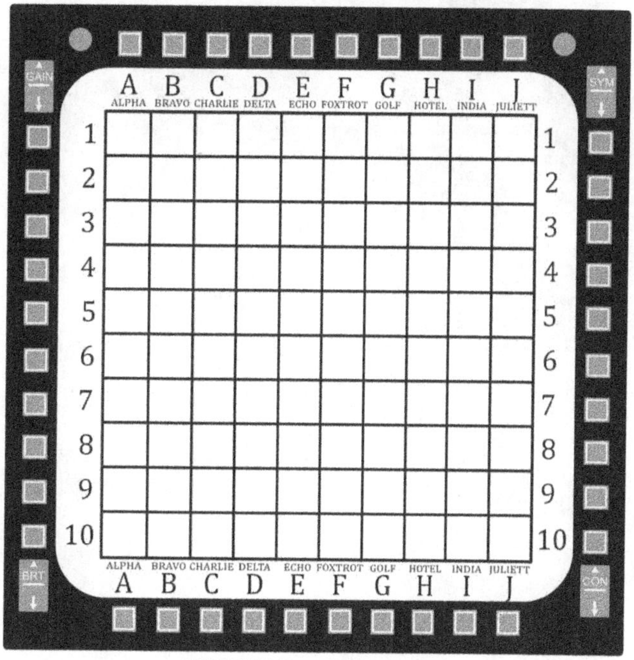

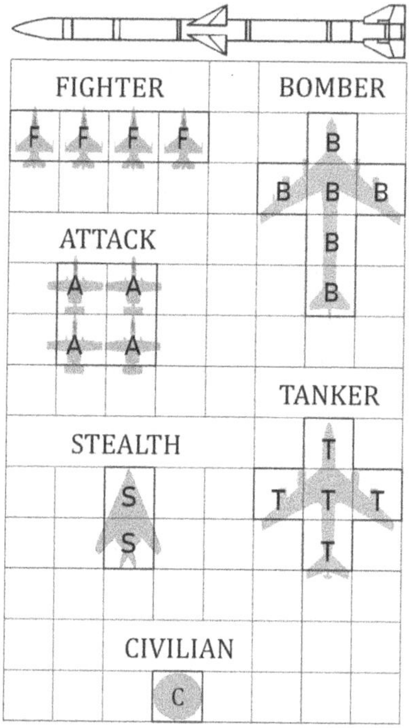

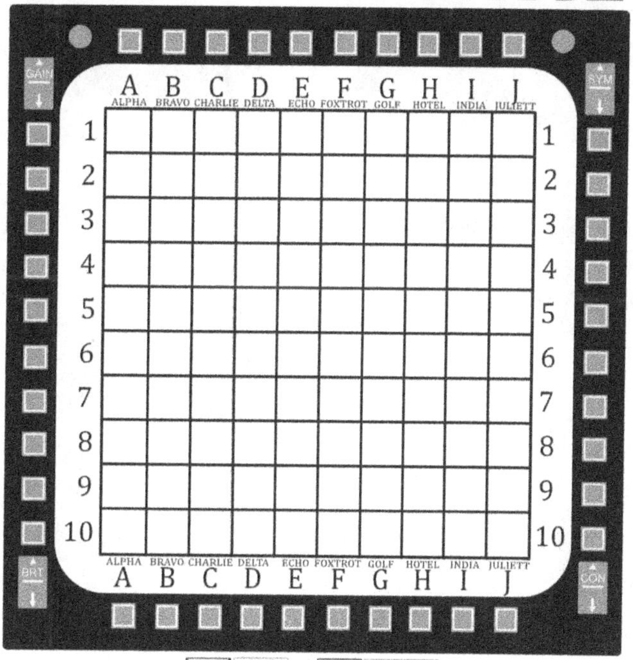

☒ HIT   ◯ MISS

UNCLASSIFIED

Fuel Up with Extra game sheets:

AIR BATTLE

FOLD ALONG DOTTED LINE AND TEAR

FOLD ALONG DOTTED LINE AND TEAR

Call Sign: _____

KEY

MY AIRSPACE

FIGHTER

F F F F

BOMBER

B
B B B
B
B

ATTACK

A A
A A

TANKER

T
T T T
T

STEALTH

S
S

CIVILIAN

C

A B C D E F G H I J
ALPHA BRAVO CHARLIE DELTA ECHO FOXTROT GOLF HOTEL INDIA JULIETT

1 2 3 4 5 6 7 8 9 10

GAIN SYM BRT CON

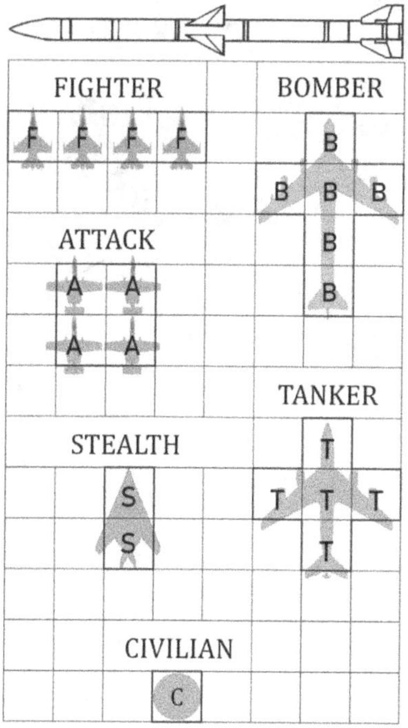

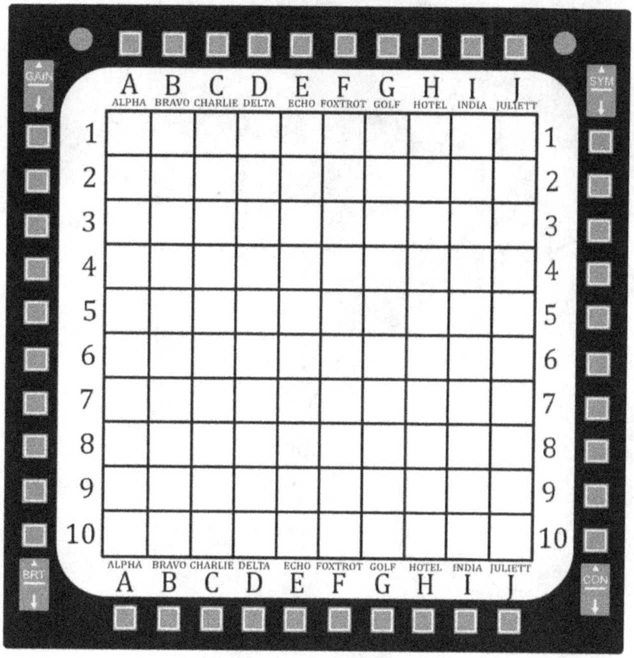

☒ HIT   ◯ MISS

Enemy Call Sign: _____

KEY

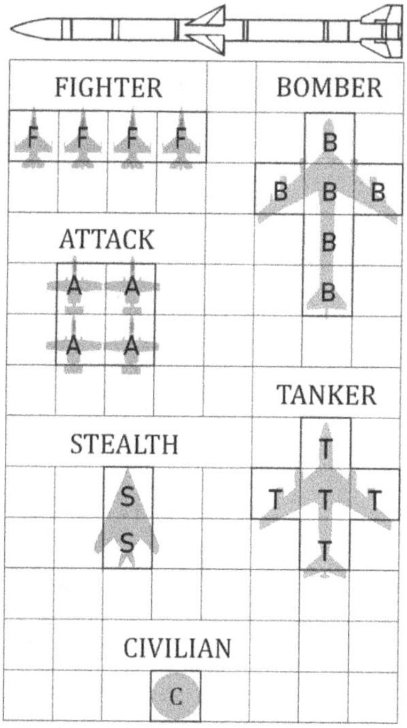

ENEMY AIRSPACE

FIGHTER

F F F F

BOMBER

B
B B B
B

ATTACK

A A
A A

TANKER

T
T T T
T

STEALTH

S
S

CIVILIAN

C

A B C D E F G H I J
ALPHA BRAVO CHARLIE DELTA ECHO FOXTROT GOLF HOTEL INDIA JULIETT

1 2 3 4 5 6 7 8 9 10

GAIN SYM BRT CON

☒ HIT   ◯ MISS

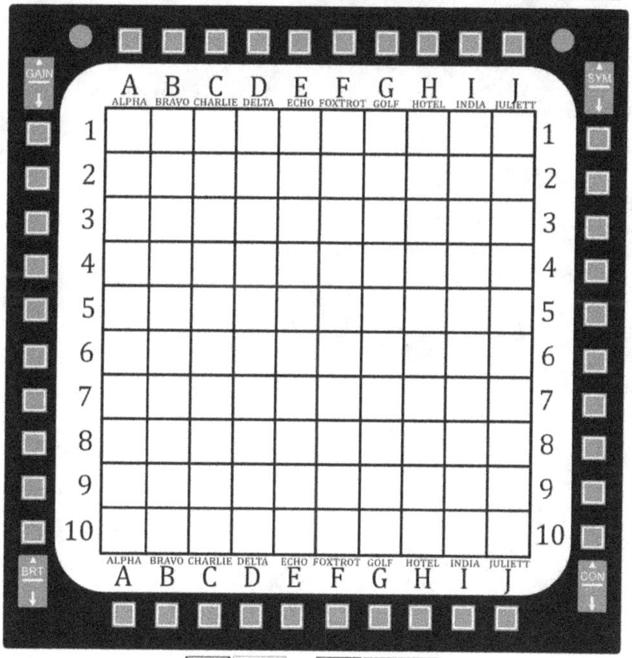

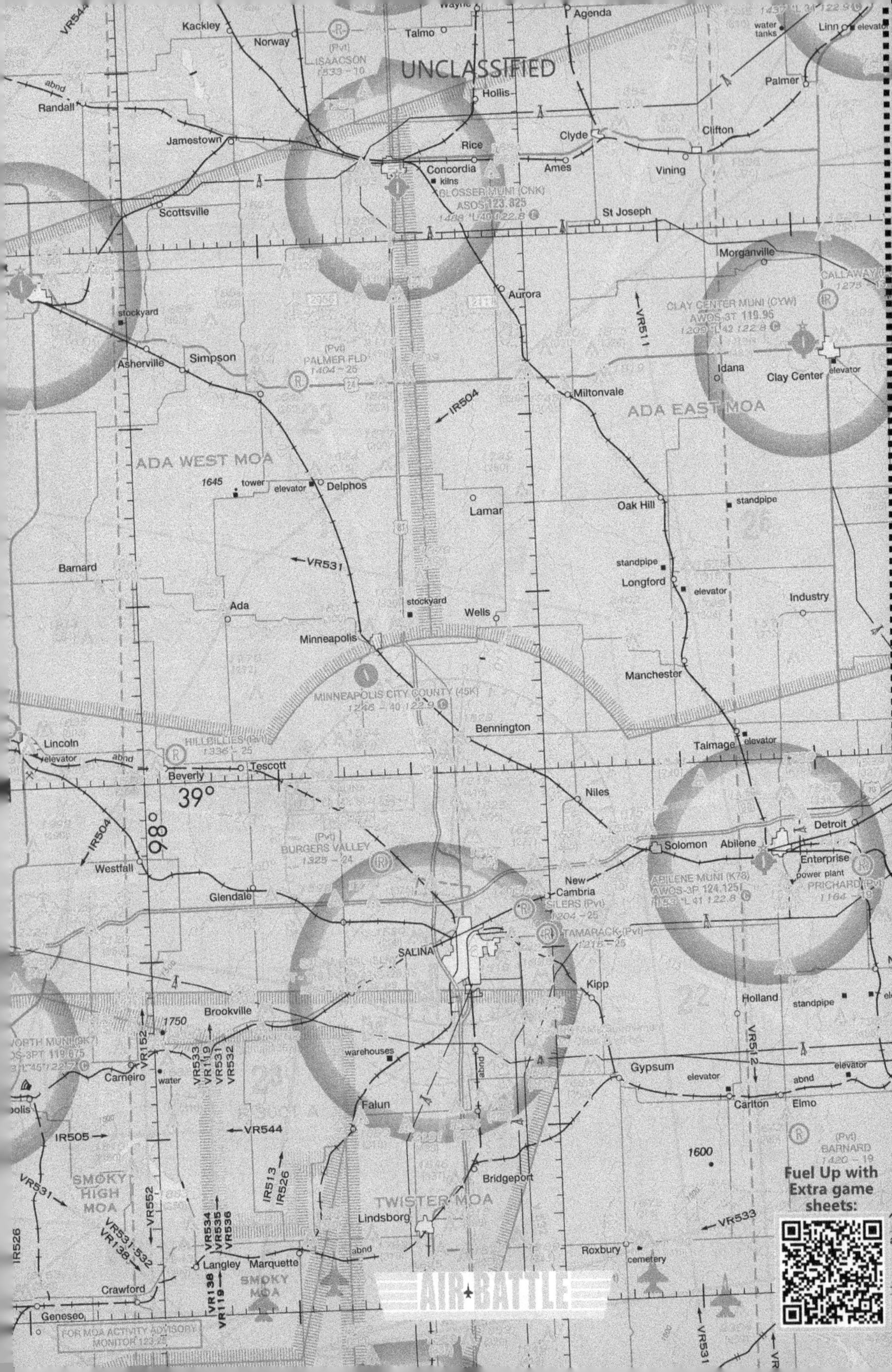
UNCLASSIFIED
Kackley
Norway
Talmo
Agenda
Linn
Palmer
Randall
Hollis
Jamestown
Rice
Clyde
Clifton
Concordia
Ames
Vining
kilns
BLOSSER MUNI (CNK)
ASOS 123.325
Scottsville
St Joseph
Morganville
CALLAWAY
stockyard
Aurora
CLAY CENTER MUNI (CYW)
AWOS-3T 119.95
VR511
Asherville
Simpson
(Pvt)
PALMER FLD
1404 – 25
Idana
Clay Center
elevator
Miltonvale
IR504
ADA EAST MOA
ADA WEST MOA
1645
tower
elevator
Delphos
Lamar
Oak Hill
standpipe
Barnard
VR531
standpipe
Longford
elevator
Ada
stockyard
Wells
Industry
Minneapolis
Manchester
MINNEAPOLIS CITY COUNTY (45K)
Bennington
Lincoln
HILLBILLIES (Pvt)
1336 – 25
Talmage
elevator
abnd
Beverly
Tescott
39°
Niles
Detroit
98°
IR504
BURGERS VALLEY
1325 – 24
Solomon
Abilene
Enterprise
Westfall
New
Cambria
power plant
ABILENE MUNI (K78)
AWOS-3P 124.125
PRICHARD (Pvt)
1164 – 19
Glendale
SILERS (Pvt)
1204 – 25
TAMARACK (Pvt)
1215 – 25
SALINA
Kipp
Brookville
1750
Holland
standpipe
VR152
VR533
VR119
VR531
VR532
VR512
warehouses
Gypsum
elevator
Carneiro
water
abnd
elevator
abnd
Carlton
Elmo
Falun
IR505
VR544
(Pvt)
BARNARD
1420 – 19
1600
SMOKY HIGH MOA
VR552
IR513
IR526
Bridgeport
VR531
TWISTER MOA
Lindsborg
VR533
IR526
VR534
VR535
VR536
VR531-532
VR138
Langley
Marquette
abnd
Roxbury
cemetery
SMOKY MOA
Crawford
VR138
VR119
AIR BATTLE
Geneseo
FOR MOA ACTIVITY ADVISORY
MONITOR 123.25
VR531

Fuel Up with Extra game sheets:

FOLD ALONG DOTTED LINE AND TEAR

FOLD ALONG DOTTED LINE AND TEAR

Call Sign: _____

KEY

MY AIRSPACE

FIGHTER

F F F F

BOMBER

B
B B B
B
B

ATTACK

A A
A A

TANKER

T
T T T
T

STEALTH

S
S

CIVILIAN

C

```
      A   B   C   D   E   F   G   H   I   J
    ALPHA BRAVO CHARLIE DELTA ECHO FOXTROT GOLF HOTEL INDIA JULIETT
 1                                              1
 2                                              2
 3                                              3
 4                                              4
 5                                              5
 6                                              6
 7                                              7
 8                                              8
 9                                              9
10                                             10
    ALPHA BRAVO CHARLIE DELTA ECHO FOXTROT GOLF HOTEL INDIA JULIETT
      A   B   C   D   E   F   G   H   I   J
```

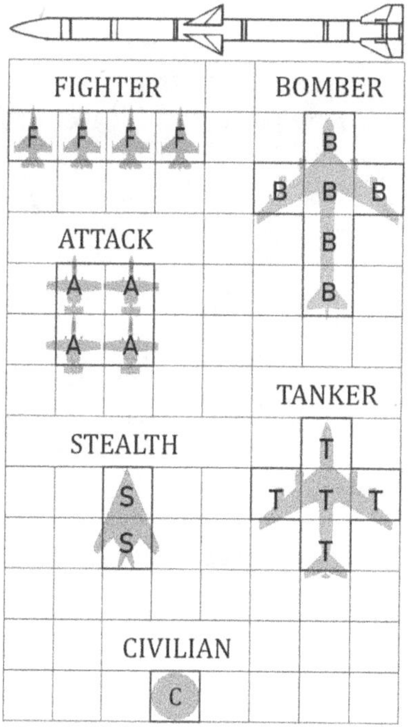

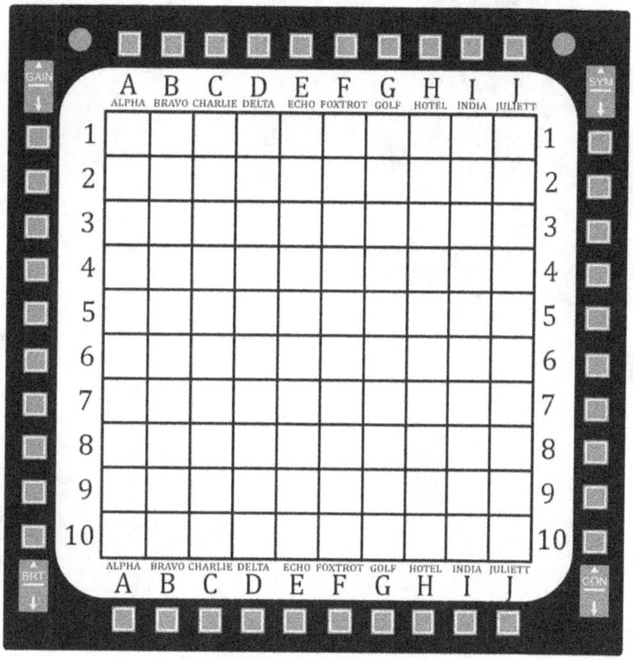

⊠ HIT   ◯ MISS

Enemy Call Sign: _____

KEY

ENEMY AIRSPACE

FIGHTER

F F F F

BOMBER

B
B B B
B
B

ATTACK

A A
A A

TANKER

T
T T T
T

STEALTH

S
S

CIVILIAN

C

```
      A   B   C   D   E   F   G   H   I   J
    ALPHA BRAVO CHARLIE DELTA ECHO FOXTROT GOLF HOTEL INDIA JULIETT
 1                                              1
 2                                              2
 3                                              3
 4                                              4
 5                                              5
 6                                              6
 7                                              7
 8                                              8
 9                                              9
10                                             10
    ALPHA BRAVO CHARLIE DELTA ECHO FOXTROT GOLF HOTEL INDIA JULIETT
      A   B   C   D   E   F   G   H   I   J
```

⊠ HIT   ◯ MISS

FOLD ALONG DOTTED LINE AND TEAR

FOLD ALONG DOTTED LINE AND TEAR

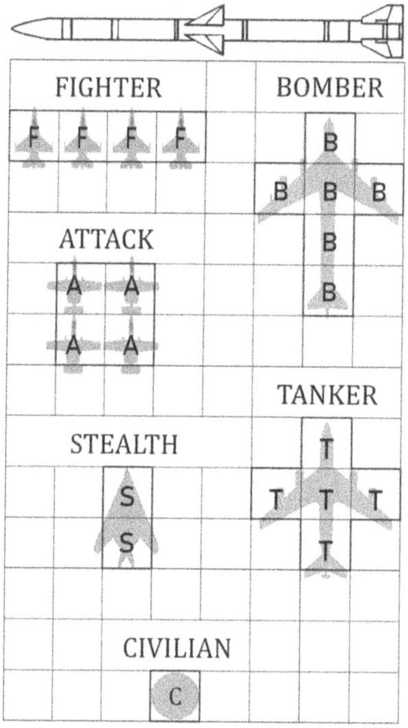

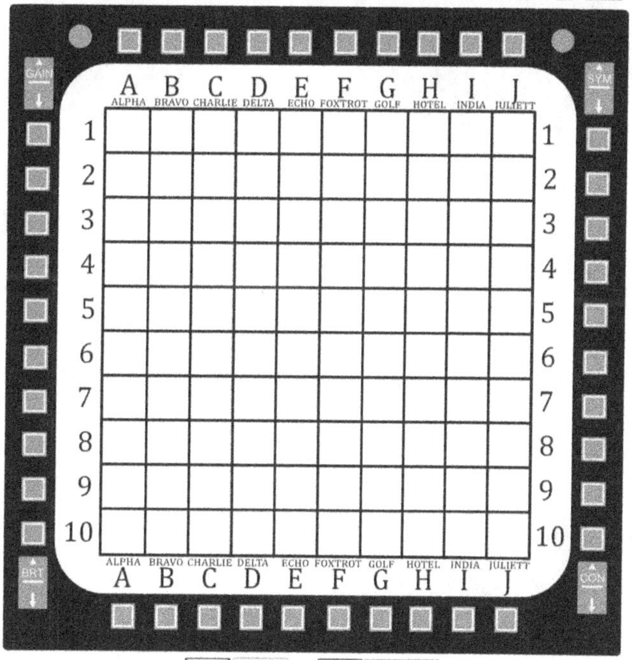

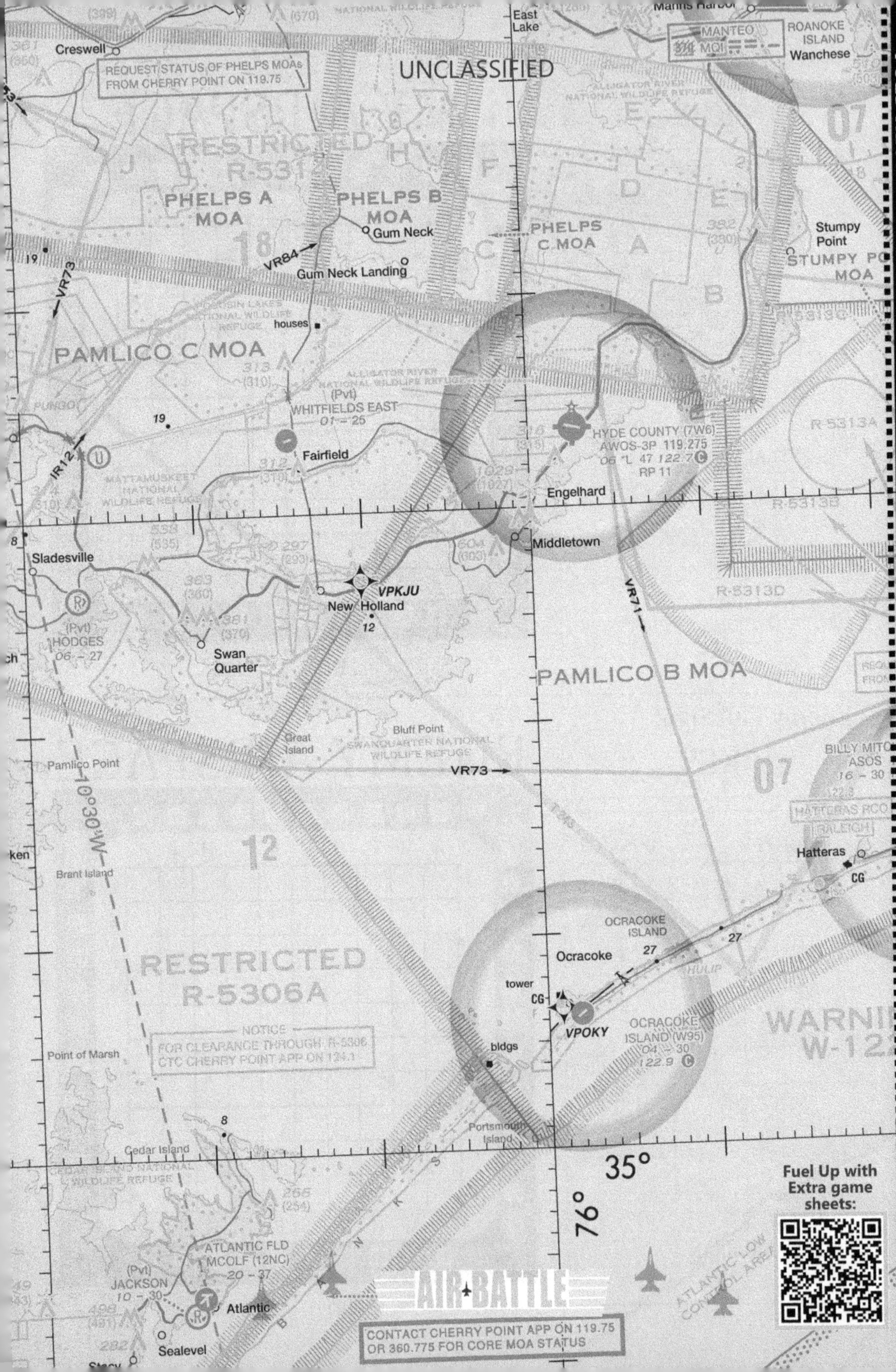

UNCLASSIFIED
East Lake
Manns Harbor
MANTEO MQI
ROANOKE ISLAND
Wanchese
Creswell
REQUEST STATUS OF PHELPS MOAs FROM CHERRY POINT ON 119.75
RESTRICTED R-5312
PHELPS A MOA
PHELPS B MOA
PHELPS C MOA
Gum Neck
Gum Neck Landing
VR84
VR73
Stumpy Point
STUMPY PO MOA
R-5313C
houses
PAMLICO C MOA
ALLIGATOR RIVER NATIONAL WILDLIFE REFUGE
(Pvt) WHITFIELDS EAST 01 – 25
Fairfield
HYDE COUNTY (7W6) AWOS-3P 119.275 06 L 47 122.7
RP 11
R-5313A
IR12
MATTAMUSKEET NATIONAL WILDLIFE REFUGE
Engelhard
R-5313B
Middletown
Sladesville
VPKJU
New Holland
VR71
R-5313D
(Pvt) HODGES 06 – 27
Swan Quarter
PAMLICO B MOA
Great Island
Bluff Point
SWANQUARTER NATIONAL WILDLIFE REFUGE
Pamlico Point
VR73
BILLY MITC ASOS 16 – 30
HATTERAS RCO
RALEIGH
10°30'W
Brant Island
Hatteras
CG
OCRACOKE ISLAND
Ocracoke
RESTRICTED R-5306A
tower
CG
VPOKY
NOTICE FOR CLEARANCE THROUGH R-5306 CTC CHERRY POINT APP ON 124.1
OCRACOKE ISLAND (W95) 04 – 30 122.9
WARNI W-122
Point of Marsh
bldgs
Portsmouth Island
Cedar Island
CEDAR ISLAND NATIONAL WILDLIFE REFUGE
35°
76°
Fuel Up with Extra game sheets:
ATLANTIC FLD MCOLF (12NC) 20 – 37
(Pvt) JACKSON 10 – 30
Atlantic
Sealevel
AIR BATTLE
ATLANTIC LOW CONTROL AREA
CONTACT CHERRY POINT APP ON 119.75 OR 360.775 FOR CORE MOA STATUS

FOLD ALONG DOTTED LINE AND TEAR

FOLD ALONG DOTTED LINE AND TEAR

Call Sign: _____

KEY

FIGHTER
F F F F

BOMBER
B
B B B
B
B

ATTACK
A A
A A

STEALTH
S
S

TANKER
T
T T T
T

CIVILIAN
C

MY AIRSPACE

	A	B	C	D	E	F	G	H	I	J	
	ALPHA	BRAVO	CHARLIE	DELTA	ECHO	FOXTROT	GOLF	HOTEL	INDIA	JULIETT	
1											1
2											2
3											3
4											4
5											5
6											6
7											7
8											8
9											9
10											10
	ALPHA	BRAVO	CHARLIE	DELTA	ECHO	FOXTROT	GOLF	HOTEL	INDIA	JULIETT	
	A	B	C	D	E	F	G	H	I	J	

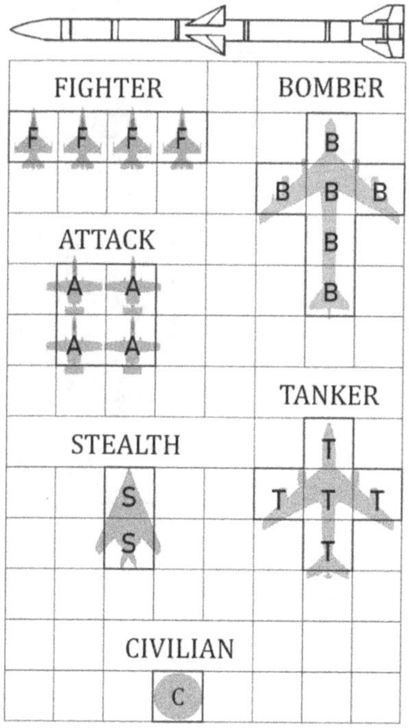

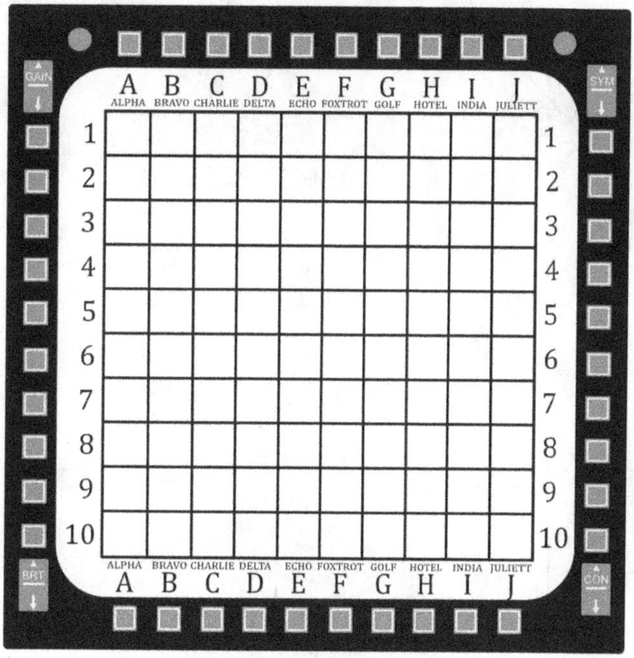

☒ HIT   ◯ MISS

Enemy Call Sign: _____

KEY

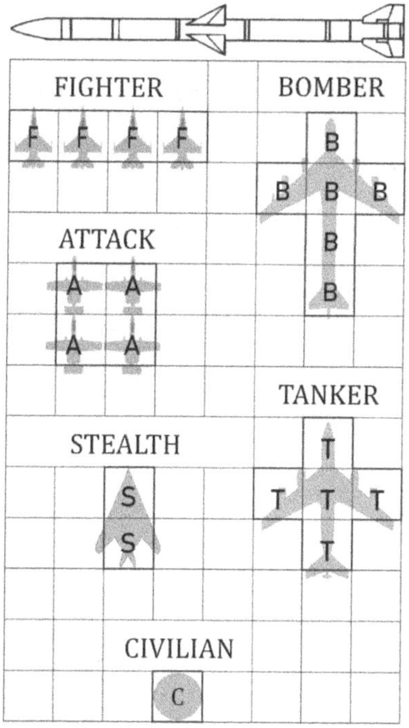

FIGHTER
F F F F

BOMBER
B
B B B
B
B

ATTACK
A A
A A

STEALTH
S
S

TANKER
T
T T T
T

CIVILIAN
C

ENEMY AIRSPACE

	A	B	C	D	E	F	G	H	I	J	
	ALPHA	BRAVO	CHARLIE	DELTA	ECHO	FOXTROT	GOLF	HOTEL	INDIA	JULIETT	
1											1
2											2
3											3
4											4
5											5
6											6
7											7
8											8
9											9
10											10
	ALPHA	BRAVO	CHARLIE	DELTA	ECHO	FOXTROT	GOLF	HOTEL	INDIA	JULIETT	
	A	B	C	D	E	F	G	H	I	J	

☒ HIT   ◯ MISS

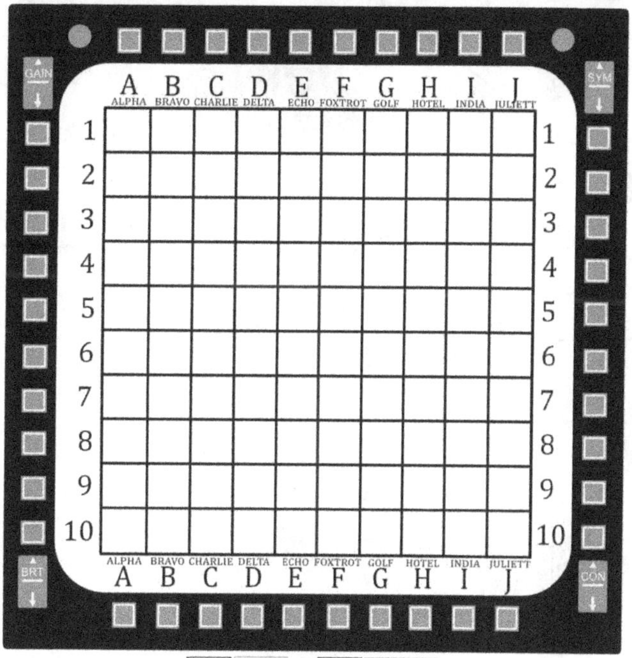

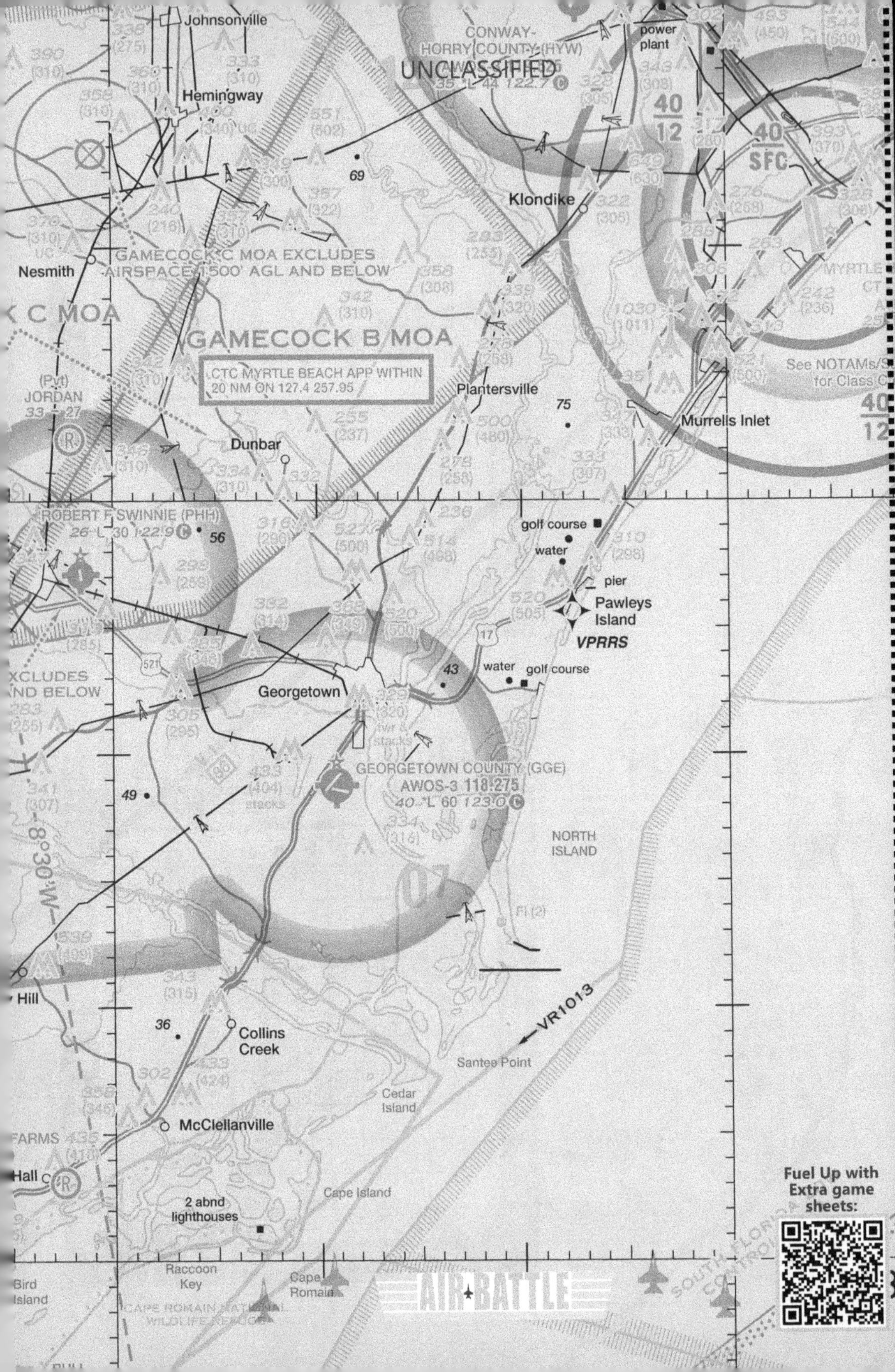
UNCLASSIFIED
Johnsonville
Hemingway
CONWAY-
HORRY COUNTY (HYW)
35 L 44 122.7
power
plant
Klondike
Nesmith
GAMECOCK C MOA EXCLUDES
AIRSPACE 1500' AGL AND BELOW
C MOA
GAMECOCK B MOA
CTC MYRTLE BEACH APP WITHIN
20 NM ON 127.4 257.95
(Pvt)
JORDAN
33 27
Plantersville
Dunbar
Murrells Inlet
See NOTAMs/S
for Class C
MYRTLE
ROBERT F SWINNIE (PHH)
26 L 30 122.9
golf course
water
pier
Pawleys
Island
VPRRS
XCLUDES
ND BELOW
water
golf course
Georgetown
twr &
stacks
GEORGETOWN COUNTY (GGE)
AWOS-3 118.275
40 L 60 123.0
stacks
NORTH
ISLAND
FI (2)
78°30'W
Hill
VR1013
Collins
Creek
Santee Point
Cedar
Island
McClellanville
FARMS
Hall
Cape Island
2 abnd
lighthouses
Raccoon
Key
Cape
Romain
Bird
Island
CAPE ROMAIN NATIONAL
WILDLIFE REFUGE
AIR BATTLE

Fuel Up with
Extra game
sheets:

FOLD ALONG DOTTED LINE AND TEAR

FOLD ALONG DOTTED LINE AND TEAR

Call Sign: _____

KEY

MY AIRSPACE

FIGHTER
F F F F

BOMBER
B
B B B
B
B

ATTACK
A A
A A

STEALTH
S
S

TANKER
T
T T T
T

CIVILIAN
C

My Airspace grid:
A B C D E F G H I J
ALPHA BRAVO CHARLIE DELTA ECHO FOXTROT GOLF HOTEL INDIA JULIETT
Rows 1–10

ALPHA BRAVO CHARLIE DELTA ECHO FOXTROT GOLF HOTEL INDIA JULIETT
A B C D E F G H I J

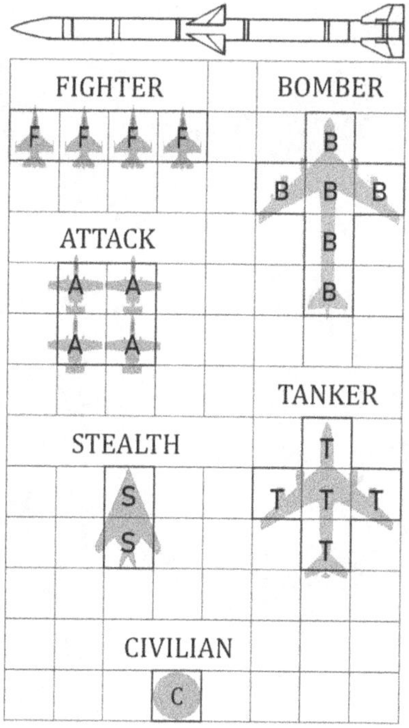

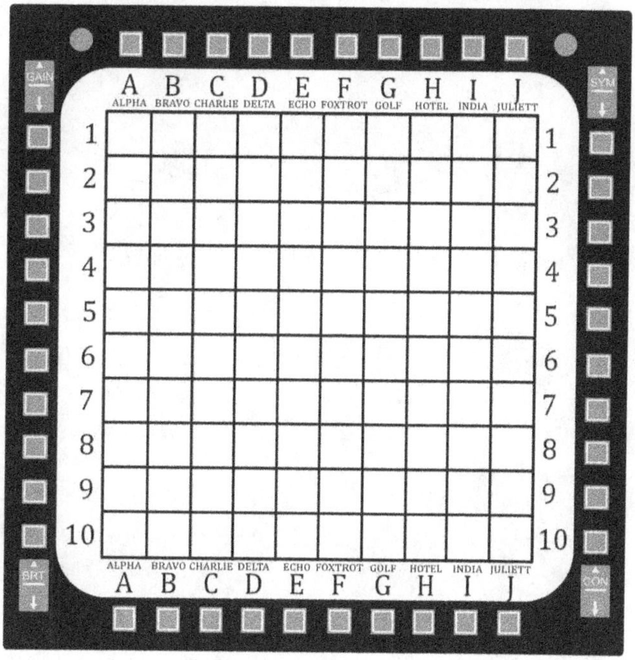

⊠ HIT   ◯ MISS

Enemy Call Sign: _____

KEY

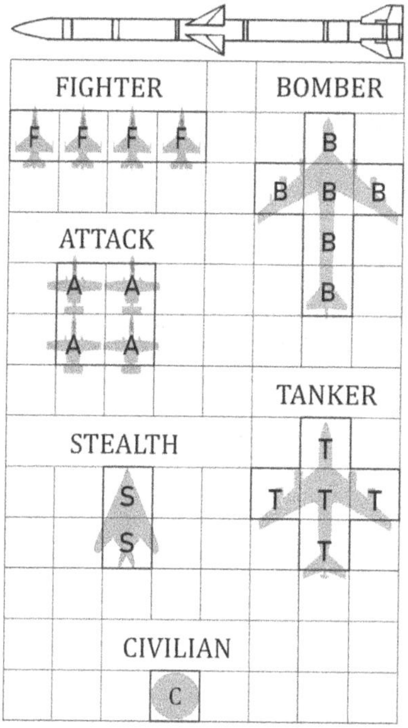

ENEMY AIRSPACE

FIGHTER
F F F F

BOMBER
B
B B B
B

ATTACK
A A
A A

STEALTH
S
S

TANKER
T
T T T
T

CIVILIAN
C

Enemy Airspace grid:
A B C D E F G H I J
ALPHA BRAVO CHARLIE DELTA ECHO FOXTROT GOLF HOTEL INDIA JULIETT
Rows 1–10

ALPHA BRAVO CHARLIE DELTA ECHO FOXTROT GOLF HOTEL INDIA JULIETT
A B C D E F G H I J

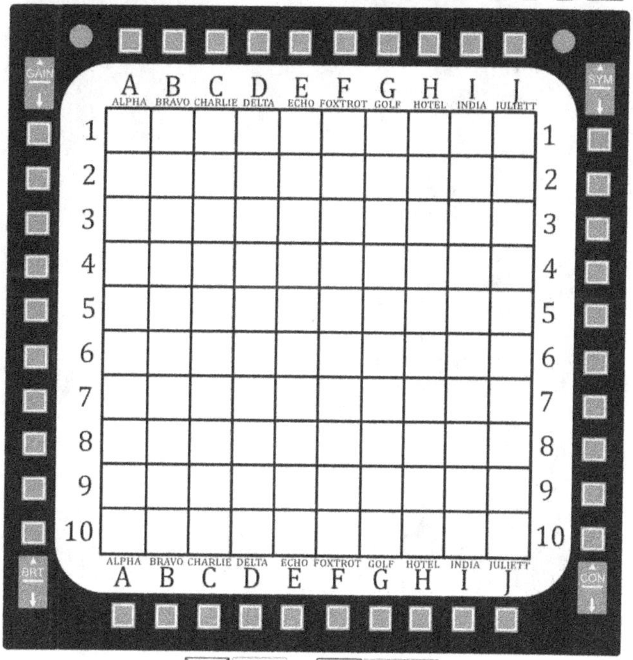

⊠ HIT   ◯ MISS

FOLD ALONG DOTTED LINE AND TEAR

UNCLASSIFIED

FOLD ALONG DOTTED LINE AND TEAR

FOLD ALONG DOTTED LINE AND TEAR

UNCLASSIFIED

FOLD ALONG DOTTED LINE AND TEAR

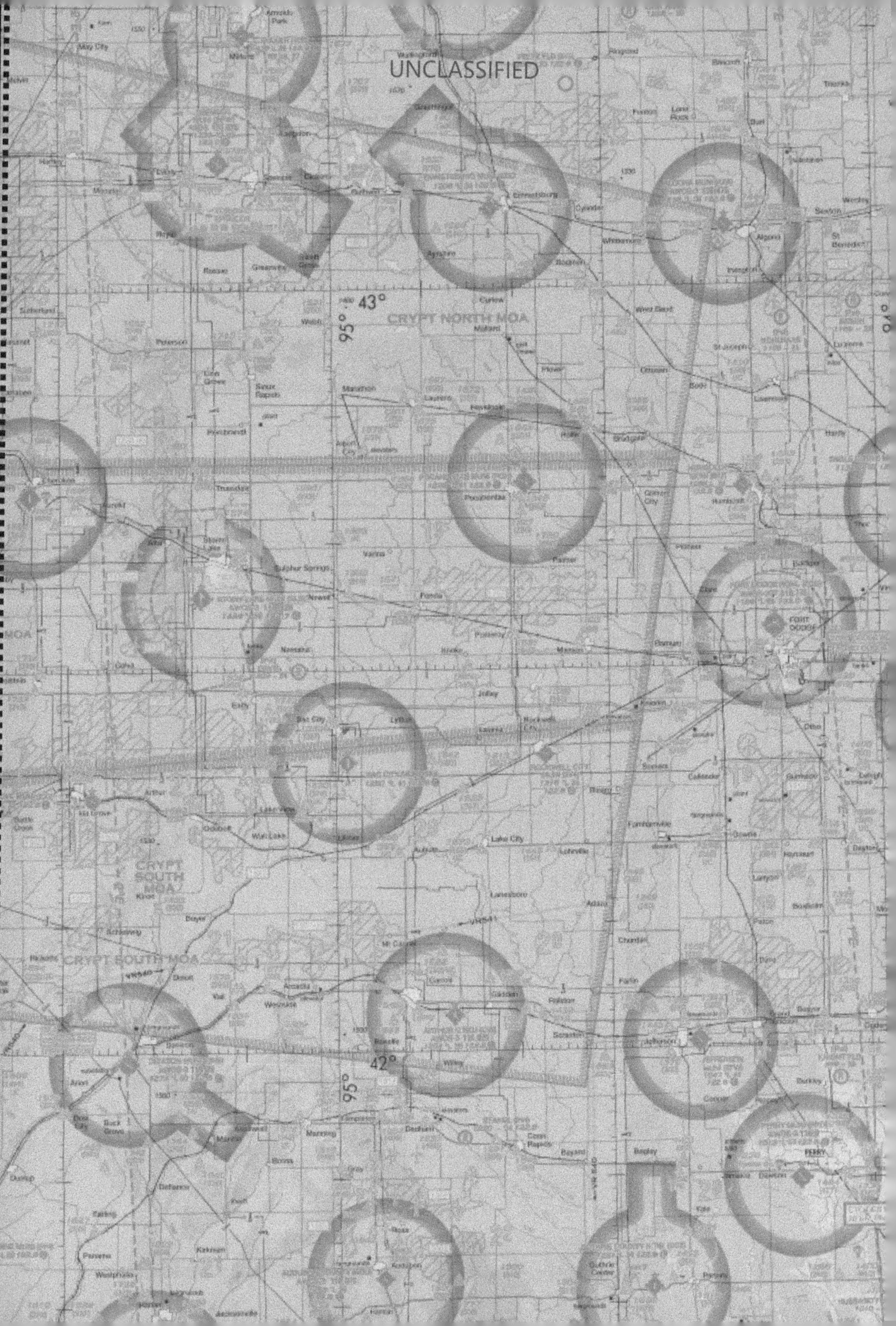

43°
95°
CRYPT NORTH MOA
CRYPT SOUTH MOA
CRYPT SOUTH MOA
42°
95°

FOLD ALONG DOTTED LINE AND TEAR

UNCLASSIFIED

Call Sign: ____________

MY AIRSPACE

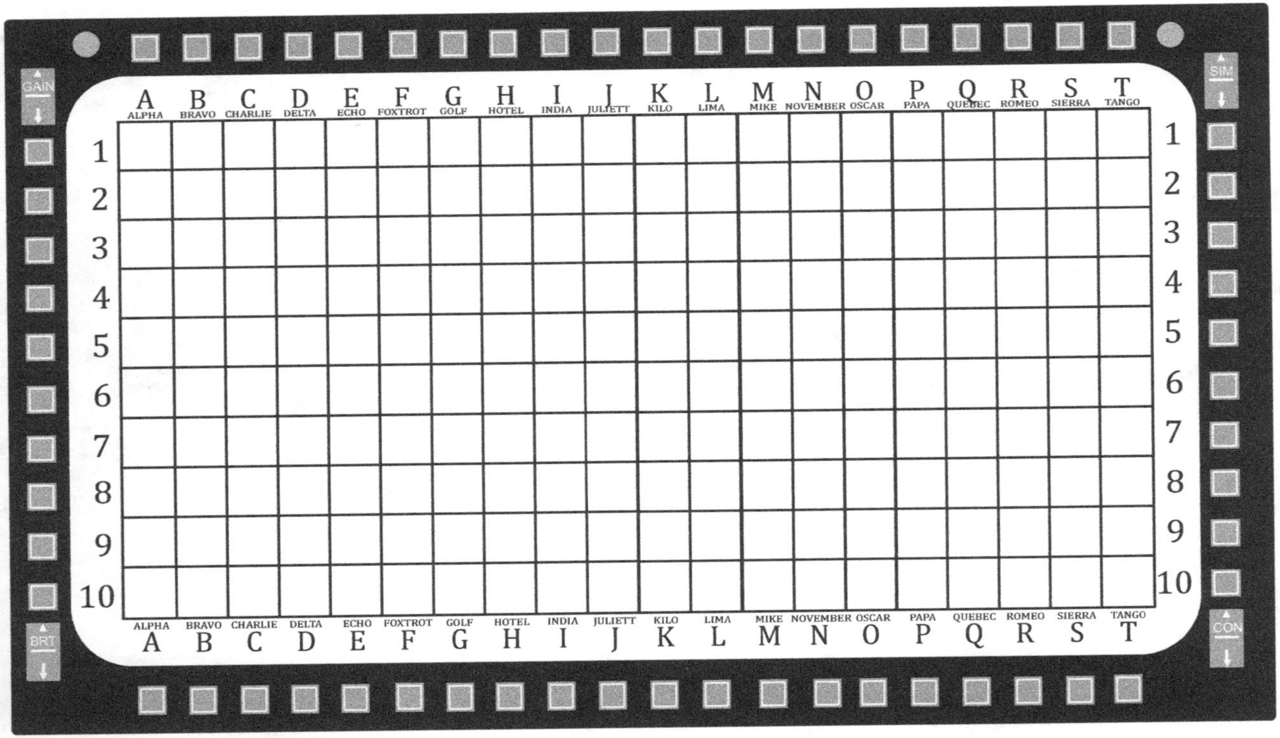

	A ALPHA	B BRAVO	C CHARLIE	D DELTA	E ECHO	F FOXTROT	G GOLF	H HOTEL	I INDIA	J JULIETT	K KILO	L LIMA	M MIKE	N NOVEMBER	O OSCAR	P PAPA	Q QUEBEC	R ROMEO	S SIERRA	T TANGO	
1																					1
2																					2
3																					3
4																					4
5																					5
6																					6
7																					7
8																					8
9																					9
10																					10
	A ALPHA	B BRAVO	C CHARLIE	D DELTA	E ECHO	F FOXTROT	G GOLF	H HOTEL	I INDIA	J JULIETT	K KILO	L LIMA	M MIKE	N NOVEMBER	O OSCAR	P PAPA	Q QUEBEC	R ROMEO	S SIERRA	T TANGO	

GAIN SIM BRT CON

DRAW 2 OF EACH
(10 PIECES+ 2 CIVILIAN)

KEY

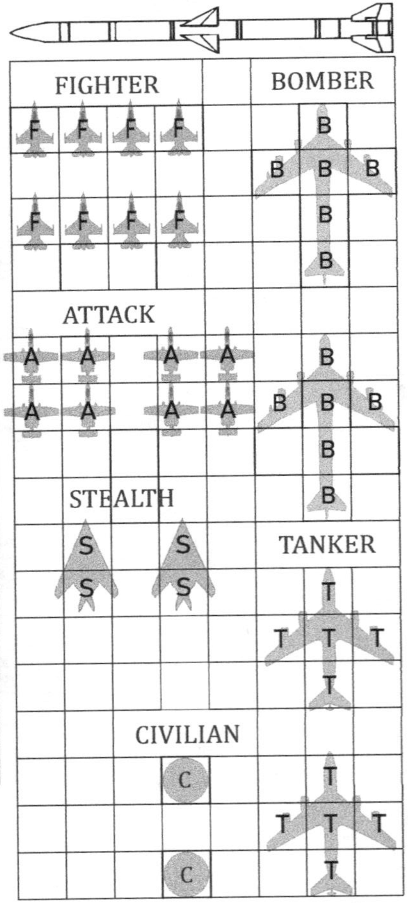

FIGHTER
BOMBER
ATTACK
STEALTH
TANKER
CIVILIAN

FOLD ALONG DOTTED LINE AND TEAR

FOLD ALONG DOTTED LINE AND TEAR

FOLD ALONG DOTTED LINE AND TEAR

FOLD ALONG DOTTED LINE AND TEAR

Enemy Call Sign: ____________

UNCLASSIFIED

ENEMY AIRSPACE

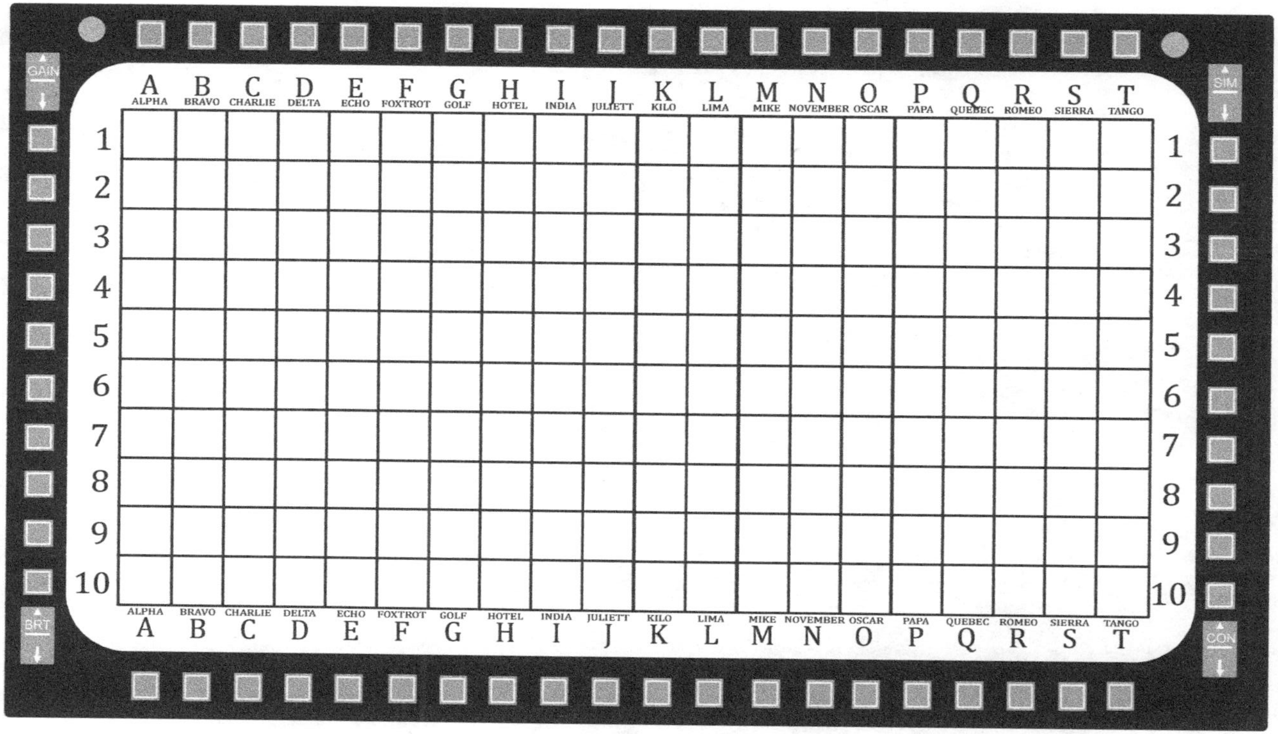

HIT 2 OF EACH

(10 PIECES)

(AVOID TWO CIVILIAN)

KEY

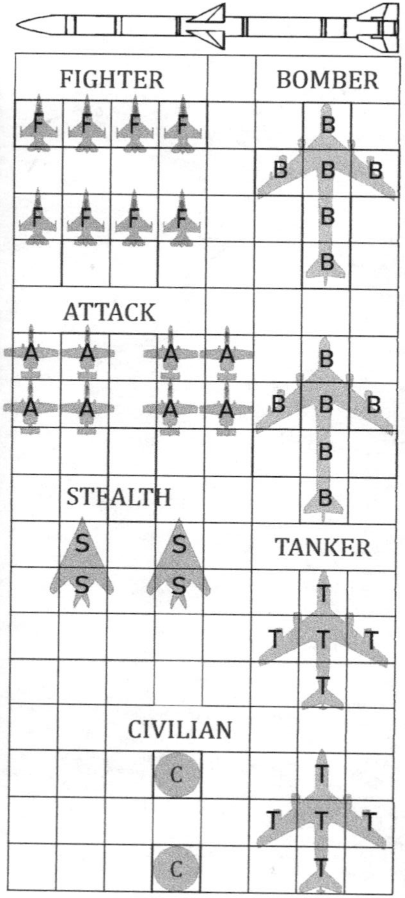

FIGHTER
BOMBER
ATTACK
STEALTH
TANKER
CIVILIAN

UNCLASSIFIED

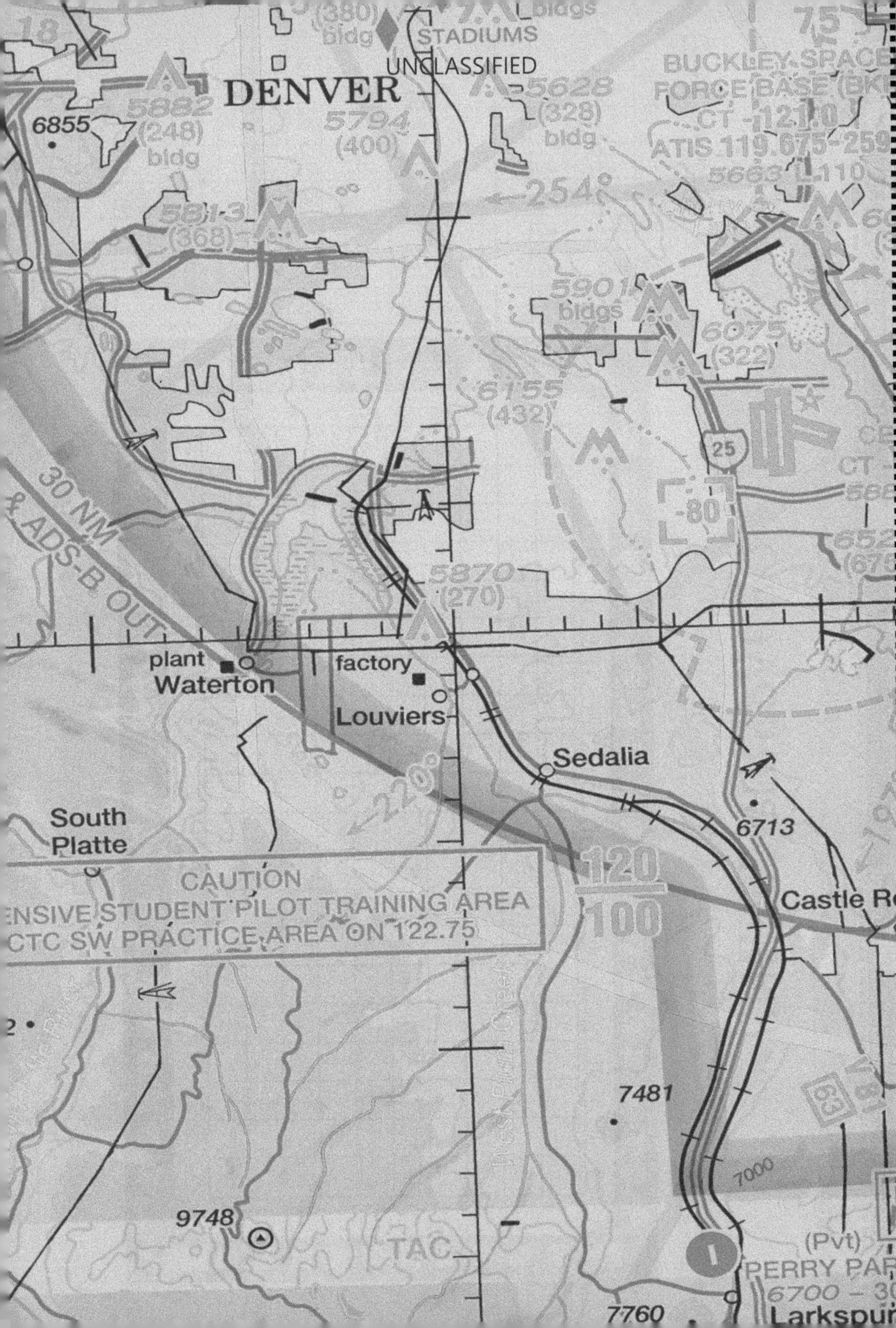

DENVER
STADIUMS
bldg
bldgs
BUCKLEY SPACE FORCE BASE
CT 121.0
ATIS 119.675
6855
5882 (248) bldg
5794 (400)
5628 (328) bldg
5813 (368)
5901 bldgs
6075 (322)
6155 (432)
254°
25
80
5870 (270)
30 NM & ADS-B OUT
plant
Waterton
factory
Louviers
Sedalia
6713
South Platte
220°
CAUTION
ENSIVE STUDENT PILOT TRAINING AREA
CTC SW PRACTICE AREA ON 122.75
120
100
Castle Ro
63
7481
7000
9748
TAC
(Pvt)
PERRY PAR
6700 – 30
7760
Larkspur

FOLD ALONG DOTTED LINE AND TEAR

FOLD ALONG DOTTED LINE AND TEAR

FOLD ALONG DOTTED LINE AND TEAR

FOLD ALONG DOTTED LINE AND TEAR

70
(Pvt)
VAN SLYKE FLD
25
120
70
6147
(304)
078°
FALCON
116.3 Ch 110 FQF
5949
(268)
5758
(210)
See NOTAMs/Supplement
for Class D eff hrs
HARRINGTON (Pvt)
5975 – 35
68
5962
(312)
120
100
6529
(225)
LEVERITT (Pvt)
6295 – 22
6230
6820
(309)
7049
120
90
CAUTION
INTENSIVE STUDENT PILOT TRAINING AREA
CTC SE PRACTICE AREA ON 122.75
fairground
Elizabeth
Kiowa
6811
(210)
6450
(Pvt)
DIETRICHS
6780 – 25
(Pvt)
CIRCLE 8
6650 – 37
(Pvt)
COMANCHE
CREEK
6620 – 31
7020
(210)
(Pvt)
D BAR D
6752 – 30
TAC
(Pvt)
FLYING G
6911 – 38
6447
(350)
Fondis
Elbert

UNCLASSIFIED

Call Sign: ____________

MY AIRSPACE

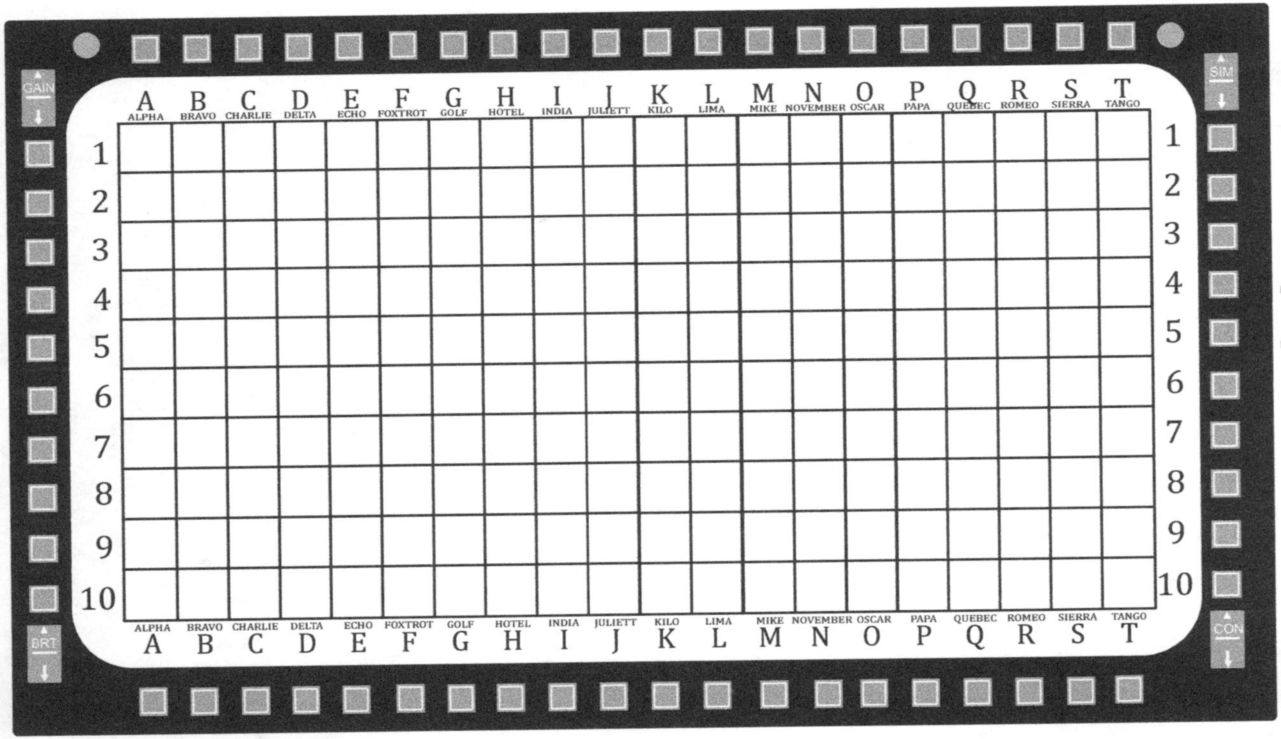
GAIN
SIM
BRT
CON
A ALPHA
B BRAVO
C CHARLIE
D DELTA
E ECHO
F FOXTROT
G GOLF
H HOTEL
I INDIA
J JULIETT
K KILO
L LIMA
M MIKE
N NOVEMBER
O OSCAR
P PAPA
Q QUEBEC
R ROMEO
S SIERRA
T TANGO
1 2 3 4 5 6 7 8 9 10

Draw 2 of Each
(10 pieces+ 2 Civilian)

KEY

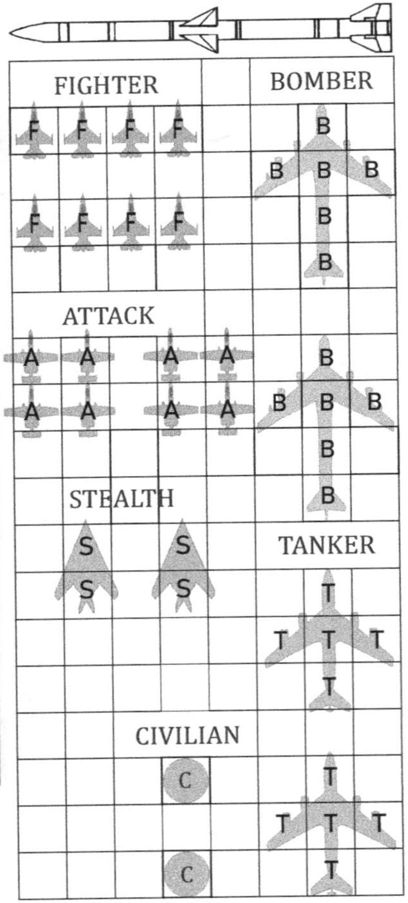
FIGHTER
BOMBER
ATTACK
STEALTH
TANKER
CIVILIAN

FOLD ALONG DOTTED LINE AND TEAR

FOLD ALONG DOTTED LINE AND TEAR

FOLD ALONG DOTTED LINE AND TEAR

FOLD ALONG DOTTED LINE AND TEAR

Enemy Call Sign: ____________

UNCLASSIFIED

ENEMY AIRSPACE

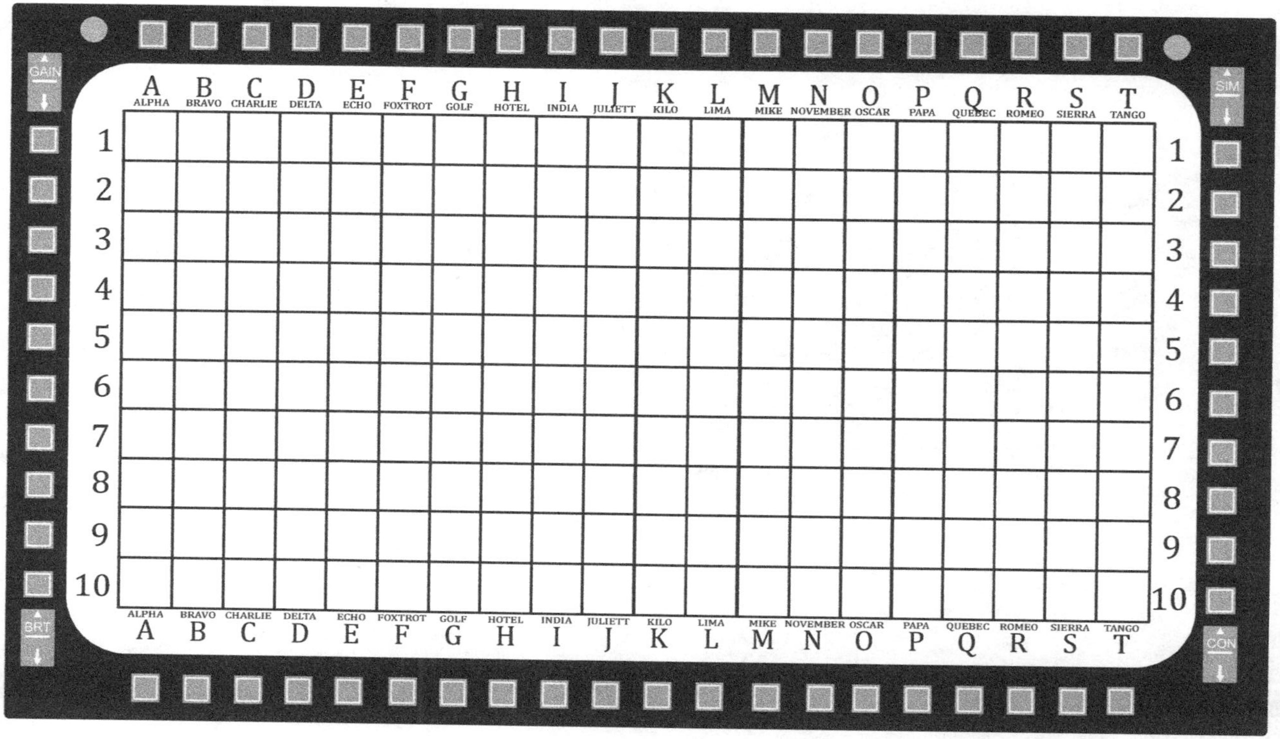

HIT 2 OF EACH
(10 PIECES)
(AVOID TWO CIVILIAN)
KEY

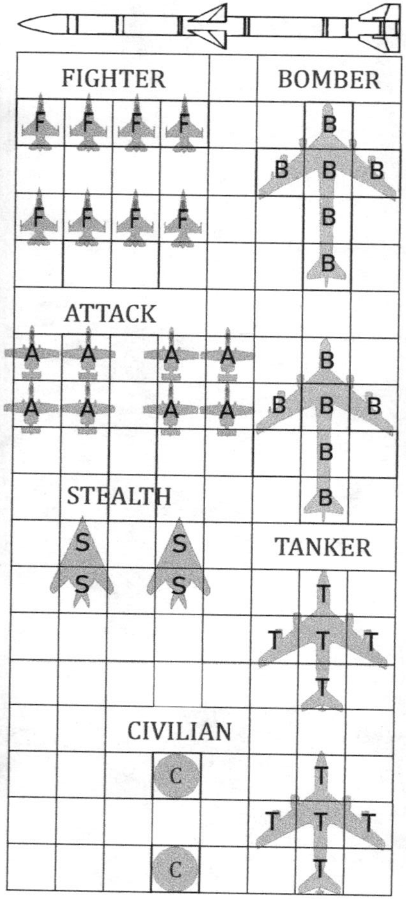

FIGHTER
BOMBER
ATTACK
STEALTH
TANKER
CIVILIAN

UNCLASSIFIED
WINDSWEPT
710 - 23
Deshler
1817
(1090)
Belmore
775
1010
(263)
1005
(265)
1021
(242)
1024
(279)
McComb
1050
Leipsic
1026
1039
PUTNAM COUNTY (OWX)
AWOS-3 120.525
764 *L 45
122.7
FINDLAY (FDY)
ASOS 132.85
813 *L 65 122.725
122.4
Ottawa
Gilboa
Benton Ridge
964
FINDLAY RCO
CLEVELAND
OBJECTIONABLE
41°
84°
1271
(497)
1105
(300)
1097
UC
1104
1099
(280)
Pandora
1069
Mt Cory
SCHALLER (Pvt)
830 - 26
75
1129
(300)
1070
(295)
1153
Bluffton
FLAG CITY
108.2 Ch 19 FBC
BLUFFTON (5G7)
243°
1123 851 *L 41 122.8
1156
(307)
1164
1254
(320)
30
Beaverdam
ADA (ØD7)
949 - 19 122.8
1122
(250)
1171
(260)
1185
Dunkirk
1215
(260)
Dola
1206
(264)
LIMA ALLEN
COUNTY (AOH)
ASOS 128.725
Lafayette
Ada
1448
1274
(300)
1268
1370
(345)
Harrod
Alger

FOLD ALONG DOTTED LINE AND TEAR

FOLD ALONG DOTTED LINE AND TEAR

FOLD ALONG DOTTED LINE AND TEAR

TORONTO FIR CZYZ
UNCLASSIFIED
CANADA
(ONTARIO)
UNITED STATES
(NEW YORK)
MISTY 1 MOA
LAKE ONTAR
Magnetic disturbance of as much as 7° exists at lake level at latitude 43°28'N and extends from longitude 78°05' to 78°45'W.
(Pvt) TIGER PAW 295 - 28
settlement
Olcott
Appleton
Lyndonville
abnd
GAINES VALLEY AVIATION 380 - 40 122.8
Gaines
Morton
MAYNARD'S (Pvt) 342 - 30
HILTON
marina
Ridgeway
Murray
BROCKPORT
HOLLANDS INTL FLD (85N)
KNOWLESVILLE (Pvt)
prison
Albion
Holley
SPENCERPORT AIRPARK (D91)
SPENCERPORT
ROYALTON (9G5) 628 - 25 122.8
MEDINA
Middleport
Barre Center
PINE HILL (9G6)
LOCKPORT
LEDGEDALE (7G0)
CTC ROCHESTER APP WITHIN 20 NM ON 123.7 322.3
CHURCHVILLE
IROQUOIS NATIONAL WILDLIFE REFUGE
CLARENCE AERODROME (D51)
Bergen
GENESEE COUNTY (GVQ) AWOS-3PT 127.525
stack
AKRON/JESSON FLD (9G3)
plant
POTOCZAK (Pvt) 582 - 22 122.9
Scottsville
CLUNG
STAFFORD
BUFFALO
Le Roy
43°
78°
LE ROY (5G0)
CALEDONIA
Clarence
BUFFALO-LANCASTER RGNL (BQR)
CTC BUFFALO APP WITHIN 20 NM ON 126.15 263.125
BATAVIA
BETHANY AIRPARK (Pvt)
Darien Lake Theme Park
WOZEE
DARIEN
Alden
Alexander
Bethany
Pavilion
Avon
CAUTION LASER LIGHT ACTIVITY See Supplement
Lancaster
Attica
Linden
prison
Piffard
Wyoming
CUMMINGS AIRFIELD
(Pvt) TRUMP MTN
GENESEO (D52)
LAKEVILLE (Pvt)
GENESEO
EAST AURORA
VARYSBURG
PERRY-WARSAW (01G) AWOS-2 118.525
Leicester
Orchard Park
plant
Warsaw
Perry
(Pvt) BLOECHER FARM
West Falls
S Wales
Mount Morris
SEVEN GULLS (Pvt)
Java Village
N Java
Rock Glen
SCOTT'S SKY RANCH (Pvt)
Sonyea
Groveland
ski area
prison
Silver Springs
TUSCARORA PLATEAU (Pvt)
Colden
Holland
Castile
Gainesville
Tuscarora
CLASS E eff SR-SS
(Pvt) HIGH ACRES
ARCADE TRI-COUNTY (D23)
abnd
Nunda
(Pvt) KEYSA
Portageville

FOLD ALONG DOTTED LINE AND TEAR

Call Sign: ____________

MY AIRSPACE

	A ALPHA	B BRAVO	C CHARLIE	D DELTA	E ECHO	F FOXTROT	G GOLF	H HOTEL	I INDIA	J JULIETT	K KILO	L LIMA	M MIKE	N NOVEMBER	O OSCAR	P PAPA	Q QUEBEC	R ROMEO	S SIERRA	T TANGO	
1																					1
2																					2
3																					3
4																					4
5																					5
6																					6
7																					7
8																					8
9																					9
10																					10
	A ALPHA	B BRAVO	C CHARLIE	D DELTA	E ECHO	F FOXTROT	G GOLF	H HOTEL	I INDIA	J JULIETT	K KILO	L LIMA	M MIKE	N NOVEMBER	O OSCAR	P PAPA	Q QUEBEC	R ROMEO	S SIERRA	T TANGO	

GAIN SIM BRT CON

DRAW 2 OF EACH
(10 PIECES+ 2 CIVILIAN)

KEY

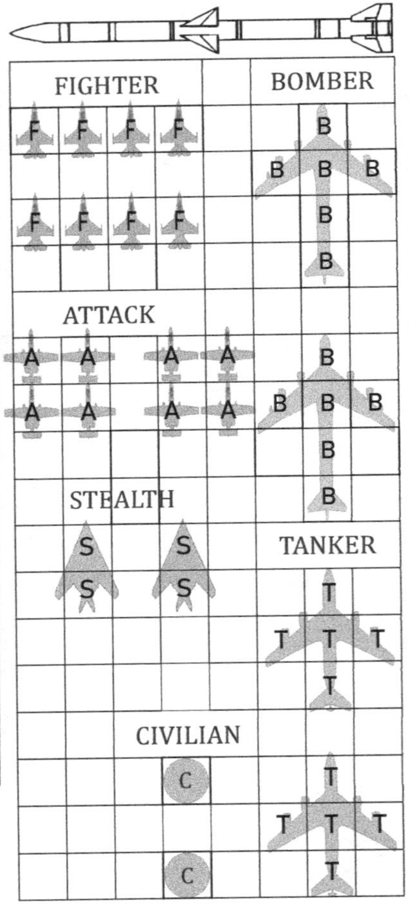

FOLD ALONG DOTTED LINE AND TEAR FOLD ALONG DOTTED LINE AND TEAR

FOLD ALONG DOTTED LINE AND TEAR

FOLD ALONG DOTTED LINE AND TEAR

Enemy Call Sign: ____________

ENEMY AIRSPACE

	A ALPHA	B BRAVO	C CHARLIE	D DELTA	E ECHO	F FOXTROT	G GOLF	H HOTEL	I INDIA	J JULIETT	K KILO	L LIMA	M MIKE	N NOVEMBER	O OSCAR	P PAPA	Q QUEBEC	R ROMEO	S SIERRA	T TANGO	
1																					1
2																					2
3																					3
4																					4
5																					5
6																					6
7																					7
8																					8
9																					9
10																					10
	ALPHA A	BRAVO B	CHARLIE C	DELTA D	ECHO E	FOXTROT F	GOLF G	HOTEL H	INDIA I	JULIETT J	KILO K	LIMA L	MIKE M	NOVEMBER N	OSCAR O	PAPA P	QUEBEC Q	ROMEO R	SIERRA S	TANGO T	

GAIN BRT SIM CON

HIT 2 OF EACH
(10 PIECES)
(AVOID TWO CIVILIAN)

KEY

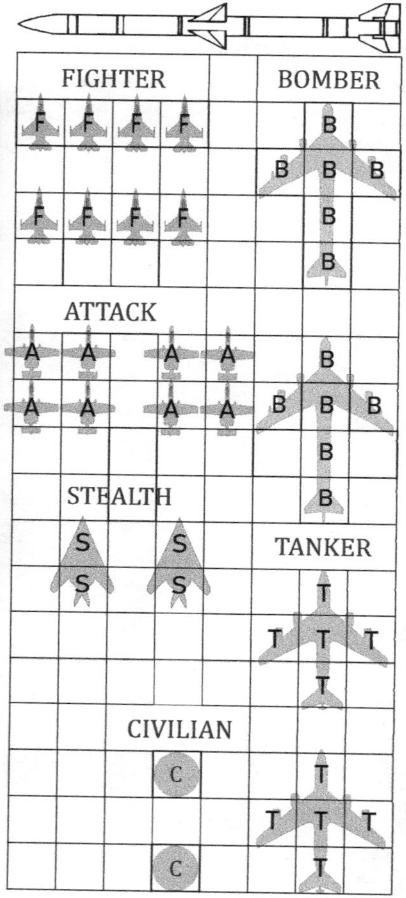

FIGHTER
F F F F
F F F F
BOMBER
B B B B B B
B B B B B B
ATTACK
A A A A
A A A A
STEALTH
S S S S
TANKER
T T T T T T
T T T T T T
CIVILIAN
C C

UNCLASSIFIED
R-4806W
AYSEES PEAK
6268
5280
towers
bldgs
bldgs
6412
6804
SPOTTED RANGE
INDIAN SPRINGS VALLEY
PINTWATER
6574
bombing and gunnery range
targets
5725
6060
4780
target
6043
disposal
water
Mercury
6078
CREECH AFB (INS)
CT - 118.3
ATIS 290.45
3134 *L 90
bldgs
See NOTAMs/Supplement for Class D eff hrs
DESERT NATIONAL WILDLIFE RANGE
tower
4819
targets
Indian Springs
95
57
FOR ADVISORIES IN THIS AREA CTC NELLIS APP ON 119.35
MODE C & ADS-B O
30 NM
IR286
CAUTION: Extensive unmanned aircraft activity within 6nm of INS below 7500' MSL. Traffic advisories available from Creech ATCT 118.3
6567
8218
6496
SPRING MTNS
9168
Cold Creek
A-481
HIGH PERFORMANCE CLIMBS & DESCENTS BY NELLIS AFB TRAINING MISSIONS
8756
10745
4984
street pattern
camps
camps
radome
11548
6100
11915
Mt Charleston
(Pvt)
THE AIRPORT CLUB
2736 - 25
10014
bldgs
NORTH LAS VEGAS
8154
Pahrump
6089
8468
street pattern
racetrack
houses
bldgs
VORTAC
LAS VEGAS
tower
CAAS (Pvt)
2800 - 18
SEE LAS VEGAS TERMINAL AREA CHART FOR CORTEZ, ROCKS & GYPSUM VFR TRANSITION ROUTES
4980
PAHRUMP VALLEY
Blue
plant

FOLD ALONG DOTTED LINE AND TEAR

FOLD ALONG DOTTED LINE AND TEAR

FOLD ALONG DOTTED LINE AND TEAR

UNCLASSIFIED
EXAMPLES OF CLASS B ALTITUDES
70
30
Ceiling in hundreds of feet MSL
Floor in hundreds of feet MSL
LAS VEGAS TERMINAL AREA
Pilots are encouraged to use Las Vegas VFR
Terminal Area Chart for flights at or below 10,000'
TAC
MORMON MESA
113.1 Ch 78 MMM
RENO
122.1R
15
78
85
LAS VEGAS
CLASS B
Moapa
substation
Glendale
Logandale
PERKINS FLD (U08)
1366 L 48 122.8
RP 32
Overton
5226
3230
4650
tower
93
100
75
3994
solar farms
solar farm
substation
truck
stop
100
70
3281
100
50
solar farm
MODE C & ADS-B OUT
30 NM
LAKE MEAD NATIONAL
RECREATION AREA
bldgs
solar farm
solar farm
15
100
SFC
3464
MUDDY MOUNTAINS
3947
Stewarts
Point
Echo
Bay
ECHO BAY (0L9)
1535 - 34
122.8
RP 25
100
70
5431
SPEEDWAY
NELLIS AFB (LSV)
CT - 132.55
ATIS 270.1
58
plant &
strip mine
3484
FRENCHMAN MTN
100
60
4080
3310
WYLND
NEVADA
ARIZONA
resort
100
45
100
65
3917
LAKE MEAD NATIONAL
RECREATION AREA
HENDERSON
transformer
2057
5340
6471

FOLD ALONG DOTTED LINE AND TEAR

Call Sign: ____________

MY AIRSPACE

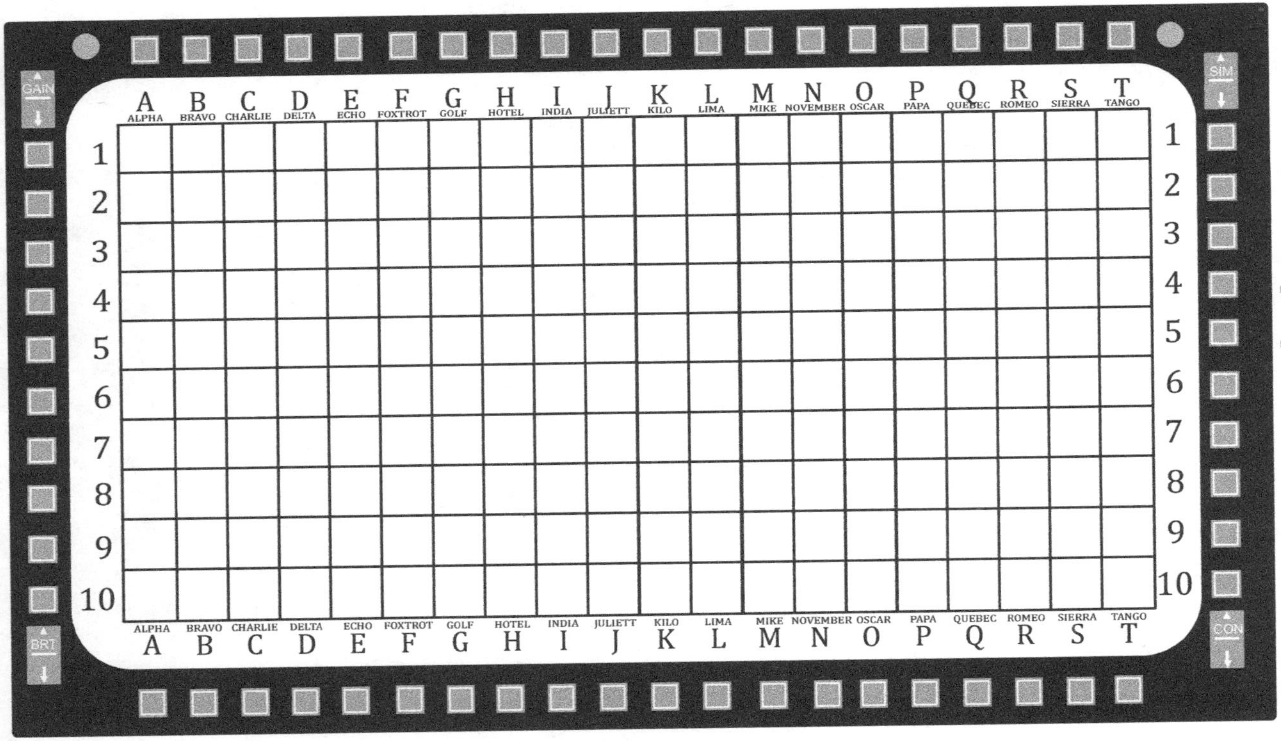
GAIN
SIM
BRT
CON
A B C D E F G H I J K L M N O P Q R S T
ALPHA BRAVO CHARLIE DELTA ECHO FOXTROT GOLF HOTEL INDIA JULIETT KILO LIMA MIKE NOVEMBER OSCAR PAPA QUEBEC ROMEO SIERRA TANGO
1 2 3 4 5 6 7 8 9 10

DRAW 2 OF EACH
(10 PIECES+ 2 CIVILIAN)

KEY

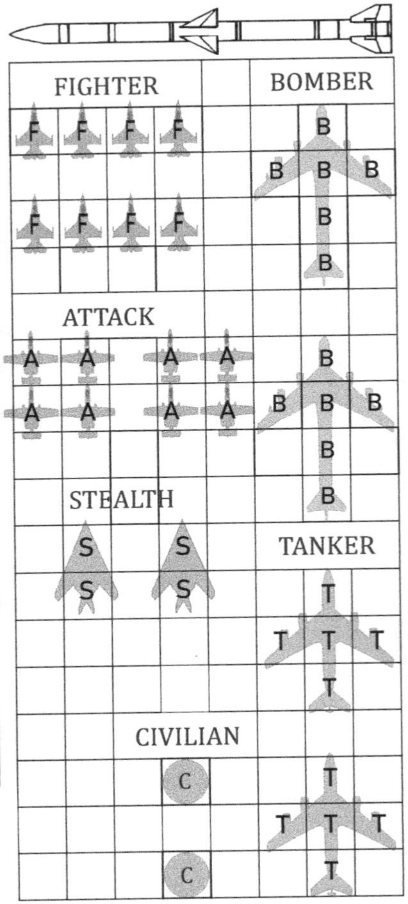
FIGHTER
BOMBER
ATTACK
STEALTH
TANKER
CIVILIAN

FOLD ALONG DOTTED LINE AND TEAR

FOLD ALONG DOTTED LINE AND TEAR

Enemy Call Sign: _____

ENEMY AIRSPACE

HIT 2 OF EACH
(10 PIECES)
(AVOID TWO CIVILIAN)
KEY

FIGHTER	F F	F		**BOMBER**	B B	B
	F F	F			B	B
					B B	B
ATTACK	A A	A			B B	B
	A A	A		**TANKER**	T T	T
	A A	A			T	T
STEALTH	S	S			T T	T
	S	S		**CIVILIAN**	C	
						C

	A	B	C	D	E	F	G	H	I	J	K	L	M	N	O	P	Q	R	S	T
	ALPHA	BRAVO	CHARLIE	DELTA	ECHO	FOXTROT	GOLF	HOTEL	INDIA	JULIETT	KILO	LIMA	MIKE	NOVEMBER	OSCAR	PAPA	QUEBEC	ROMEO	SIERRA	TANGO
1																				
2																				
3																				
4																				
5																				
6																				
7																				
8																				
9																				
10																				

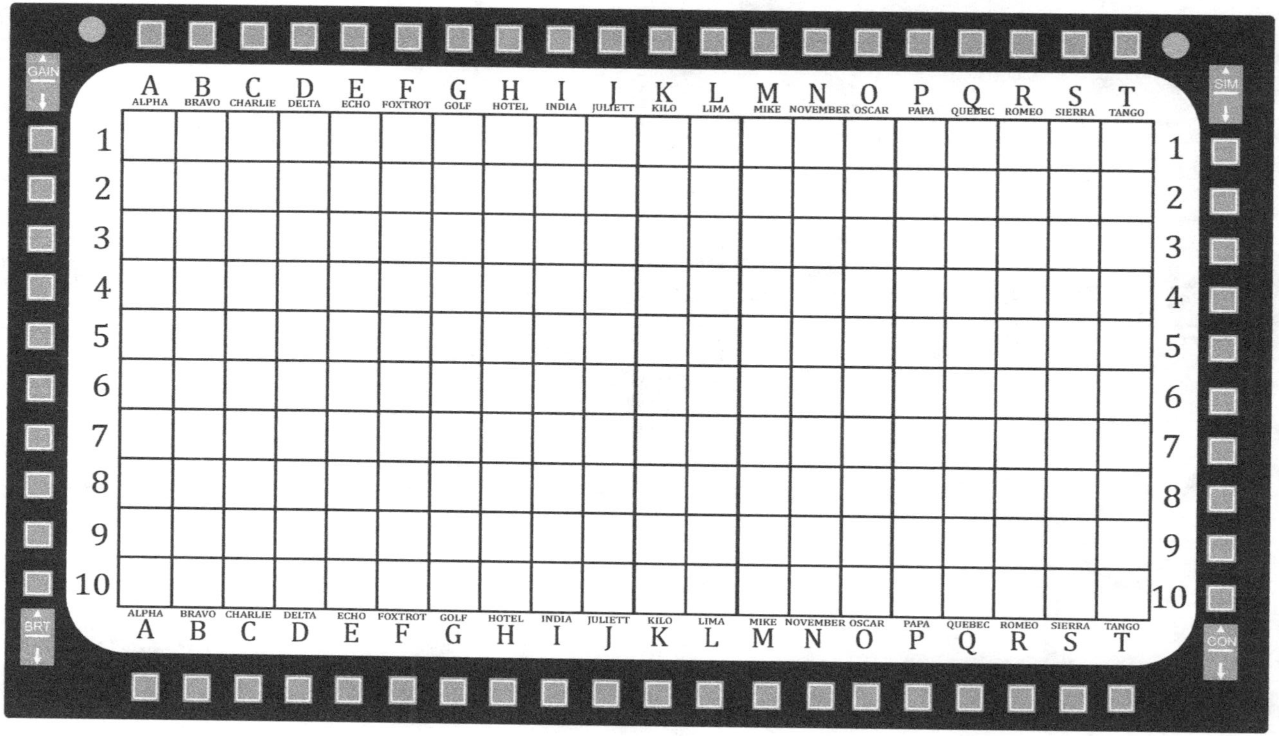

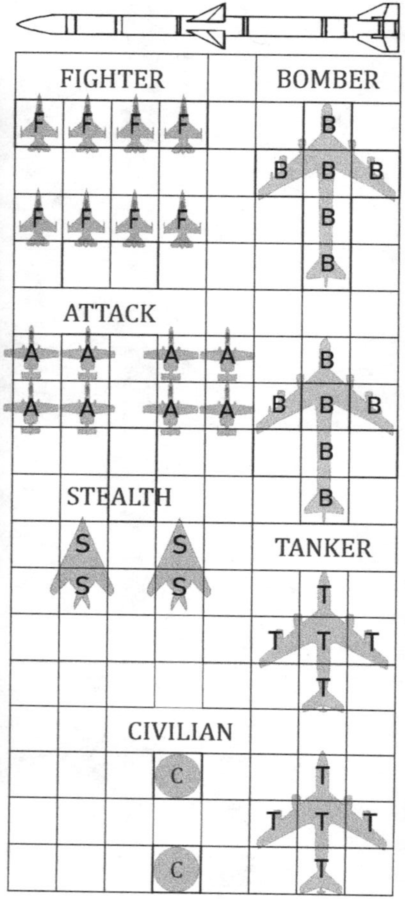

(301)
JOE FOSS FLD (FSD)
T - 118.3 ★ C ATIS 126.6
1430 *L 90 122.95
1678
092°
1774
Brandon
1652
(236)
39
1800
(290)
INTER
SIOUX FALLS
3427
(1999)
1961
(465)
1635
(224)
1652
(260)
1935
(490)
1857
(306)
Y14)
Harrisburg
IOWA
SOUTH DAKOTA
29
1754
(395)
A
Creek
1532

FOLD ALONG DOTTED LINE AND TEAR

FOLD ALONG DOTTED LINE AND TEAR

Tournament Bracket

FOLD ALONG DOTTED LINE AND TEAR

FOLD ALONG DOTTED LINE AND TEAR

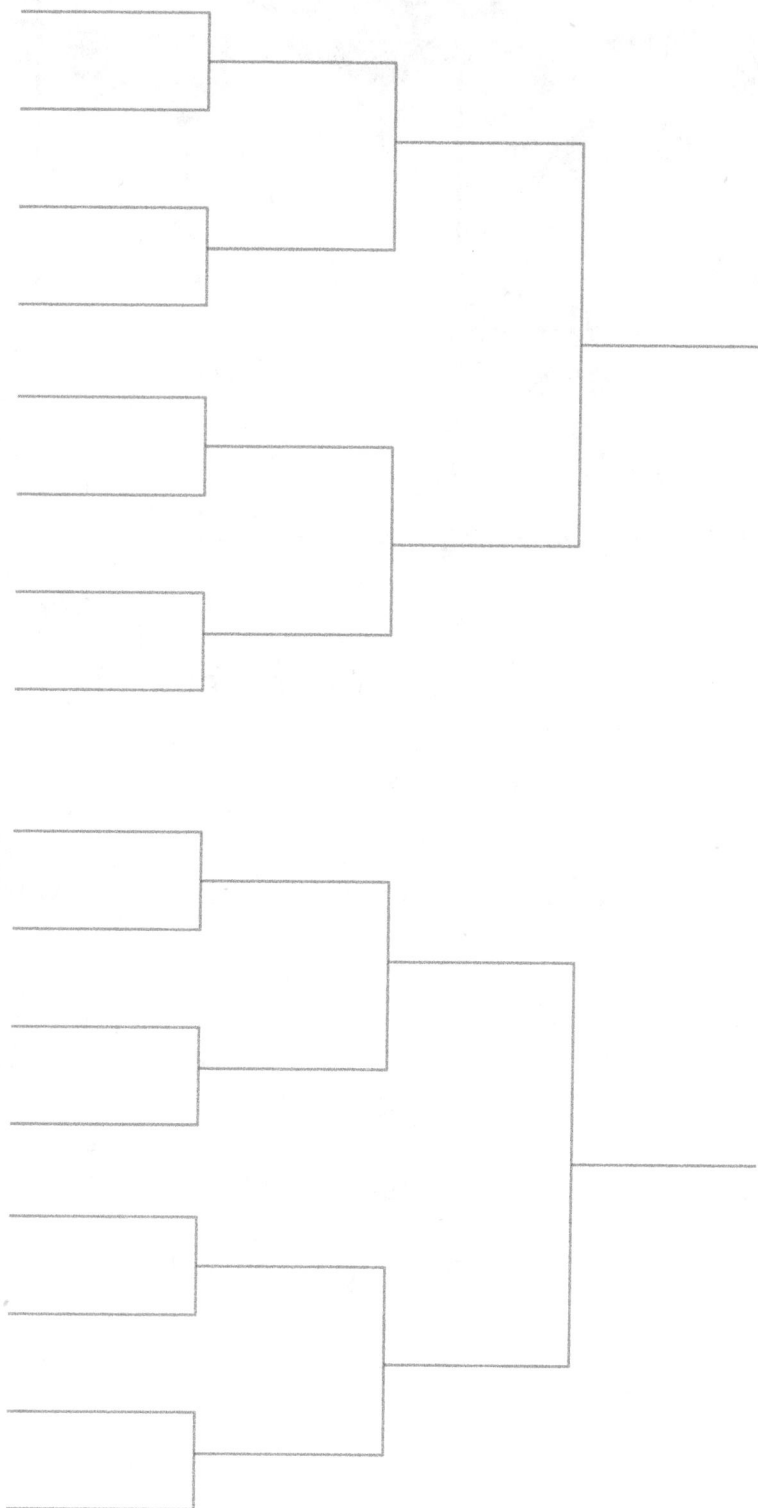

IOWA
SOUTH DAKOTA
1520
1386
(270)
1677
(309)
Jefferson
1445
(334)
1770
(375)
1620
GRAHAM FLD (7K7)
109 – 32 122.9 C
RP 15
N Sioux City
1684
1321
1700
1630
SIOUX CITY
S Sioux City
(306)
(496)
1305
(206)
(303)
KRISTIJANTO AIRSTRIP (Pvt)
Sergeant

FOLD ALONG DOTTED LINE AND TEAR

FOLD ALONG DOTTED LINE AND TEAR

Tournament Bracket

FOLD ALONG DOTTED LINE AND TEAR

FOLD ALONG DOTTED LINE AND TEAR

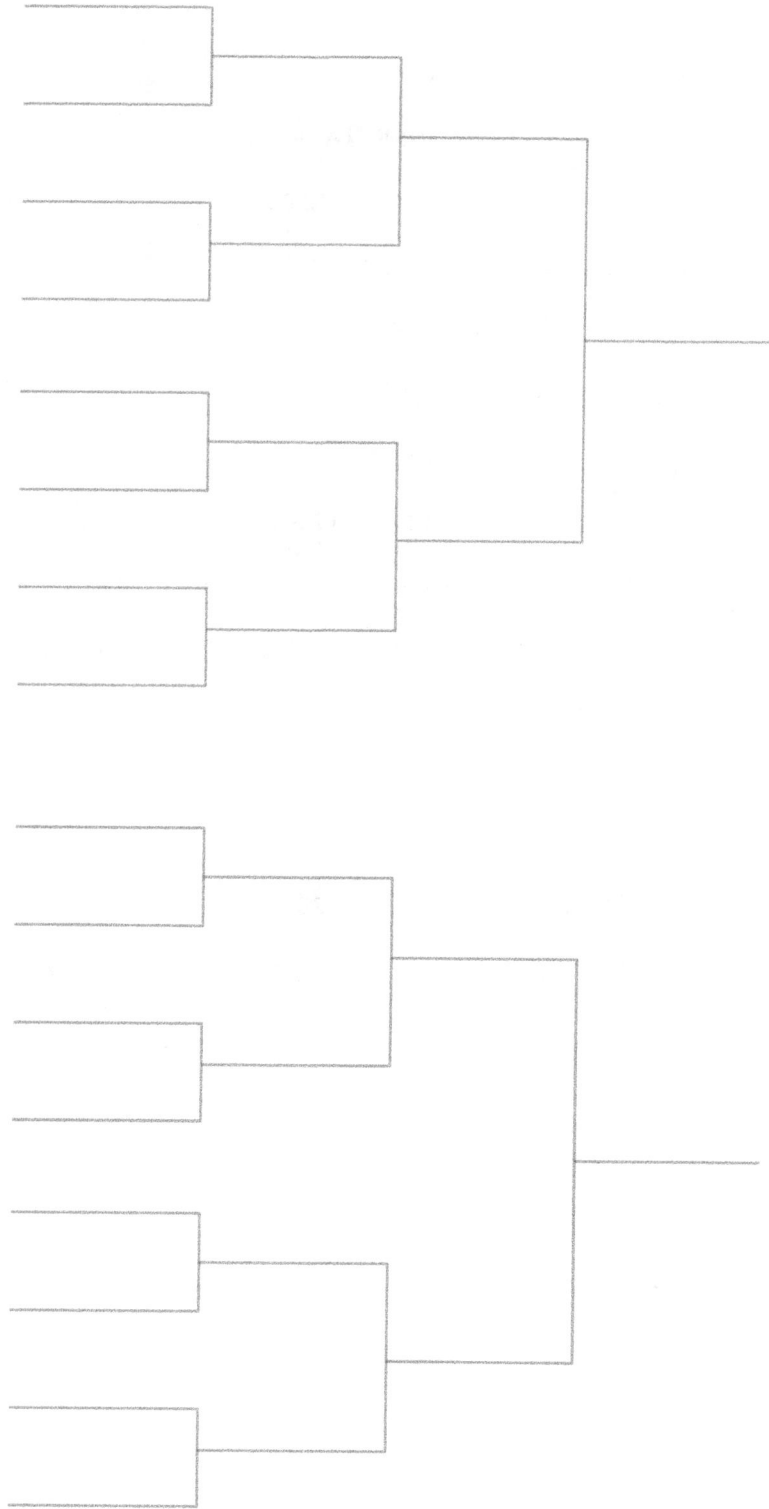

Movie Quotes to Defeat (Frustrate) your Enemy

Searching:

"Talk to me Goose, Talk to me Goose"

"What's the vector Victor?"

"What's the clearance Clarence"

"Dark Star bogey dope"

On the Offensive:

"It's a target rich environment"

"Too close for missiles switching to guns"

"I feel the need, the need for speed"

"I've got tone, I've got TONE"

"Jester's dead"

"It's time to Buzz the tower"

On the Defensive:

"This bogey is all over me"

"Your ego is writing checks your body can't cash"

"The force is strong with this one"

"I'm going to hit the Brakes, You'll fly right by"

"Negative Ghost Rider, the pattern is full"

After Losing:

"You can be my Wingman Anytime"

"Crashed and Burned"

NATO Brevity Code Words to Use During The Game:

Bingo: Outta Gas, Gotta Go

Bogey: Unidentified aircraft

Bogey Dope: Information on location of Bogey

Contact: Have radar hit of target

Cease Buzzer: Stop jamming

Fox Three: Launch of radar-guided missile (AIM-120 AMRAAM)

Fox Two: Launch of infrared-guided missile (AIM-9 Sidewinder)

Hostile: Confirmed enemy aircraft

Knock it Off: Stop the entire fight

Lufbery: Prolonged horizontal fight where neither fighter gains an advantage

Picture: Request for all enemy positions

Tally: Visual confirmation of target

Terminate: Stop the current engagement

Tumbleweed: Total loss of situational awareness

Spike: Enemy radar has a locked friendly

Splash: Enemy aircraft destroyed

Winchester: Out of weapons

ADVANCED RULES

(PICK ANY OR ALL)

TOP GUN RULES:

EACH PLAYER GETS 1 "JAMMER ON" CALL PER GAME

THIS CALL WILL ALLOW THE DEFENSIVE PLAYER TO *RE-DIRECT* A MISSILE TO ANY GRID (MAKING IT A MISS)

EXAMPLE: OFFENSIVE PLAYER CALLS A SHOT "A-2"

DEFENSIVE PLAYER CALLS " JAMMER ON, J-10, MISS" (MAKING SHOT A MISS)

AND

EACH PLAYER GETS 1 "SECOND SHOT" CALL PER GAME

THIS CALL ALLOWS OFFENSIVE PLAYER TO IMMEDIATELY FIRE A SECOND MISSILE.

EXAMPLE: OFFENSIVE PLAYER CALLS A SHOT "B-5"+"SECOND SHOT, B-6"

DEFENSIVE PLAYER CALLS "HIT, HIT" (AS APPROPRIATE)

MINE SWEEP RULES:

IF YOU HIT THE CIVILIAN AIRCRAFT YOU LOSE - "GAME OVER"

MULTI-PLAYER RULES (A LITTLE COMPLEX):

RED TEAM VS BLUE TEAM

2 v 2

3 v 3

4 v 4 ...

FILL OUT MY AIRSPACE GRID NORMALLY

ENEMY AIRSPACE GRIDS WILL BE SHARED WITH YOUR TEAM

FOLD AND TEAR ALL "ENEMY AIRSPACE" GRIDS FROM GAME SHEETS

- LABEL ENEMY CALL SIGNS ON "ENEMY AIRSPACE" GRID
  (YOU SHOULD HAVE 1 GRID FOR EACH ENEMY PLAYER)
- SHARE THE ENEMY AIRSPACE GRIDS AMONG YOUR TEAM MARKING HITS/MISSES ON EACH ENEMY PLAYER AS APPROPRIATE

EACH PLAYER CAN SHOOT AT ANY OTHER PLAYER ON OPPOSITE TEAM

ALL RED PLAYERS TAKE A TURN (ONLY ONE SHOT) THEN ALL BLUE PLAYERS TAKE A TURN

HOUSE RULES: ____

____

____

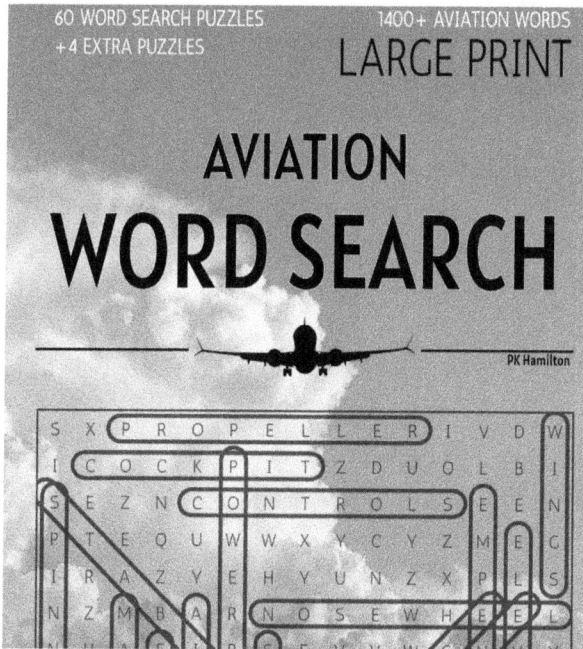

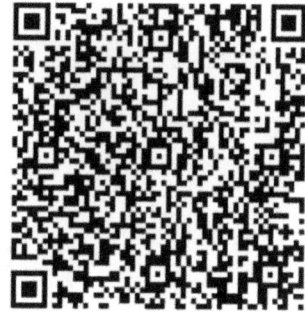

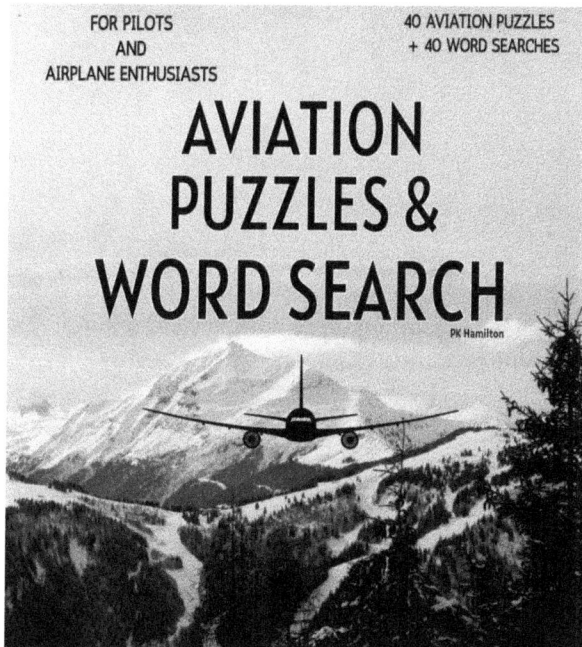

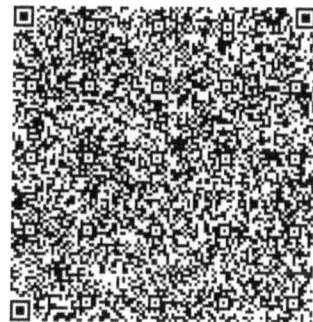

UNCLASSIFIED

SPECIAL MILITARY ACTIVITY FOR IR200, IR425 CTC JOSHUA CON ON 126.55 FOR ACTIVITY STATUS
CTC NELLIS APP ON 126.65 OR FLIGHT SERVICE PRIOR TO ENTERING MOA
VR209-1259
IR425
IR200
IR286
VR1253
TEMPIUTE MTN
MOUNT IRISH
microwave tower
ranch
houses
farms
Ash Springs
MOA EXCLUDES AIRSPACE 1500' AGL & BELOW
ALAMO LANDING
Alamo
letter "P"
BALD MTN
EMIGRANT VALLEY
R-4808 N
windmill
water
sand
T I K A B O O
V A L L E Y
P A H R A N A G A T
R A N G E
PAHRANAGAT NATIONAL WILDLIFE REFUGE
target
targets
DESERT NATIONAL WILDLIFE RANGE
bldgs
37°
116°
towers
Mercury
disposal
tower
R-4806W
R-4806 E
AYSEES PEAK
SPOTTED RANGE
bombing and gunnery range
INDIAN SPRINGS VALLEY
PINTWATER RANGE
CREECH AFB
See NOTAMs/Supplement for Class D eff hrs
HAYFORD PK
SHEEP RANGE
Indian Springs
FOR ADVISORIES IN THIS AREA CTC NELLIS APP ON 119.35
MODE C & ADS-B OUT 30 NM
IR286
Cold Creek
A-481
HIGH PERFORMANCE CLIMBS & DESCENTS BY NELLIS AFB TRAINING MISSIONS
SPRING MTNS
street pattern
camps
radome
Mt Charleston
THE AIRPORT CLUB
Pahrump
racetrack
CAAS (Pvt)
LAS VEGAS
RACEWAY
SEE LAS VEGAS TERMINAL AREA CHART FOR CORTEZ, ROCKS & GYPSUM VFR TRANSITION ROUTES

OUTTA GAS, GOTTA GO!!

AIR BATTLE
A Paper Game
of Strategy, Search, and Destroy
Includes 80 Game Sheets
Ages 8-108

Suggestions and Corrections:
PKHamilton@SmartSwitchPublications.com

Smart Switch
ON
Publications

www.ingramcontent.com/pod-product-compliance
Lightning Source LLC
Chambersburg PA
CBHW081641040426
42449CB00015B/3413
* 9 7 9 8 9 9 2 2 4 3 2 4 6 *